MW01008016

# *Pride and Tradition*

# Pride and Tradition

## More Memories of Northeast Minneapolis

GENNY ZAK KIELEY

*Best wishes!*
*Genny Kieley*

NODIN PRESS

Copyright © 2000 by Genny Zak Kieley

All rights reserved. No part of this book may be reproduced
in any form without the permission of Nodin Press
except for review purposes.

ISBN: 0-931714-85-0
First Edition

Library of Congress number: 99-068391

Nodin Press, a division of Micawber's, Inc.
525 North Third Street
Minneapolis, MN 55401

This book is dedicated to my grandsons, D.J.
and Anthony and for my future grandchildren.
You are my inspiration for recording these memories.

"A nation can be the victim of amnesia. It can lose
the memories of what it was, and thereby
lose the sense of what it is or wants to be."

*With Heritage So Rich*

U.S. Conference of Mayors
Special Commission on Historic Preservation

# Acknowledgments

I would like to thank the following:

The Northeast community for all their help in gathering information and their willingness to share rare family photos. And for leading me to others who had information. Your direction helped me to shape and create this book. And some gave a little extra, put up with numerous phone calls and were always enthusiastic. Irene Spack, John Dady, Walter Warpeha, Kay McFarland, Jack Kabrud, Jude Honigschmidt, Roxanne Jorgenson and Grace Sharp.

My wonderful family who shared in my joy, spread the word, and have been genuinely supportive. I don't think you realize how much this means to me. My brothers and sisters and their (spouses), Don and (Alice) Moss, John and (Ruth) Maslowski, Pat Steinke and her late husband, (Les) Steinke, Bob and (Ceil) Maslowski, Josie and (Gary) Kvistberg, Phyllis and (Dick) Hackbarth, Dorothy and (Neil) Doebbert and my late brother, Raymond Zak. And my in-laws, Gerald and Vivian Kieley, Nancy and Bob O'Dette and Roger and Betty Kieley.

Shelly Halford, you have been a lifesaver for me on both of my books. Thank you for your creative thinking ability, and your willingness to drop everything in your own life to help a bewildered aunt.

Joe Noble, your research and writing on the Northeast bars put an extra zing into my book. You were also a great source of support.

For almost twelve years I have been meeting with a group of writers at the Writing Center that have become a surrogate family. They listened, read and commented on portions of my book, helped me with titles, listened to me whine, and continually encouraged me. They are very creative and inspiring people. Bernie Becker, Bob Cambanes, Stephanie Derhak, Siana Goodwin, Judy Granahan, Dave Hannula, Linda Herkenhoff, Ruth Jurisch, Janet Kramer, Christina Potyondy, Lyn LaCoursiere, Kim Sanford, Sandy Swanson, and Ross Tarantino. A special thanks to Meg Miller who kept us all together and had faith in me and in all of us.

Most of all to my husband, Doug, who took many of the photos and at a critical point he read several portions of the book and made many helpful suggestions. He also valued my love of history and nostalgia enough to allow me to quit my job; no questions asked and encouraged me to continue my dream of writing a book. This book would certainly not be possible without him.

# Contents

Foreword ix

How My First Book "Heart and Hard Work" xi
    Was Received

1  Front Porch Memories    15

2  Streets Named After Presidents    29
    Boundaries
    Why President Streets?
    Main and Marshall
    Central Avenue
    East Hennepin
    13th Avenue

3  Churches on Every Other Corner    51
    Nineteen Neighborhood Churches

4  Immigrants, Steamers, Trolleys
    and a French Explorer    103
    Pierre Bottineau
    Immigrants
    Ship Enterprise
    Sandy Lake
    Gerber Baths
    Trolleys
    Great Northern Station

5  Connections, the Places We Remember    129

6  Alleluia! Nazdrowie!    169
    Bars
    Drugstores
    Schools
    Diners
    Movies

7  The Homefront During World War II
    in Northeast Minneapolis    201

8  The Ma and Pa Stores
    Are All Gone Now    211
    Fifteen Interviews with Northeast Residents
    My Aunt was hit by a stray bullet
    People used tar blocks from the street
    19th Avenue and Sixth Street
    Pizza was unknown in Minnesota
    I wasn't Catholic or Irish
    I held a run on the streetcar mainline
    What kind of American farm is this?
    Don't build a house, unless it is on a hill
    We used magazines as shin guards
    Aunt Leda became a dressmaker
    Five Generations were raised
    The Grain Belt Beer sign had an arrow
    The Ma and Pa stores are all gone now
    Our uncles would tell us wild tales
    Ma the Streetcar is coming

# Foreword

This book is a continuation of my first book, *Heart and Hard Work: Memories of Nordeast Minneapolis* and was born out of people's claims that there were things missing in my first book. "You didn't include my church or you didn't include the little store, just down the corner from us that everyone loved." So like the first book I tried to include places that people felt connected to.

People would ask me where do you find your information or how can I get in your book? The answer is that whoever had information and was willing to share it could get into the book. For the people I've spoken with, it's whatever their memories are and the places they hold dear to their heart that are important.

Some people thought that I focused on a certain part of Northeast, like the neighborhoods west of Central in my first book and that I would focus more on the neighborhoods east of Central in my second book. That really isn't true. I simply collected as much information as I could. All of it was random. Back when I first started I tried to get businesses that were 100 years old and tried to represent all ethnic groups that settled in earlier times and the churches that they built. But some had no information to give me. With the second book I had to stop taking information even though I was still getting calls. The information had to end at some point. It could not go on forever.

At any rate I have added two volumes of history to Northeast Minneapolis that didn't exist before in the library or in the bookstores. It was also my mission to collect as many photos as I could.

I did a great deal of my work through letters and by phone. I used specific criteria and specific questions, everything that was used in the interview had to have a connection to Northeast. I did research at the Minnesota Historical Society, Special Collections of the Minneapolis Public Library and the Hennepin County History Museum. The rest was done through personal interviews.

The years covered in this book are from the story of Pierre Bottineau in the 1840s through the interviews of people who grew up in the 1950s and '60s.

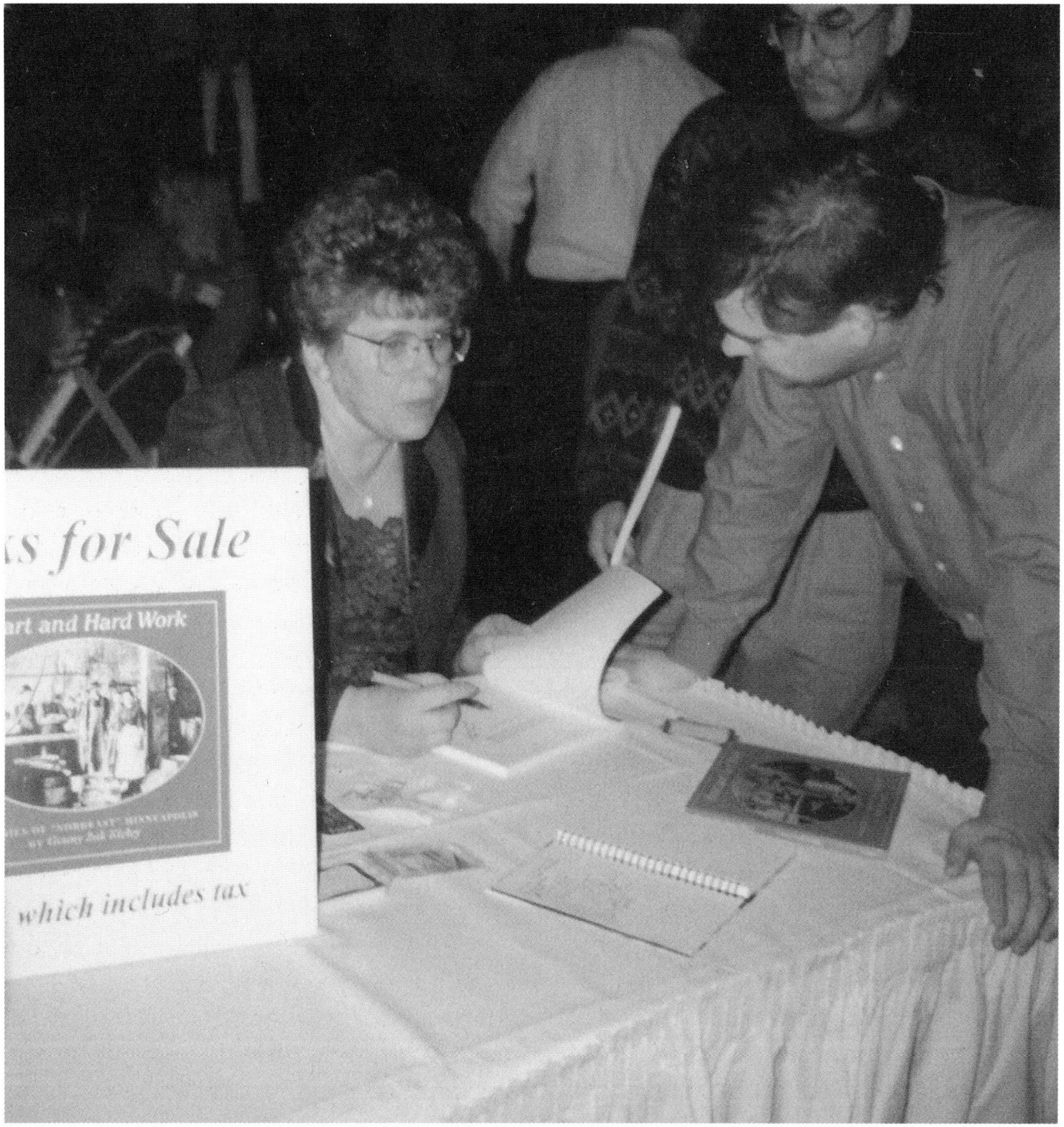
ks for Sale
art and Hard Work
which includes tax

# How my first book, *Heart and Hard Work* was received and the infamous "Kramarczuk's Book Signing!"

My book came out on December 4th, 1997 and we had a party at Little Jack's to celebrate. On Monday after the autograph party, I had my first TV interview for Channel 2, Newsnight with Cathy Wurzer. I really was reluctant to do this. My publisher laughed and said, "You're life is going to be filled with all kinds of new experiences." It ended up being an exciting day, but the camera lights made me a little nervous.

On Wednesday of that week I got a call from Chuck Haga. My publisher had told me that he was going to call, but I didn't believe it. He wanted to interview me for the *Star/Tribune.* We met at Mill City Coffee Shop. The interview went well and he took a few photos of me walking on the railroad tracks by Bottineau Park near where my aunt lived.

The next day the article came out in the morning paper. My husband called from work and woke me up at 7:30. "Get up and go down to the store," he said, "You're in the paper." So between the two of us we bought twelve copies. Then the lady at the Food and Fuel gave me six free copies and was so happy for me that she cried before I left the store. That night my friend, Bob who works for the Star/Tribune gave me 75 copies of the Metro section.

Then came the day of the infamous "Kramarczuk's book signing" that was listed in the Star/Tribune along with my interview with Chuck Haga. I arrived early at 10 AM to get things set up. My husband came with me, but he wasn't planning to stay. Coming in the door I was greeted by the wonderful smell of sausages and fresh bakery bread. And three people who were waiting. By the time I finished signing their books and had a nice chat with them I noticed there were more people waiting and before long—a line had formed. But from my end, I couldn't really tell how long it was.

Two of my aunts and cousins had come down. Friends from the old neighborhood were there, schoolmates, people I hadn't seen in thirty years, and thought I'd never see again. When I saw the Dziedzic girls who used to visit their grandma who lived next door to us and Mrs. Kubinski's granddaughter, I got so excited I almost cried. Then a woman came up to the table and said, "My husband used to date you."

"Oh no, you must be mistaken," I said. "I only dated a few guys." After talking with her for awhile, I realized that sure enough I did date him. Imagine the guy who dumped me was showing my picture all over town.

The day became a swirling sea of activity—writing long Slavic names, and trying to spell them. Before I knew it, I looked up and the line had extended to the end of the room. But after awhile I realized we were blocking the lunch counter. I asked my husband a couple of times to try to move the line, he said he tried but couldn't get their attention. So I had to stop signing books, get up on a chair and start yelling at the crowd. Then I had to march and lead them all into re-forming a line, toward the west wall and away from the lunch counter. They all followed me and I felt like we're doing 'the wave' at the ball park.

I sat down again, continuing to sign books and listen to the people share their memories. When I looked up the next time, I saw the line that wound all the way around the restaurant and the meat market, then out the door and down the sidewalk. Then things started to get a little crazy. People were knocking stuff off of the Christmas tree. Some were buying a whole stack of books for Christmas presents and wanted me to write long verses. And the owner was telling me I needed to speed things up. One guy said he had a number that was over 100 and found out he was in the meat line instead of the book line.

It was hard for me to watch others getting their sausage and pierogis and I could sure smell it, but I didn't have time to eat lunch. It was comforting to hear the ethnic elevator music over the loud speaker. They were Polish Christmas songs that I remembered from my childhood. I told my husband to call rein-forcements. So he called up every number he knew by heart and told them to come down and help. It was about that time that the little grandma came from be-hind the lunch counter. She had on one of those little white chiffon aprons. "This is our busiest day of the year and people can't get their food. They are opening and closing the door." Then she lifts her hands up in frustration, "Even my bread won't rise!" she said.

We ended up staying there for seven hours and fi-nally the line died down. At the end of the day I was exhausted. And I finally got to eat my lunch. I looked around and my husband, Doug, was no where to be found. I thought for sure they had taken him away in a paddy wagon. It seems while he was opening a case of books, someone from the crowd bumped him and he cut his finger, right to the bone. So my son drove him to the store for a bandage. He said next time he's going to put on a red wig and sign books so he can get the line going and I'm going to do crowd control.

Before the end of the day the little grandma from behind the lunch counter came out and said to me, "Did you save one of your books for me. Could you sign one for me?"

One of the comments that people love to tell me is that "I was in that line" or someone in their family had stood in the line at Kramarczyks. Some came from long distances and some stood in line for two to three hours. All this when they could have been out doing their Christmas shopping. People came from as far as Forest Lake, Greenfield, Lauderdale, Lino Lakes, Still-water and Zimmerman in Minnesota and Marine on St. Croix and Ellsworth, Wisconsin plus Des Moines, Iowa.

My books have gone to about fifteen different states and even a few foreign countries. People have used my books at family reunions, pointing out people they know that are in the book. It has brought together many friends and family members that haven't seen each other in twenty-five years or more.

The next few weeks went by quickly. One thing I remember about that time is that after the book came out, my next dream was to see it on the shelf at the book store. I first went to B. Dalton in Brookdale. I saw a book the same size and color of mine on the regional shelf and I got excited. But it wasn't mine. So I went to the front counter. Trying not to look too conspicuous, I asked, "Do you have that book, *Heart and Hard Work-Memories of Nordeast Minneapolis?*"

"Oh, you mean by Kieley." After checking the computer he said, "We don't have it, we ordered it, but it sold out." "It just came in a week ago," I said. "Are you sure there aren't any in the back room?" He checked and there wasn't. So I began a mission. I started calling other book stores. And couldn't find anyone that had a copy on the shelf.

Meanwhile, what I didn't realilze was that people from my family and friends were calling and also asking about it. They'd say,"You should really get that book." Before long it was getting to be well known at the bookstores. Another thing that was going on was that friends, relatives, and even people that I didn't know were going to bookstores, straightening my books and even moving it to other nearby shelves so that it could be seen easier.

And this is how it has all come to be. I have had many joys since this book came out. I have received cards and letters from all over the country. My husband and I have had a lot of good laughs over all that's gone on. People fighting over my book, so many told me about how their sister, or wife or neighbor took their book and they had to buy another one. One guy called me up and said,"Guess what I'm having right now? Pig's feet." And guys calling and saying they used to date me. One guy 85 years old.

But the best part is how supportive the people have been to me. They wanted me to succeed and were willing to do what they could to help. It may sound strange but my book has taken on a life of it's own. Something much bigger than the fact that I put it together. People see things in this book that I didn't plan on. I think they are adding their own memories to it. I just wanted to pass on memories to my own family, not realizing that so many others like the same thing as I do. The people of Northeast are lovers of history and nostalgia. Some people gave me gifts and invited me for a special dinner. One lady knitted me a shawl and gave me a brick from my old school. One lady gave me a glass door knob from her old house.

It's been a wonderful experience. Somehow through the grace of God—people from all over the country have read and are talking about Northeast Minneapolis—a very special place.

*Our house on California Street*

*My two aunts in the 1930s*

# 1 Front Porch Memories

Some people have asked me why would I write a book about Northeast Minneapolis. For those who live or grew up there it's obvious. It's because of the changes. We live in such a fast paced society that driving over to Northeast where I was raised is a comforting experience for me. But sometimes when I go back there, I feel the pangs of loneliness for the old days—the way things were. Why were those days so great? I guess it's just because it was my little place in history, my world and my universe, the streets, the porches, the corner mom and pop stores and all the memories.

We all have a place that is special to us, a place that we keep near to our heart. It can be a place where we discover who we are. The place we think about when we need comfort and freedom to be ourselves. A place that holds memories. For me those memories go back to a time and place in the sixties.

From the age of six until I was married at twenty-one, I lived in Northeast Minneapolis. I live in the suburbs now and I don't get back to the old neighborhood as often. Most of my family members and friends have moved away. But when I do go back the feelings still return as I approach the Wickes Furniture store that sits on the hill where 694 meets East River Road. The Mississippi bends there, opening up its view slowly. The water sparkles in the sunlight, giving me a warm feeling. It's at that point I realize I'm going home. The FMC factory and what used to be the Minnesota Linseed Oil Company stretch out on my left. So many friends and neighbors worked there. As I coast down a hill of single lane highway and swing under the Soo Line railroad bridge, I am reminded that I'm entering the old part of town—city limits of Northeast Minneapolis.

*Railroad bridge on Marshall Street*

*Near California and Grand Streets at 30th Avenue NE, 1910*

The streets are lined with the nuts and bolts of commerce—auto parts stores, welding suppliers and lumber companies. The machine shops and metal fabricators make it Minneapolis' most industrial community. Wide-open spaces of railroad yards cut into the land, with rows of standing freight cars for as far as the eye can see. Abandoned gas stations and grain elevators remind me of another time period when life was a little simpler. The sound of the train whistle and the smell of grain will remain in my memory forever. The NSP plant towers above the river with Marshall Terrace Park beside it. The lush green border of trees that line the river's edge add a touch of beauty against a backdrop of fences and black mounds of coal. Looking at the park I am reminded of long summer days playing on the swings and parallel bars, enjoying games of four square and softball followed by a quick dip in the wading pool. Then hurrying home before the 9:00 curfew whistle blew.

Coasting down Marshall Street and then to 27th and Grand, the streets are quieter than I remember. Turning on to the avenue and then on to California

Street, I begin to search for things that look familiar. My childhood home is in the middle of the block of California Street. There it stands, gutted and barren; nothing left inside but cold and empty walls. The outside is really showing its age. It had always been old, but somehow I never noticed. The stucco has grayed and yellowed over the years, and the trim paint is cracked and chipped. It's hard to tell the original color, but I remember the turquoise that was always a favorite of mine. A stray cat wanders over to sit on the front step. Does he know that there is no longer anyone living here? He seems to know he has free reign; there is no longer a little dog to bother him.

I sit and stare from the car window, afraid to approach the house. I wonder if there might be a few things left inside. I wonder if the old brown leather couch on the front porch is still there. I have the overwhelming urge to go inside. Stepping out on the pavement, I cross the street and slowly walk up the small pathway. Although the yard was never perfect, it was never like this. Young tree saplings grow tall in the cracks of the sidewalk, and the weeds are taking over the irises in the front yard. Walking around the house, I pass the peonies, lilies, and irises that had been there for so many years; many are gone now, taken by the family. The ones that remain are no longer nurtured and cared for by gentle hands.

When I reach the backyard, I begin to look around. Most of the old elm trees are gone now, replaced by young seedlings. The lilac bush that separates the backyard from the alleyway behind it still stands magnificently. While guarding intruders from entering the yard, the lovely lavender flowers fill the air with fragrance and mark the beginning of spring. The deep pink Victorian rosebush and white peony bush were planted by my grandmother long before I was born. Gently touching one of the roses, I inhale the fresh fragrance, close my eyes, and think about my grandparents and how it all began.

*Grandma's rosebush and my mother's peony bush*

My grandparents built the house in 1914, the first one on the block of California Street in old "Nordeast" Minneapolis. It was the first and only house they ever owned. Starting with nothing and working their way up, they must have been proud to own their own house more sections. Nine children grew up here. After they were gone, as fate would have it, my mother brought her family to live here. Nine more children grew up here and went off to face the world. I was the last one.

I begin to feel a little tired. So I decide to sit down on the old swing hanging from the clothespole. Out of the corner of my eye, I glance at the back door and feel a slight shudder. Resting awhile with my eyes on the house and the back steps, I remember the morning glories stretching and attaching themselves to the railing and wrapping around the clothesline. They always seemed to be reaching toward the warmth inside the house.

Through the years this house was always full of life and joy, many times bursting with people. During the time my grandparents lived, it was a favorite meeting place for neighbors, friends, and family. Parties with polka dancing and live music, provided by my uncle,

*Grandma and Grandpa Koniar, 1930s*

in America, something next to impossible in their native land, Poland. It was a small house with a sturdy frame. Later, as their family got larger, they added on

*Uncle Frank's wedding, 1942*

were a regular occurrence. My Grandma and Grandpa with their large family were the only ones on the block who had the paper delivered. Grandma always made sure it was left on the front porch. Everyone was welcome to walk in and read it. Irene Lunewski and Alice Kaczor told me when they were young girls roller-skating down the sidewalk in front of my grandparent's house, they would stop and read the paper, they knew they'd be welcome. I can just imagine the result if my neighbors found me on their front porch reading the paper. Years later Irene Lunewski married my Uncle Benny and became my aunt.

With the next generation, which was mine, we continued celebrating many christenings, showers, weddings, birthdays, and holidays. Christmas and Easter were the ones I enjoyed the most. My family's favorite pastime was to sit around the kitchen table and recall the memories we shared together. We even enjoyed painting and cleaning the house. My family found humor in almost everything. Something would always happen that kept us laughing. Mixing up words, teasing, and practical jokes were quite natural for us. An example of this was when my mother once moved a big heavy dresser, which several of us couldn't budge, across the room. After that we teased her about having super powers.

Still resting on the swing, I notice the sun is beginning to slip behind the clouds, casting a shadow on the back of the house. I sense the stillness around me, and feel an emptiness inside. I remember my mother.

After all the kids were gone, my mother lived alone in the house, and everything inside was a reflection of her. Each room had a charm and character of its own. Edged with dark-stained molding, thick and beveled.

The high ceilings and old-fashioned wooden archways and built-in glass bookcases between rooms reflected the style that was popular in 1914 when the house was built. The living room and dining room might have been considered a hodgepodge of decorating; old and new pictures of family members arranged everywhere, and in every corner knickknacks and souvenirs. Each item had special meaning, having been given to her by those who were dear to her, most from her cherished children and grandchildren. The furniture was a reflection of the past: old handmade desks and ornate pedestal tables covered with fringed scarves and old lace doilies. Plants were everywhere.

A favorite room of my mother's, and perhaps the most used, was the large kitchen with a cubbyhole pantry behind it. My mother was still using a wringer washer in the sixties and drying all the laundry outside on a line. I can still remember the rustling sound of the lace curtains on a breezy day as the smell of fresh poppyseed bread filled the house.

After I left to get married, I often came back to visit my mother. These were our special times together when we shared secrets and talked of the latest happenings in the family. It was hard to resist the lure of the coffeepot and Mom's cookie jar in the pantry. Her aprons always hung neatly on a hook in one corner, behind the doorway of the pantry.

I get off the swing and walk toward the back steps. As I approach the back door, I half expect to see Mom in one of her aprons standing near the coffeepot. Then I notice the glass of the back door is gone, replaced by a large piece of plywood. In all the years I had lived here, the door was never locked. As I stare at the boarded-up door, I remember the sound of breaking

*Pinning a corsage on my mother on my wedding day at St. Hedwig's Church, 1970*

glass and feel an awful pain as the events of the dreadful day flash before me. My mother was slumped in her rocking chair, waving her arm. The doors were locked, and no one could get inside to help her. Then the paramedics came, broke the glass, and took her away to the hospital.

I bang on the door until my fists are sore, my heart beating faster and faster. I wish it had never happened and that she could still be inside. I sit down on the steps and cry. When there are no more tears, I get up to walk around the house. I'm now ready to move on.

On my way back to the car, I decide to take one last peek in the porch window. The front porch was a comforting place where I always felt special and unique; I was safe and shielded from the rest of the world. The old brown leather couch with the afghan thrown across the back was my solace in times of trouble. My mother and I spent many hours on that couch talking things out. Then I could go home to my family and face whatever problems I had. Once she mentioned that she and her mother used to sit on the porch together and do the same thing. This little room surrounded by windows, letting in the cold of the winter and the warmth of the sun in the summer, was always my sanctuary. Somehow I don't even remember the winters.

I yearn to go inside and turn the clock back so I can once again experience that same feeling of safety. Why can't the coffeepot still be there, perking in the pantry waiting for me? Why can't the couch on the front porch continue to be my solace in times of trouble? My heart aches desperately to go inside, but I know I cannot go back. The couch is no longer there. But the love that bound us together will always be with me.

After crossing the street I look back at the row of sturdy framed stucco houses, each with windows all the way across the front porch and small tidy yards with barely enough room for a small sidewalk between them. Dalecki's house where my first playmates lived looks smaller than it used to and the wooded lot across the street where we used to play remains empty. The trees near the middle of the field were the most intriguing. Our gateway leading into the trees was a giant weeping willow with sagging branches that hung clear to the ground. It was tricky getting in, but once we were there, it was worth it. We could stay hidden for almost an entire afternoon without our parents having the slightest inkling of where we were or what we were up to. The trees and surrounding bushes became an imaginary world filled with wonder, a look out for Cowboys and Indians, a fortress for Castles and Kings, or an island to explore.

This lot was also where all the neighborhood gardens were grown. Mrs. Kubinski was always out there weeding. Sometimes we would run through the garden that was at the edge of the trees. Mrs. Kubinski wore a beige cotton sweater, pulled tightly over her flowered dress, thick support hose and an old fashioned babushka. She would point her hoe at us and mumble something in Polish. Even when she was mad at us she always gave us fresh carrots to eat, straight out of the garden.

Two blocks west of here is Grand Street, the bus route leading to downtown Minneapolis. There are so many abandoned storefronts along the route. This street was once the trolley car line before the advent of buses. When I first moved to Minneapolis in 1956 there was still the remains of streetcar tracks and red bricked cobblestones at the corner of 27th and Grand where the Second Street bus route began. I often imagined what life was like back in the early era when streetcars, gas lamps and dirt roads existed.

*Polish store owned by Zawislak family on 27th and Grand Street*

My old school located on 26th and Grand is gone. I didn't think much about it when they tore it down. My mother said they were having a big closing ceremony and selling all the desks and equipment. I didn't understand her concern. It wasn't until about ten years later that I realized what that school meant to me. I had a dream one night that I was on the school's front steps. Standing there gave me a sense of security. It was on those steps that my dreams were in the beginning stages. When I awoke, I felt sad that those steps were gone forever. Over the years it was a comfort just to know I could drive by Schiller School whenever I felt a pang of nostalgia. But now Schiller is gone. In the 1970s others suffered the same kind of loss when seven schools were torn down.

Going up Grand Street, I turn on Lowry, the corner where Bautch's and Koscielek's Stores stood. The buildings are still there but they are used for other businesses. These stores were the only ones in the neighborhood that were not closed on Sundays. It was

*Koscielek's Store, 1997*

*Bautch's Store, 1997*

nice to have them there for those little necessities for dinner. But having been raised Catholic in that era, I would be slightly uneasy about going to a store that was open on Sundays. The Catholic belief was no business on Sabbath day. Two nice ladies ran Koscielek's Grocery and Bautch's was a family run store with a huge meat counter in front. These stores had ceiling fans that hummed, wood floors that creaked, spacious shelves with very few brands, screen doors that slammed and bells that tinkled when you entered.

From these stores I drive down to Lowry and Second Street, the corner of Lowry Liquor and Little Jacks, both still standing. When I was growing up, there was a drugstore on the corner next to Lowry Liquor and a hardware store across the street. I loved to look at the toy section with gaily-colored cellophane wrapped packages: pink jump ropes, toy Jax, and bags of cats eye marbles. And my favorite, a set of toiletries especially for little girls, pink bottles with toy lipstick, nail polish and tiny bottles of perfume labeled toilet water. Ptak's, a small dry goods store on 24th Avenue and Second Street sold fabrics on huge bolts. Two matronly ladies with sweet faces ran the store. And when you went there you were often the only customer in the store so you got individual attention. They sold sewing supplies and embroidery thread, nylons, handkerchiefs, housedresses, wool scarves, aprons and orthopedic shoes. Everyone went there to have their communion veils custom made.

The memories flood past as I drive further down Second Street and past Bottineau Park, my old skating hang out. I'd walk up to Bottineau no matter how cold it was because that was the best skating park and kids

*Ptak's Dry Goods Store*

came from all over just to skate there. There were always games going on, crack the whip and Red Rover, pom pom pullaway. And the boys would always steal your hat, which was good for a little chase. Sometimes we'd watch the boys play hockey.

Then I pass 13th Avenue. I remember going down there every day after school. We'd stop for a coke at Rolig Drug. I always loved the red twirling seats, the shiny fountain and the loud whir of the malt machine. I sat mesmerized as the waitress took the malted milk shake out, poured half into a glass with a metal base holder, then topped it off with whipped cream that came from a pressurized steel can. It was also fun to see who was there. A big crowd always gathered here after Friday night dances at Sheridan School. Some were lined up in Smoker's Alley. Sheridan dances were the best. On Friday nights when they turned down the lights and played a slow song, if you were lucky enough to have a partner, it was like being in heaven. I can still remember when I was a mere seventh grader and a ninth grade boy asked me to dance. I was wearing my white ruffled Ben Casey Blouse and a green wool plaid jumper. His name was Johnny Pachorak, one of the most popular boys in school. We danced the "Coliseum" or the "Walk" to the Lion Sleeps Tonight. It was instant love.

We also hung out at Dady's Drugstore, which was on the other end of 13th Avenue. We'd have a coke or a flavored charged-water fizz. My friend Jeannie always ordered some strange concoction like chocolate or lime coke. Drinking a charged water fiz was a real symbol of being in the "in crowd."

*Teenagers eating lunch at Rolig Drug in the 1960s*

Pretty soon I'm driving by St. Cyril's Church and the Polish White Eagle Hall, where everyone from the neighborhood had their weddings.

*My five sisters at Josie's shower: Phyllis, Pat, Josie, Genny and Dorothy. My mother is sitting in front, 1958*

The Polish Wedding was a custom brought over from the old country. With our large family of nine kids, there was usually a wedding about every two years, at which we partied and feasted for several days. It was the event of the year. We'd start out a few months ahead with a shower for the bride. We had many wedding showers at our house. The women from our family and several of the neighbors would be packed into the living room and dining room. It was traditional to fill the house with crepe paper and white bells saved from the last shower. And also my Auntie Ann's umbrella would be covered with tissue paper decorated with flowers and crepe paper and hung above the bride's head. It was tradition. The bride's mother always gave pillows, home made by Mrs. Dziedzic and the groom's mother gave a clothesbasket filled with spices and household staples.

It was not unusual for the lights to go out during these showers. With the overloading of circuits, lights, coffee makers and crock-pots the evening often ended with the lights going out and women screaming. It was hard to find fuses for this house with its inferior wiring and old-fashioned fuse box located on the back porch. There were only a few outlets in the house. So Uncle Fred came over and jimmied up the wiring system. There were extension cords going all over the place. We all thought it was amazing that Uncle Fred never electrocuted himself.

The wedding day began with the ceremony at St. Hedwig's Church followed by a breakfast feast at my Auntie Vicki's house. We didn't have groom's dinners, we had bridal breakfasts. For Catholic weddings, we fasted all morning before communion. The lay out of this breakfast was something for the wedding books. Her beautiful dining room table covered with hand made lace and adorned with every kind of food you can think of, Polish sausage, pierogis, and home made cinnamon rolls. And the centerpiece was always a colorful bouquet of Uncle Fred's roses. It was so elegant.

The wedding reception at about 4 or 5 P.M. was usually in someone's basement or one of the regular Northeast halls: Polish National Alliance, Polish White Eagle or Kaneski Loss. Most of our family's were at the Polish White Eagle. With the smell of sauerkraut bubbling, turkey roasting and sausages stewing, men in gabardine suits and women in flowery dresses stood around waiting for dinner. Portraits of Pulaski, and Pilsudski were on one side of the shiny-floored hall and George Washington and Woodrow Wilson were on the other.

Uncle Joe would always call out, "Zeby cie kaczka kopta." It's an oath that means a duck will kick you. It brings luck. The Polish band consists of a threesome, always with an accordion, drums and maybe a guitar. We often used Jolly Joe's Polka Band. The rooms would fill with the familiar music playing in 2/4 time, and the calling out of Yessinasa! A few of the favorite tunes were *Who Stole the Kieska and Wedding in the Cemetery*. And they all lined up for polkas like *Hupaj Siupaj, Green Meadow Polka* and *Roll out the Barrel*. Everybody joined in. The kids knew how to keep the beat, even toddlers. This was the way we all learned how to dance. Many met their intended this way at the weddings. No male partner available? Just grab your sister or your aunt. In the olden days a plate had to be broken with a silver dollar, followed up by a shot of whiskey and a dance with the bride. Now we just have the dollar dance. Of course, there are plenty of polkas and waltzes. But the favorites are the Schottische, Butterfly and the Bunny Hop. These are the ones that require real stamina. Sometimes if we felt the urge, we'd hop right out into the parking lot and then hop back again through the side door. One time I was on my way to the bathroom and the line came by. I had to join in. Later, women would fight over the bouquet and then we all went home exhausted.

The next day everyone was invited over to the bride's mother's house for "popravinie." This is a gathering where we'd eat and drink up all the leftovers. And of course the kids shiveree the bridal couple. They pound on pots and pans until the bride and groom throw coins at them to make them stop. Nowadays the popravinie includes the opening of gifts by the bride and groom. We opened them at the reception.

*Uncle Abbie's wedding: Red Koniar, Abbie Koniar, Mary Linder, Bill Yurch, Frank Koniar,*
*Ann Koniar, Gladys Koniar, Margaret Frenzel, Vicky Koniar, 1929*

*NSP sign on the river near East Hennepin*

After leaving the Polish White Eagle Hall and the memories of Polish weddings behind I pass Boike's Barbershop, Leitschuh's and Dr. Zaworski's office. Then I pass the building of the Little Sisters of the Poor, which was always a little scary. This huge castle-like building surrounded by black iron fences seemed like a guarded fortress to me. I had heard stories about teenagers sneaking in there at night and never coming out again. Going down further to Eighth Avenue and Second Street there is St. Anthony of Padua Church, where my sister was married and my brother and I made our first communion. East Hennepin is not at all the same as it was. The department stores and drugstores are all gone now. It is no longer the thriving shopping center that it was in the '60s.

To outsiders of Northeast Minneapolis the Grain Belt Beer Sign on the river and the Brewery are probably the most notable landmarks. But as a child what I remember is taking the bus downtown and going across the Third Avenue Bridge. Crossing the Mississippi we loved to see Ready Killowatt, who was a lightbulb with a big nose and the "electricity is penny cheap," sign that always flashed the time and temperature. The Minnegasco's Indian Maiden was there too. Then going across the bridge and over the river, I can still remember the humming sound the bus made as it crossed the open steel gridded bridge. It was a long bridge. And the excitement of the beauty, mixed with a little bit of fear of this great body of water, would overtake me. The Coca-Cola building on First Street and Central was always a beautiful site, especially at night because it was so huge and lit up the surrounding sky with a glow. And the Great Northern Depot with people and tracks going everywhere was so impressive.

The depot is where Northeast Minneapolis ends, so I head for home. I realize each generation makes a place of their own in history. The older generation lived with a Northeast I never knew and can only imagine through their stories. Just like I can only tell stories to my children and hope they get a glimpse of what it was like when I was young. But the young people of today will have their own special places and memories that go with them. I wonder if they will value the old churches, the neighborhood parks, theaters and the old schools that were so special to us. I hope so.

*Aerial view of Northeast Minneapolis in 1948, includes Lowry Avenue Bridge and Gluek Brewing Company at 2000 Marshall Street NE*

# 2 Streets Named After Presidents

## Boundaries

Northeast's boundaries are the city limits on the north and east and the Mississippi River on the west. The southern boundary is somewhat more complex, being Hennepin Avenue for the greatest extent, except for a distance of five blocks where Central and 9th Street Southeast meet. The small area of Southeast Minneapolis now north of Hennepin resulted when Hennepin and the old Division Street, now East Hennepin were connected. Boom Island and the north end of Nicollet Island are also in Northeast.

The original town of Minneapolis was on the west bank of the river, while St. Anthony stayed close to the east bank. When the two towns incorporated in 1872, the northern boundary reached about six blocks north of Broadway. The eastern edge was approximately at what is now Stinson Boulevard. By 1883, the northern boundary stood about five blocks beyond Lowry Avenue. In 1887 the boundaries attained their current shape.

## President Streets

Immigrants were required to take a test to receive their American citizenship papers. As part of this test they were asked to list the American presidents. So the streets were named after the presidents to help them remember. So the streets running north and south are all president streets and are in the order of when they were in office. So when asking for directions in Northeast Minneapolis, it is important to know your Civics.

Starting from University Avenue, then Fourth, Fifth, Sixth and Seventh Avenues, then starts Washington, Adams, Jefferson, Madison, Monroe, Quincy, Jackson, Van Buren, Harrison, Tyler, Taylor, Fillmore, Pierce, Buchanan, Lincoln, Johnson, Ulysses, and Hayes.

## Main and Marshall Streets

The roadway that edges the Mississippi River on the east bank has three names, Main Street, Marshall Street and the East River Road. It is thought to be the oldest street in town. Historical accounts state that Father Hennepin viewed St. Anthony Falls in 1680 and was probably the first white man to walk that roadway, then a trail used by Indians.

It was also the Old Red River Ox Cart Trail and the principal street of St. Anthony. As the hub and business district it was also the site of the first railroad station when the first train came into St. Anthony on June 28, 1862. It was a well traveled road for the Red River Carts from St. Paul to Pembina, North Dakota.

*View of the falls from Main Street of St. Anthony,*
*land office and fur carts in foreground from daguerreotype, 1854*

This trail started with six carts in 1844 and by 1858 more than 600 carts were seen and counted carrying furs to the St. Paul markets.

The first street sign calls the roadway "Main Street" and starts near Father Hennepin Bluffs by the Tenth Avenue Bridge in Southeast Minneapolis. On one side utility towers and railroad tracks and on the other, the Pillsbury "A" Mill. From there the cobblestone street climbs toward East Hennepin, a glimpse of Nicollet Island just visible through the trees.

Once across Hennepin it becomes Northeast Marshall Street and travels 1½ miles up hill. This is the area where one sees the skeleton of the B.F. Nelson Company, one of Northeast's largest employers before the 1970s. It was torn down to make an exit for highway I-94. The "Pioneers" statue of four generations of immigrants resides over the intersection where Main and Marshall split.

New homes, 49 of them, fill the blocks near Fourth Avenue Northeast as the street turns gently to the right, still following the river's edge. All were torn down and rebuilt during urban renewal in 1964. The deteriorated homes were part of Old St. Anthony and originated in the mid-19th century.

*"Old Foster House" the second oldest house on the Eastside of Minneapolis, 427 Main.*
*Later owned by Alexander and Catherine Erb. Grandma Catherine is sitting on front porch*

Three miles north of Fourth Avenue, Marshall Street becomes East River Road. 37th Avenue is the county line, the boundary between Hennepin and Anoka counties. The three miles up Marshall present the contrast of the old and new. The Grain Belt Brewery with the turn of the century tower still dominates the skyline. Marshall was once a grand street in its day. There were grand mansions of Civil War days, the horses and carriages, the stepping stones and curbside for ladies when they alighted from their riders. The sawmill near the Plymouth Bridge employed many men and the Siwek Lumber Company manufactured herring tubs. The commerce created by the railroads and lumbering gave the road its character.

## Main Street Businesses

Joseph M. Bochnak, Tailor—1016 Main Street

Herman Burkhardt Plumbing Shop—1018 Main Street

Henry Mengelkoch Hide and Tallow—1013 Main Street

Main Drug Store—1011 Main Street

Mauren & Karow Hardware—1019 Main Street

Otto Forthmiller, Taxidermist—1009 Main Street

Hans Baumeister, Upholsterer—1005 Main Street

St. Chris Mergen Department Store—10th and Main Street

John F. Wallerius, Wholesale Notions—1007 Main Street

Main Street Theater—Broadway and Main Street

## Marshall Street Businesses

3rd and Marshall Robert & Lum Ice Depot

639 Marshall Valentine Wojcik Shoe Repair

704 Marshall Frank Boyda Butcher Shop

721 Marshall T.S. Krawczyk Meats

729 Marshall Lawrence Leitschuh, Manufacturer of wagons and carriages

801 Marshall Town Pump

804 Marshall St. Anthony Pottery

930 Marshall J.P. Engtrom Lumber (Now Grayco)

10th Marshall City Sash and Door (Later Carr Cullen)

1215 Marshall Orth Brewery (Later Grain Belt)

13th and Marshall Minnesota Soap Company

1312 Marshall Kraus & Friedrich Hardware, Gus Kraus operated the hardware and Pete Friedrich was the harness and saddle maker.

1428 Marshall Northeast Feed Mill

2201 Marshall Kampff-Warneke Capitol Store

2610 Marshall Marshall Block (Formerly Betzler, then Flittie)

Herdey Barbershop

*Home of Mary Jane Hannon, whose mother*
*Elizabeth Daly Smith carved the first street sign in*
*Minneapolis with a pitchfork (Washington Avenue).*

*Inside of Hannon home on 927 Marshall Street NE*

*Central Avenue and University in the 1930s. The Cataract Masonic Lodge, now Aveda is on Fourth.*
*A gas station, car lot, the White House and Jim's Coffee Shop were behind the row of duplexes,*
*now the site of the present Union Building, 312 Central. Photo by Joseph Zalusky.*

## When Central Avenue was Called New Boston

Even before the turn of the century, Central Avenue was destined to become the most important business street in Northeast Minneapolis. It was strategically located, being in a direct route from many of the small northern towns to downtown Minneapolis. In the early days, the business district was known as New Boston; after the city had planted elm trees along the streets it was also referred to as Elmwood.

The Soo Line Railroad was one of the earliest and largest employers in Northeast Minneapolis and was in large part responsible for helping to build that part of town into the thriving and hardworking community it has become. On Soo paydays, all the merchants in the Central Avenue community did a thriving business.

At one time there was a fire station on the northwest corner of 24th and Central. Four beautiful and powerful horses drew the fire rigs. Seconds after the gong sounded in the tower, these beautiful horses would go galloping down the street with the fire rigs and everyone on the avenue would stop to watch. Perhaps not many remember the livery stable which was located where the Central Northwestern Bank now stands. The stable, built in 1908, rented out hacks and buggies which were used for funerals, weddings and pleasure riding. As there were few if any cars in those days, the hacks and buggies were the taxis of their day. Before 1914, the livery stable burned one night. The stable was never rebuilt after the fire.

In the 80-plus year history of Central Avenue, which was formerly known as Harrison Street, it would be difficult to recall all the business people who have come and gone during the years but the following are some of them:

Aaron Carlson Millwork on 1505 Central
Northern Pump (FMC) on 920-18th Avenue
Minar Ford on 1710 Central
Olson's Hospital on 1828 Central.
Nels Swanson Fuel & Transfer on 1831 Central, coal, oil, and wood, transfer and ice business.
Elmwood Café on 1846 Central, run by Mrs. Gertrude Stadig
George O. Hart Groceries 1824 Central
Louis Egler Harness business 1848 Central, later became Central Avenue Hardware.
Schmidler Meat Market, 1919 Central, in the early 1900's, they would fill up their horse-drawn wagon with meat and then go door-to-door selling meat right off the wagon.
Misses Johnson's Department Store, 2027 Central, owned by the sisters, Freda, Ellen and Olga Johnson, the largest women's department store on the East Side
Martinsen Brothers Grocery, 2201 Central
Emil Gustafson Jewelers, 2201 Central
Walter and Philip Johnson Real Estate and Insurance, 2215 Central.
Gust Johnson Grocery, 2220 Central
Goodwill Store, first floor, 2220 Central
Edith Larson Millinery Shop, 2222 Central
O.E. Larson Mortuary, 1911 Central Provo Building
Williams Electric Co., 2300 Central
Louis Lietzke Bakery, 2302 Central

*Philip Johnson delivering groceries with "Billy" for Gust Johnson, his grandfather*

*Gust Johnson Grocery Store on 22nd Central Avenue NE. Robert, Harding and Gustav Johnson about 1920*

*Earlier store on Monroe Street owned by the Johnson family*

Arion Theater, 2316 Central

Danielson Drug, 2339 Central

Central State Bank, 2329 Central, they became a national bank and later affiliated Northwest Bank Corporation. They have expanded their building a few times.

Fidelity State Bank, 2400 Block on Central

Billman's Hardware, 2506 Central. His sons Dan, Sam and Paul ran the business for many years, and added the furniture line. Some years later the business was run by the third generation of the Billman family. The store was later sold to Bonhus Hardware.

L.W. Northfield Fuel Business, 2542 Central, later added the transfer Business and building supplies.

Christ Fageros Meat and Groceries, 26th Central

Central Floral, 26th and Central owned by Oscar Magnuson and S.T.Hopper

Anchor Laundry, 2300 Central owned by Ira Towle, later turned into Despatch Laundry.

Carl Wegner Law Office, 24th and Central, above Woolworth's, later moved above Danielson Drug.

Hedean's, 1901 Fillmore Street

Harry Johnson Drugstore, Lowry and Central

P.H. (Perly) Nordland Jewelry, Lowry and Central

Eastside High, 4th and Central

Eastside Precinct. The Second Precinct Police station moved from the 400 block to 19th and Central Avenue in 1933.

Two libraries— the Pillsbury Library is at Central and University. The Carnegie Library at 22nd and Central was built in 1915. But was torn down and rebuilt in 1972.

*Rose Drugs and Medicines, Perfumery and Fancy Goods, 208 Central Avenue, 1881*

*Women chasing chickens at Central Avenue picnic, 1926*

*Enjoying the festivities at the Central Avenue picnic, 1926*

*The first suspension bridge extending from Nicollet Island to East Hennepin at Main Street.*
*The store building on the right once constituted the main shopping center for the town of St. Anthony, about 1872.*

*East Hennepin near Fourth Street dressed up for the holidays, 1928*

# East Hennepin

Many of Northeast's long time residents remember East Hennepin as a mini downtown from the 1930s to the 1960s. Families spent hours getting everything they needed within walking or streetcar distance from home. The streetcar power barns were located on Fourth Street and University. The Central/East Hennepin area was the "crossways" for a lot of different streetcar lines. During the Depression, people were always on the lookout for specials. Most didn't have cars so they'd bring their children's wagons. They'd load up their groceries and haul them back home. During the late 1940s when there were more cars, people would double park and run in to do their shopping. Horn honking was common. The men in their business suits stood three-deep at the local bars on Friday nights, all waiting for their wives to finish their shopping. Friday nights were so crowded, you couldn't even walk on the sidewalks.

From Main to Fifth Street there were stores on both sides. Most of these businesses are long gone from "the avenue." Eklund's Clothing was always an anchor. The main stores were J. C. Penneys and Sears Roebuck. The S. S. Kresge and F. W. Woolworth Dime Stores were located on the same block. Walgreens and National Tea Grocery Company were mainstays.

There were once eleven furniture stores in a six-block radius including Rainville, Cashway, Truman, Midland, Northwestern, Krome's and East Hennepin Furniture. The area became a furniture center and drew customers from as far as the suburbs. They knew that they could get fine furniture at a value. Grocers also did well on East Hennepin. Sidney Spielberg's fa-

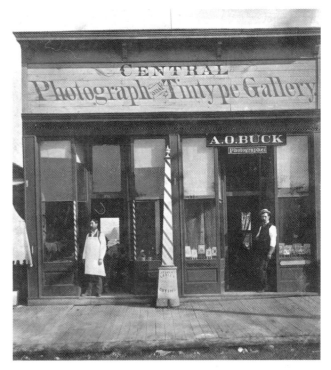

*Central Photography and Tintype Gallery,*
*27 Central Avenue now East Hennepin, 1881*

ther opened a small fruit and vegetable market on Nicollet Island in the early 1900s and eventually moved his business to 223 East Hennepin, calling it Jacob O. Spielberg Groceries. The customer would give the order and the clerk would run back and forth retrieving the items. Then all the groceries on the counter were totaled up on a paper bag. The business was mostly credit and delivery. Other grocers were Red Owl, Crystal Market and Cooper's Market. The meat markets made their own sausage and hung fresh fowl and rabbit in their windows including Blue Ribbon Meats with it's golden bull sign and St. Anthony Meats.

The Ryan Hotel at 219 East Hennepin had 40 single units on the top floor, eight apartments on the second floor and four stores downstairs.

**List of Stores**

Bars/Restaurants—East Hennepin Café, Chris Anos Café, Hurdle Bar, Red E. Bar, Garden Restaurant, and the Huddle Bar run by the Brisky Brothers, Surdyk's and East Side Liquors owned by Kid Cann.
Photography Studios—Liebig , Kierski
Jewelry Stores—Pomerlau, Olsen.

Banks—St. Anthony Falls (First National) and Third Northwestern Bank.
Other stores—Scott Five and Dime, Egekvist Bakery, Columbia Department Store, doctor's office, Roses' Drugstore, later Falls Pharmacy, Brody Drygoods, Western Auto Shop, Sparta's Store, Hum Yum Chinese Laundry, and a barbershop that gave haircuts for 19 cents.

The 1960s saw a flight to the suburbs. J.C. Penneys after almost 40 years of business closed in 1963. Some of the big stores left because they wanted more space and more parking. The business dropped off. This area suffered from the association with flophouses that were

*Third Northwestern Bank at 430 East Hennepin. Crowd gathered on street during Christmas season in 1933*

*F.W. Woolworth at 309 East Hennepin, 1924*

on nearby Nicollet Island. Many of the stores sold out to Riverplace in the 1980s.

## Princess Theater

The Princess on Fourth Street between University and First Avenue featured both vaudeville and movies during it's hey-day in the 1930s and 1940s. Roy Secrest was the last one to run it. They had promotions and jackpots. They raffled off furniture and other things. Saturday matinees cost five cents and Sundays were ten cents "All Quiet on the Western Front" was a popular movie from the 1930s starring Lew Ayres. They also had cowboy movies, serials, cliffhangers and "The Phantom" on Saturdays. The Andrew Sisters won Amateur Night at the Princess Theater in the 1920s.

*East Side Cycle and Repair 105 East Hennepin Avenue in 1956.*
*Elvin, Francis and Roger Rodengen and Ludwig Drellack.*

*Hy's Men's Store at*
*314 East Hennepin in 1948*

*Hotel on 41 East Hennepin in 1922. From 1888–1930 it was the*
*French Hotel, Laliberte. From 1946–1969 it was the Sherwood Hotel*
*that advertised cozy air-conditioned rooms and*
*pleasing rates from $1.25. In 1970 the building was razed.*

*People waiting in line at the Ritz Theater Cooking School in 1952*

## 13th Avenue Businesses

In the early days of St. Anthony, Thirteenth Avenue NE was the beginning of the prairies and was known as "New Boston." This name was applied to all territory outside the congested districts of the East Side. Orth Brewing Company at Marshall and Thirteenth Avenue was one of the first breweries of the city. There was even a streetlight on the corner in front of the brewery. Later the Ritz Theater drew crowds to the Avenue. With two drugstores, one on each end, the PNA and PWE Halls, the neighborhood churches and schools, and some of the finest restaurants in town, it became a natural roadway that extended from the levee on the river where steamboats once docked in the early days of St. Anthony to Jackson Street. The PNA building housed a short-lived National Tea Store which became a drugstore. Joe Magiera owned it in the '30s and was said to be one heckuva guy. He had a great personality and did stuff for the kids. It became Debelak Pharmacy in the 40s and then Rolig's in the '50s. Thirteenth Avenue was also an early boundary of the city in the 1870s. Thirteenth and Second Street was where the streetcar lines crossed and it developed into one of the most popular places where everyone came on the weekdays and weekends. Thirteenth Avenue was repaved in the 1970s. The project included removal of the old streetcar tracks, buried under the asphalt, the planting of 50 trees and replacement with concrete.

Kapala Funeral Home, 230–13th

Sampson's Grocery Store, 300–13th (Now Lucille's Flower Shop(originally next door to Lazarz Liquor, building burned in 1952)

Northeast Meat Market, 302–13th

R.F. Bertch & Company, 325–13th

331 Club Bar (used to be Andy and Vic's), 331–13th

Auguston's Phillip "66", 332–13th

Rabatin's (formerly Northeast Ice Cream Bar), 337–13th

Northeast Radio and TV owned by John Hemak (formerly Standard Glass & Screen, then Dymanyk Electric), 339–13th

Chet Mady's Snackshop, (Earlier this was John Libman's Restaurant, then Walter J.Duggan Fuel and Transfer)

Therres and Sons Gas Station (Conoco), 339–13th

Favorite Café then Grossy Café, 341 13th Avenue

Ritz Beauty Shop, owned by Betty Dormer, 345–13th

Ritz Theater, 345–13th

Ritz Barbershop, 345–13th

Frank Kozlak Insurance (A shoe shop in 1915), 349–13th

Murlowski Hardware, 355–13th

Ludwig Bakery (former owners, Warmings before 1950, then Nicholas Semotiuk (Dr. Thysell upstairs), 355–13th

Lazarz Liquor Store, 358–13th

Doctors and Insurance Building, Dr. Dargay, Dr. L. A. Borowicz

Dentist upstairs, Dr. Walter Krawczyk, Art Shasky Insurance

Rolig Drugstore (Magiera Pharmacy), 359–13th

PNA Hall (Upstairs), 359–13

The Hamburger Shop (Later became the Sandwich Shop), 360–13th

Kurmachek Popcorn Shop with penny candy

Ladies Dresshop, Drycleaners and Drygoods-Marie Harasyn

Home Bakery (called Polski Bakery or Pani Donut Shop)

J. Boike and Sons Grocery and Meat,1235–4th Street

Bolduc Grocery Store, (now across from Malone Auto Works; later became Carpentier's Dairy Store), 13th and 5th Street

Kolodjski's Barbershop, 1306–4th Street

**Shoe Repair Shops**

Wagners, on 13th and 6th Street

Andrew Manshak, 13th and 2nd Street

Kulig Shoe Repair, 13th and 5th Street

*Boike's Barbershop on 13th Avenue and Second Street. Peter Hnath (on left with visor) established the shop in the late 1920s with partner Alf Mork. Peter Hnath, Jr. took over when his father died in 1944. Later owned by Joe Ptak in about 1954. Art Boike bought it in 1958.*

*The Laskowski wedding party in 1942 at the Polish White Eagle Hall on 13th and Second Street NE. Very well known place to have weddings.*

*Some doings at the PNA Hall in the mid-1920s. A lot of familiar faces. Fraternal organization of the Polish National Alliance located on 13th and Fourth Street above Rolig Drug.*

*All Saints Church, 1999*

# 3 Churches on Every Other Corner

In *Heart and Hard Work,* I included eleven churches. This book includes nineteen other churches that do so much to define the people and landscape of Northeast Minneapolis.

## ALL SAINTS CHURCH
*435 Fourth Street NE*

The church of All Saints was organized in September of 1916. The first mass was celebrated in the Church of Our Lady of Mt. Carmel, 627 Main Street NE. They rented the building for $30 a month using it as a temporary church until the All Saints Church and School was under construction. The first parish meeting was held and the assessments were levied for the purchase of property. Each family was assessed $50, single men $30 and single women $15. Two lots on Fifth Street and Fifth Avenue and one corner lot on Fourth Street were purchased. The two lots on Fifth Street were stone quarries. The lot on Fourth Street was where three houses and a large barn in the rear stood. This belonged to former Mayor William H. Eustis of Minneapolis.

The Young Ladies Sodality and the St. Casimir's Society was organized and held their first meeting. The first janitor was Michael Fudali and the organist was Anna Magiera. The first servers were Frank Fudali,

Edward Gable, Frank Narog, Stanley Czyscon, Frank Kowalczyk, and Andrew Wojciak. The first wedding on October 16, was between William Muchlinski and Anne Kocik, first baptism was Julyana Rosalia Smyruk on November 5th and the first funeral was for Anna Bierski on October 9, 1916.

The Sacred Heart Society and the White Eagle, Group IV was organized. During the groundbreaking ceremony, Pastor Francis T. Matz turned the first spade. Work on the building continued through the winter months. Early treasurers were Valentine Miskowiec and Matthew Rybarczyk.

A Sacred Concert was held for the benefit of the new parish. It was assisted by Mr. & Mrs. Robert Gehan of St. Paul, F. J. Gehan, Reverend Missia, and other notable Twin City singers. The building committee was selected. The All Saints Society, the Polish Union and St. Rita Court was organized. Each of these helped to raise money for the church.

The first Forty Hours Devotion of the parish was held in the rented church. The house and the lot at 428-Fifth Street NE was purchased to be used as a convent for school teachers. The cost of the lot, house and large barn was $15,000. On May 19, 1918 the ceremonies for the laying and the blessing of the cornerstone were performed. The sermon in Polish was delivered by Father Matz and in English by Reverend P. Roy. All

*All Saints Sodality, 1935*

neighboring priests and parishes attended. Two large bands furnished music. All the societies from Polish parishes with insignias and banners served as guards of honor. About twenty boys and girls of All Saints made their First Holy Communion at the Church of Our Lady of Mt. Carmel.

All Saints School opened for the first time under the supervision of the Sisters of St. Francis from Sylvania, Ohio. The members of the first faculty were Sisters: M. Evangelist, M. Salome, M. Judith, M. Wilfreda, M. Ethelreda, M. Francesca, and M. Jolenta.

The first mass in the new combination building of the church of All Saints was celebrated on September 29, 1916 by Father Matz. One week later, the first confirmation of five hundred was held. In October of 1916 no masses were held in any Catholic churches in Minneapolis for two weeks by order of the Health Board. They were closed on account of the "Influenza" that was raging in the city. Wydzial Narodowy was organized for the purpose of the newly organized or freed Poland and the poor in Poland. A public parade of people marched to Union Depot to greet those who enlisted to go to fight for Poland. The Red Cross organization unit in All Saints finished all their World War labors and disbanded.

Early members of All Saints were: Frank Bochnak, Casimir Chorzempa, Michael Czyscon, Mrs. Mary Ford, Mrs. Hencinska, Joseph Klempka, A. Kozlowski, John Kozlak, John Kuczek, Mrs. H. Kurpiesz, Stanley Lijewski, Ignatius Liberkowski, Stanley Lijewski, Joseph Matula, Joseph Micek, John Muskala, J. Niznik, Adam Razwicki, Mr. and Mrs. Matthew Rybarczyk, J. Roskowiak, F. Styliski, Paul Sienko, John Sutkowski, F. Stylski, Adam Steczek, Paul Tromniczak, John Teca, Mrs. S. Witkowska, Mrs. C. Zmuda, Matthew Zelazny. Other members were Jacob Murzyn, Dr. E. A. Zaworski, John Rapacz, Henry Kontorowicz, Steve Pelawa, John Sczislowicz, Valentine Miskowicz, Michael Fudali, Frank Gehan, Martha Matz, and Mary Schipritt.

In 1919 the parish bought the house at 435 Fourth Street NE to be used as a temporary parsonage. On May 13th the first public Novena to St. Rita was held. Hundreds of people attended the Novena and the annual Novena was held every year for many years that followed. According to the parish growth, it became necessary to have three masses on Sunday mornings. Reverend W. B. Jensen, Chaplain of the Little Sisters of the Poor acted as the first temporary assistant.

On May 31st a procession of school children was held for the crowning of the Blessed Virgin Mary. Anna Micek and Sister M. Agnes were chosen to represent the school children during this affair. This May procession became an annual event. In 1966 on May 3rd with the May crowning, the Millenium of Poland's Christianity was observed. In June, forty-eight children received their first Holy Communion in the newly built church of All Saints. The first school commencement was held on June 18th. The first graduates were: Francis J. Narog, Edward Gable, Anna Micek, Helen Fudale, Mary Mruz, Mary Julkowski, Mary Witkowski, and Mary Kurpiesz.

The Kolko Polek was organized to take care of the poor, which included sewing and care packages sent for the poor of Poland. A big public parade of Polish people in Minneapolis started from Thirteenth Avenue and marched up Fifth Street NE to Hennepin, then to Nicollet to the Municipal Auditorium. A reunion and reception was held for those who served in World War I from the First Ward in St. Anthony. A meeting was held at the All Saints Hall for all those who belonged to the "Sokol" in Minneapolis.

An essay contest was held in 1920 for all the parochial schools in the St. Paul diocese. All Saints School was awarded first prize to an eighth grade boy, Andrew Holewa and first prize to a sixth grade boy, John Fudali. In June of 1921 the first Parish Picnic was held at Snail Lake.

A cloud burst came in 1923 and the school building was flooded. Three feet of water and the men worked till 3:00 PM Sunday morning to clean up the slush. Pulaski Day was celebrated and the parish picnic was held at Lake Owasso in 1931.

The parish grew so much that the church proved too small to serve its purpose. A campaign began in 1933 to collect money for a new church. Plans were drawn and the firm of Devereaux and Olson Construction was selected as the contractor. Breaking of ground for the new church was in April of 1938. And the cornerstone was blessed in June. The church was built as a result of free offering of the parishioners.

A colorful new church of Spanish motif was completed. Some may wonder why is the face of Charlie McCarthy decorating the church? Charlie, who is ventriloquist Edgar Bergen's famous dummy, is carved alongside Joe Stalin, the Frankenstein monster and several bizarre animals. "They wanted gargoyles like the ones at Notre Dame of Paris," explained Barney Cullen, the stone carver who worked on the faces. "But this was in the 1930s and we didn't have pictures of those gargoyles, so they said, "carve any face you want and have fun." So when you stand in back of the church, it isn't easy to identify all of the characters, but you can spot Charlie because he's wearing his monocle and that sly smile.

Cullen also worked on the Art Deco style decorating the Uptown Theater. He first learned to carve with the traditional mallet and hammer from his father, a stone carver in Ireland.

In 1951 work on the convent was completed, the residence for the Sisters of St. Francis who served as teachers in the school since 1919. In 1961 Father Matz was honored by parishioners, relatives and the public for the celebration of his Golden Jubilee in the priesthood. In 1966 All Saints celebrated their Golden Jubilee. Then in 1968, Father Matz died and Father Edward Szymanski, a former assistant at All Saints came back and became pastor. In 1969 the All Saints School was closed and the students would now attend the Regional School at Holy Cross, a consolidation of most of the Catholic parochial schools in the area. A Father Matz Scholarship Fund was established shortly after.

*Figure at right is likeness of Edgar Bergen's Charlie McCarthy*

Although many folks have moved away, they still come back to the old neighborhood on the weekends. There is a group of parishioners who are at the 8 AM Mass every weekday, rain or shine. According to Father Kovalik, they call themselves "the daily Mass family" and that's what they are to each other, family. With an annual style show and other events, the people of All Saints also participate in a parish wide effort to send medicine and medical supplies to Poland for that nation's relief effort. Many of the All Saints parishioners have Polish ties.

In 1972 Father Henry J. Sledz was assigned as pastor. In 1976 the church's stained glass windows were completely restored and reinforced. Invasion of hornets in the choir loft alerted the congregation to the buckled condition of the windows. Delores Klimek was chosen to head the parish council, one of the first chairwomen in the diocese. Later that year, the school building was repaired. The exterior was stuccoed; new windows, security doors, second floor acoustical ceiling tiles and new lighting were installed.

In November of 1977, flood waters struck again. "Pro" vandals pulled the water sink off the kitchen wall and flooded the entire school building. Lord have mercy! A very tragic Sunday! Six very zealous parishioners mopped and drained for hours, but in vain. The floors buckled and the walls and ceilings cracked. However, fast work on the part of the "Flood Fighters" saved the building from wire shortages and resultant fire.

The festival of 1978 was well attended in the renewed school building. With bingo in the main auditorium, the entire festival was the best ever, spiritually, socially and financially. Bishop Richard Ham was appointed as pastor of All Saints in 1980. Father Henry J. Sledz celebrated his 50 years of ordination in 1983 and a Blessed Virgin Shrine was placed in the church in his honor. He died on June 9, 1991. The present pastor, Reverend George J. Kovalik was installed at All Saints in 1984. In 1991 All Saints celebrated their 75th Anniversary.

*Sacred Heart, 1999*

## SACRED HEART OF JESUS POLISH NATIONAL CHURCH
*2200 Fifth Street NE*

The origin of the church goes back to 1897 when there was chaos in the mining towns of Pennsylvania. After Father Francis Hodur was ordained in 1893, and he became the Vicar of a church in Scranton, Pennsylvania, he organized youth societies, theatrical groups, and began publishing a Polish language paper. He became known as the "People's Priest." His next assignment was Pastor of Holy Trinity in Nanticoke, PA. While at Nanticoke, the people of Scranton came to him for counsel because of problems with the local church hierarchy. They wanted to have "lay involvement in parish life." Father Hodur listened to their requests and pleaded with the local hierarchy for their cause. He was not successful.

In March of 1897, he began to give stronger leadership to the Polish Catholics of Scranton; asking the local Roman leadership to let them maintain the Catholic Tradition, but have lay involvement and hear Mass in Polish. The local Bishop refused to grant these requests and the Polish people asked Father Hodur to help them to construct a building for their own use.

Father Hodur went to Poland and Rome in 1898 to plead the cause of the Polish Catholics. His pleas were denied. He was told the rules of Rome were for all Catholics and those who could not abide by them would be outcasts. Fr. Hodur came back to Scranton, excommunicated from the Roman Church. So he and his faithful followers began to organize the Polish National Catholic Church. And so, the new spirit began in Scranton, and soon it spread to Chicago, Buffalo, and other places in the United States.

In 1900 on Christmas Eve the Mass was sung in Polish, translated from Latin to Polish by Father Hodur. Also, the church newspaper, "Straz" was established. Later, the "Rola Boza" (God's Field) succeeded "Straz." In 1907 on September 29th, Fr. Hodur became Bishop Hodur. He was consecrated by the 'laying of the hands' of three bishops, in Utrecht, Holland, thus establishing Apostolic succession in the church.

In 1914, just ten years after Fr. Hodur was elected Bishop, his work and leadership spread to Minneapolis, and on March 23, 1914, Sacred Heart of Jesus Parish was brought under the jurisdiction of the Polish National Catholic Church and guidance of Bishop Hodur.

In June of 1916, Bishop Hodur made his first visit to Sacred Heart to celebrate the Sacrament of Confirmation and confirmed the first class of youngsters. He was assisted by Fr. Plaga of Chicago; Fr. Bonczak of Milwaukee, and Fr. K.Sokolinski of Minneapolis.

A Ladies Altar Society, a Senior Choir, a Christmas Fair Club, a Youth Club and Sunday School, and a newly organized Men's Club are among the parish's organizations. A medical outreach called "Bridge to Poland" has been going continuously for the last ten years and the church sends supplies, medicine and medical equipment. Between the years of 1916 through 1935 there was a parish school for kindergarten through sixth grades. Sacred Heart Cemetery is located on 54th and Fifth Street in Fridley.

There are several feast days with a nationalistic flavor. During the Christmas season, a Shepherd's Mass, featuring Koledy or singing carols is celebrated. And a traditional Oplatek Dinner is held after Christmas. Easter still involves the tradition of blessing of Easter Baskets filled with food and the sharing of eggs (Swienconka) with horseradish for the pastor and the congregation. Eggs are the symbol for new life and the risen Jesus Christ. Other special celebrations are the Polish Fest, Polka Mass, Mother and Father's Day breakfasts, and Smorgasbord. The traditional dinner served consists of Golabki, Pierogi, Kapusta, Polish Sausage and Makowiec (Poppyseed bread).

**Memories of Hattie Bownik, August 23, 1998**

"I was asked where did my father get the idea to build a church?—When he received the Polish paper called the Kuryjer, there was an article about Scranton,

Pennsylvania and the beautiful Polish church, also the home of our Bishop, the Most Reverend Bishop Francis Hodur and Polish priests. After reading all this good news—no wonder Father wanted to build a church in Minneapolis.

Father Laszkiewicz was our first priest. That was during the time our church was being built. There was a small building across the street from our church the size of a two-car garage. It was very nicely finished, with hardwood floor and on the longer end about six inches of raised platform and a small altar. We were told that other churches were having services there until their church was finished. So on Sundays we had a short mass, sang Serdeczna Matko, blessed ourselves and went home.

The Polish families that were coming here were all looking for a Polish church and school. We had a Catholic Church but not Polish, only Latin. They wanted to be a part of the Mass and be able to pray in Polish with the priest and all the people.

*Note-It was said that Hattie's father, Jan Chmielewski came to church in a horse and buggy.

*St. Clement's, 1999*

# ST. CLEMENT'S
*911–24ᵗʰ Avenue NE*

It was originally a mission; known as New Boston, attended from St.Anthony of Padua and Mass was said for several years in a frame church at Lowry Avenue and Quincy Street NE. It became an independent parish with the arrival of Father R. J. Fitzgerald on April 2, 1902, who erected the present brick and stone trimmed church that measured 113 by 68 feet, at a cost of $45,000. It was dedicated on May 24, 1914 where a solemn mass was celebrated by Father C.F. McGinnis of the College of St.Thomas. Father Fitzgerald was appointed as the first pastor in 1902 and served 39 years. There were about 100 families attending in 1902. He died in 1941 and was succeeded by Father F. T. J. Burns, who renovated the church and pastoral residence. Henry J. Sledz was the assistant pastor at this time. Mrs. J. E Hennessy donated the main altar, in memory of her deceased husband. Other furnishings were also donated. The old church building became the first church of the newly organized parish of St. Hedwig in 1914.

Father Burns served 20 years at St. Clement. During his pastorate a stained glass window was installed in memory of 257 parishioners who died in the service of their country during World War II. Father Lawrence J. Malley was the pastor, serving 1,568 members in 1976 and Father Earl Simonson is the present pastor. Two of the parish organizations are the Holy Name Society and Rosary Guild. Trustees are Robert Howitz and Robert Roff. The first baptism was that of Mary Margaret McConville in April of 1902. The first marriage held at St. Clement's was that of Ira Collins and Mary Dearing in May of 1903. The first communion class for 52 members was in June of 1903 and the first confirmation class of 113 members in September 1909.

*St. Paul's, 1999*

## ST. PAUL'S LUTHERAN
*724 Lowry Avenue NE*

In August of 1890, the Reverend Edward Schroeder was requested by the Mission Board of the former Synod of Iowa to make a house-to-house canvass in a community of Northeast Minneapolis then known as New Boston. After Reverend Schroeder responded and worked in the neighborhood for a month, it became evident that there were quite a few German Lutheran families who were interested in forming a church. Arrangements were made to hold the first service on September 21, 1890 in a vacant store building on Central Avenue. The Reverend was not discouraged when the meeting was not well attended and worked diligently to urge and invite people to come.

After that the attendance increased so much that by the third Sunday, those present passed a unanimous resolution to organize as a Lutheran congregation. Seven men signed the constitution and became the charter members of the new congregation and they named it German Evangelica Lutheran St. Paulus Congregation. The men were Carl Henke, Ferdinand Hunke, Henry Brede, William Rahn, Gustave Plack, Henry Schlafge, and George Getschel.

After awhile it became necessary to change the place of worship to Witt's Hall on Central Avenue. Five pews and six dozen chairs were purchased. Some of the members built a small altar and pulpit. Others made special donations to purchase a rug for the altar space, vestments, communion vessels, an almsbag, and a stove.

Eight months later they decided to erect a church and special committees were appointed to find a location and to solicit for the necessary funds. The contract was set up and in 1891 the building was completed. The church was dedicated on October 18, 1891 and Reverend Edward Schroeder served the growing community until 1892 when he accepted another position. Reverend Peter Pichler of Mazomanie, Wisconsin was called as his successor and served for the next ten years. Quite a few people were out of work during this time and the pastor's salary was very small. In spite of the difficulties the congregation continued to work together. Reverend Paul Briest took over in 1902 and he is credited with organizing the Young People's Society with the help of Conrad

Helms, Lillian Henke, and Clara Kaim. During this time, the house next to the church was purchased for $1,500 and used as a parsonage. In 1904, Reverend Alfred Wilke from Dubuque, Iowa served the church community. Shortly after he arrived, St. Paulus became a self-supporting congregation. Later that year an addition was built onto the church which was used for Sunday School, confirmation classes, German School and all the other church organizations. From that time there was a steady but gradual growth.

Early in 1914, the Ladies Aid Society purchased two lots on Quincy Street, facing 22nd Avenue, for $1,450. These lots were for the future building site of the new church. After awhile these lots were abandoned and sold to Edison High School for an athletic field. When they couldn't find another favorable lot nearby, a decision was made to tear down the old church, sell the parsonage and have it moved, and build the new church on the two lots. A building committee was elected which consisted of F. Plack, Ferdinand Hunke, Fred Law, Paul Lucas, Henry Schonebaum, Albert Krueger, and Frank Backes.

The final plans were made and the actual work began on May 21, 1922 and the new cornerstone was laid. At the dedication of the new church, the choir appeared in vestments for the first time. Valentine Schott was the first choir director and Otto Froelich was the organist and choir director at the time of dedication. Special donations to furnish the new church were made by the following: the Ladies' Aid Society purchased the new pews; the Tabea Society, the bell; the Young People's Society, the new altar; and the Rosacker family, the pulpit. All the stained glass windows were donated by individual members and bear their names. A new parsonage was built on Quincy Street in 1922. And in 1927, the Tabea Society donated a new Bennett pipe organ.

In 1939 the name was changed to St. Paul's Evangelical Lutheran Church. Beginning on May 1, 1943 the German services were limited to the second and fourth Sundays of the month. And in 1945 the congregation voted to discontinue the German services altogether. Once again in 1949 time was spent looking for a new church site. But in 1950, it was voted to add a new wing on the existing church. The church was paid in full and the mortgage was burned in 1955.

In 1953 Virginia Beehler was hired as a parish worker. Norma Turnquist Saefke was hired as full-time secretary in 1958, and Gloria Kral took over as organist in 1960. Lily Olin became full-time secretary in 1961, and Don Hall joined the staff as custodian. Mr. Hall continued his dedicated service for 29 years. Blaine Thrasher was hired as a parish worker in 1977.

In 1956 the church council started a scholarship for congregation members interested in the ministry. Over the years, the following members have become ministers: Harvey Egler, William Schonebaum, James Vadis, Albert J. Guetzlaff, and Meredith Musaus. Harold Oelschlager became assistant minister in 1956 and the church also joined the Minneapolis Lutheran Church Council. In the following year a motion was passed to have two services and Reverend Wilke retired after 53 years. Reverend Albert Guetzlaff became the new pastor.

In 1958 Reverend Guetzlaff and Virginia Beehler started a newsletter. It was also decided to have communion registration cards to keep accurate accounts of communicants. Before this communicants would just call ahead if they wanted to take communion. A meeting was held in 1960 with the president of the Minnesota District Council to discuss declining membership at St. Paul's, due to changing times and internal dissension. The decision of an area merger and parish reorganization was discussed and a poll was taken in 1963. But the congregation decided that St. Paul's should retain its current status. Church maintenance was made that year including tuck-pointing, painting, and installation of gutters.

In 1965, St. Paul's held a 75th anniversary celebration where Reverend Harold Oelschlager and Reverend Alfred Wilke preached. A potluck lunch followed the services with a reunion of former communicants attending. Reverend Guetzlaff tendered his resignation in 1969 and John Quello was ordained and became full-time pastor in 1971. During that same year railings were installed on the Lowry Avenue steps and on the Quincy Street side, and kneeling pads were added to the communion rail. Also the basement was remodeled. Members of the congregation paid for all of the improvements. Curtis Thompson, a student pastor was installed as pastor when Reverend Quello was called to Rochester, Minnesota. Then in 1975, Meg Habegger served as an intern and worked full-time the following year while attending classes at the seminary. Mike and Bonnie Ensrude were hired as student assistants for a year.

"Bible Folk," a musical performed by St. Paul's choir, was held in several locations during 1978. There were performances at Prospect Park, Ebenezer Society, Gustavus Adolphus Church, and in Paynesville, Faribault and Fergus Falls. Many changes-occurred in 1979.

During the period of 1975 through 1981 the church kitchen and the duplex at 714 Lowry were remodeled.

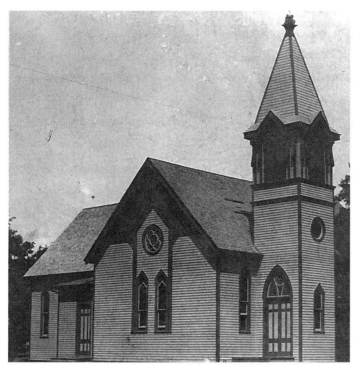
*Trinity 1893*

## TRINITY UNITED METHODIST
*2511 Taylor Street NE*

The Board of Trustees of the Taylor Street Church met at the residence of G. A. Frazer, 2223 Buchanan on May 16, 1883. The trustees were George Frazer, John D.Tolman, Daniel W. Tomkins, James W. George, Andrew Nelson, John D. Blake and John Sterling. Before that the Sunday school and church services were held in a store building at 2517 Harrison Street (now Central Avenue).

When the store was being used, the church meetings were held in people's homes until the church was established. The cost of the first church was $1200 and Reverend J. A. Wright was the first pastor. During the first year the church had 24 members and five probationers.

In 1893, there were four Sunday School rooms added to the original church and the name was changed to Trinity Methodist Episcopal Church. A new church was built in 1907 at a cost of $16,645 and the old church, which originally faced Taylor Street, was incorporated into the new building. The old church can be easily recognized by the rounded lead window on the Lowry Avenue side. In 1929, plans were made to enlarge the church. The plans set forth were as follows: leveling of the auditorium floor, raising the pulpit and organ, rearranging of the kitchen, putting cement floor in the new dining room, installing a new heating plant. The room could seat 500 people and by the use of sliding doors, Sunday School rooms could be made available on short notice. A Ways and Means Committee, consisting of V. E. Mikkelson, Doctor C. O. Cosman, F. L. Palmer, W. H. Smith and Mrs. E. L. Snyder was established. Nelllie B. Rutherford was elected as building fund treasurer. Prescott School was secured for services during the remodeling period.

In 1938 Trinity celebrated its 55th anniversary and also during this time a city-wide Methodist Mass Meeting was held to commemorate the 200th anniversary of John Wesley's heart warming Aldersgate experience and the National Witnessing Mission. During the 1930s Trinity held many social events that included plays, choir concerts, orchestra concerts and dinners. The church membership numbered 1,095 in 1938.

In the 1940s "Pennies for Bricks" began as a campaign to build a new education building and funds were started to build a new parsonage. Trinity had to be concerned about War Damage Insurance because the church was used for meetings for the neighborhood Air Raid Wardens. The church experienced a loss of membership to war service and there was a problem of fuel rationing. The women of the church made surgical dressings for the Red Cross.

In 1944, Troop 153, the Boy Scouts of America met every Monday in the basement of the church, according to Scoutmaster, Paul Guernsey who had a group of thirty scouts. Throughout the years, Girl Scouts, Campfire Girls, Cub Scouts and Boy Scouts have been an important activity in the church.

During the Korean War in the 1950s a number of Trinity men were in the service. It was a decade when church membership was increasing nationwide. At Trinity the membership remained stable. Groups in the church during this period were: 20–40 Club, Mr. and Mrs., Homebuilders, College-Career, TwoSomes, Men's Club, Ladies & Men's Bible Class and Intermediate, Senior and Post-Hi youth fellowship groups. The Wesleyan Service Guild was a vital group within the Women's Society of Christian Service. Sunday School membership was up with weekday religious classes. The Sanctuary Adult Choir numbered about 40 members and the Wesley Youth Choir averaged 15. There was also a sizable Cherub Choir, which sang monthly during worship service.

On Easter Sunday in 1953 the tower carillon bells and music were heard for the first time. Since then Trinity has come to be known as the "Church of the Tower Chimes." Then in 1955, sixteen gold robes were purchased for the Wesley Choir and a church library was established. In 1958 the focus was on Trinity's Diamond Anniversary and in May, Bishop D. Stanley Coors preached, followed by a dinner and a program.

During the decade of the 1960's and the Vietnam War, Trinity and the nation saw a declining church membership. As the demography of the city changed so did the congregation of Trinity. People began having fewer children and many young families moved to the suburbs. In 1965 the church school membership had declined 23% and church attendance 37%. An educational building was completed and classes started in 1965. In 1968 the Evangelical United Brethren and the Methodist denominations merged to become United Methodists.

In the early seventies, Trinity participated in a denominational emphasis called "Key 73" with the theme, "Calling Our Continent to Christ." And in 1975 they joined with Grace and Faith United Methodist churches in the sponsorship of a Vietnamese family. The project was called, " Northeast Methodist Project Samaritan," and they welcomed the Huan family. Later they sponsored another family who were refugees from Vietnam. Also during renovation of the education building a NEED Thrift Shop was added.

In August of 1980 Trinity became the second church in the Minnesota Conference to start a local edition of the *United Methodist Reporter,* a newsletter that comes into each home every week. The membership at the end of 1982 numbered 317.

In 1959, Trinity participated in a Convocation on Evangelism, seeking to win new members. During the 1960s, the commission on membership and evangelism became an active group. The year 1974 saw the first Lay Witness Mission and the initiation of an active visitation program. A tape ministry was started, with Sunday worship services being taken to shut-ins and to the Walker members.

Trinity has many missions. The Northeast Senior Citizens Resource Center is a service located at 13th and Monroe Street and provides housing, financial, home chore needs and volunteer drivers for health ap-

*Kitchen crew in the 1940s*

pointments. Devotional services are held in the senior citizen's highrises. The Northeast Dinner Bell provides balanced meals to shut-ins or people not able to prepare meals for themselves. Trinity is the home base for this operation. Meals are heated in the education building and delivered each weekday by volunteer drivers from the participating Northeast churches. They also participate in the Annual Christmas Card Project, UNICEF, the Nave Technical Institute in U.P., Indiana, and the Red Bird Mission in Beverly, Kentucky.

The Epsworth League was organized in 1892. The first officers of the League were L. M. Sage, F. I. Palmer, Iola Runyon, Charles W. Gray, Lottie Gray, Lena Haserick and Alma Smiley. Besides looking after the spiritual uplift of its young members, the League helped with raising money for the church and some of the young folks even helped to do janitor work and other tasks. In 1940, when the merger of the Methodist Church North and South took place, the name was changed and today we have the Methodist Youth Fellowship.

The Epsworth League at one time owned a cottage at Groveland. Today they have Camp Kingswood, a camp for youth of the Methodist Church. The goals for the senior high group in 1971 included service projects and promotion of youth-adult dialogue. Some of their activities include making of banners for the sanctuary, a spring retreat at Camp Kingswood and planning Easter Sunrise Service and serving Easter breakfast to the congregation.

Some very important early members were Edith Shufelt and Abby Sturtevant who went to China as missionaries in 1921. Reverend David Brooks was the pioneer Methodist preacher who organized the Sunday School in 1882. Their first meetings were in private homes. Some early teachers were John Vandermyde, Margaret Dingman, LoElla Briggs, Grandma Brede, and Mary Lou Anderson.

A Ladies Aid was organized at the home of Mrs. J. W. George in 1883. The officers at this time were Mrs. Frazer, Lizzie George, and Clara Tompkins. All members were to pay 25 cents dues and 10 cents each meeting. Meetings were held the second and fourth Wednesday of each month at the member's homes according to the alphabet. There were ten members at this first meeting.

The women sponsored an Ice Cream and Strawberry Festival and cleared the sum of $20.01. At one of their meetings they decided to buy carpeting for the church platform at a cost of $25.15. Since they only had $23.16 in the treasury, one of the good ladies loaned them the balance of $1.99. Mrs. Nellie Rutherford served as treasurer for 46 years. In 1940, the Women's Foreign Missionary Society and the Ladies' Aid merged into ones group called the Women's Society of Christian Service and later became United Methodist Women. They have been a strong force giving prayer, service and money contributions to the church. During World War II four women served on projects on the home field, Myrtle McQueen, Jeanne Nielsen, Lois Pestello and Beverly Troax.

In May of 1973, the theme of the spring luncheon was "Weddings Remembered," with some women still able to wear their own gowns and some finding it necessary to have a slimmer daughter model theirs. In 1979 the UMW initiated a "Bean Feed and Bake Sale" in the summer and an "Old Fashioned Chicken Dinner" with the bazaar and bake sale in the fall. More recent events have been the salad luncheon, bowling banquet, bazaar/bake sale, fruitcake sale and Harvest Dinner. They also are responsible for the United Methodist Men's dinners, Father and Son Banquet, coffee time after morning worship and serving for funerals and weddings.

Little can be found of the recorded history of Trinity Men's Club prior to World War II. A program for the Father and Son Banquet of 1930 was the earliest document discovered. At that time the officers were: A. O. Olson, Rev. L. A. Wilsey, and E. L. Snyder. In the sixties, open-pit barbecues in the church parking lot were a popular event. In recent years they have been replaced by spring ice cream socials. They have sponsored boy's interchurch athletic programs, men's bowling teams in the Northeast Church League, Boy Scout troops and an annual father-son banquet, the 59th one in 1983. They have contributed financially to various projects, such as Christmas trees for the church, Christmas gifts to Trinity's staff, sponsored members to the national UMM Congress at Purdue, all church picnics, Pastor's Emergency Aid Fund, and missionary and charitable groups, both local and foreign. They have been and continue to be a vital part of the life of the church. Their motto is, "Be ye doers of the word and not hearers only."

The needlepoint chrismons, inserted in the altar railing, were designed and made by some members of the UMW and dedicated in 1978. Vigue Sanford gave a set of figures for a creche in the late '60s and Frank Parsons made a stable of a size to match them. This lovely creche is used during each Advent season in the front corner of the sanctuary under the Memorial Niche. The "Hanging of the Greens" service is held early in the Advent Season. The paraments were made by some of the churchwomen in 1965.

*Salem Tabernacle on 18½ Central Avenue NE about 1960*

## SALEM COVENANT CHURCH
*2655 Fifth Street NW*

In Sweden beginning in the 1850s, small groups of Lutherans began meeting in homes for the reading of the Bible and enlightenment. Many lay people were dissatisfied with the established church because of its oppressive structures, the reasoning of many of its clergy, and the waning of spiritual life. This was the beginning of a folk movement that changed Swedish society, not only in giving birth to foreign mission societies but also in giving rise to the labor movement and temperance societies.

The high point of Swedish immigration came in 1887, when 46,252 Swedes left home for the "Promised Land." They were frontier people seeking a better economic life while also looking for a place of opportunity where they could exercise values of work, home and in many cases—church with a greater sense of freedom. Most of them owned no property and were from remote rural areas or expanding urban centers. Minnesota was a lot like home, both in climate and in rolling countryside marked with lakes, streams and rivers. The earliest beginnings of Salem Covenant Church in Northeast Minneapolis are in the Nils Olsson home on 17th Avenue and Monroe Street when on a winter evening in 1881, a group of seven people met for a "conventicle." They were nicknamed lasare, or readers. Those present were N. G. Johnson, Mr. and Mrs. Fran Larson, A. G. Erickson, John L. Blomquist, John Jungberg, and Mrs. Nils Olsson. They were seeking Christian fellowship through prayer, singing, reading the Bible, and examining a sermon by Luther and articles from a publication of the new movement, the Pietisten. Pastor Emil Gustaf Tornquist from the only Swedish Mission Church in Minneapolis (now First Covenant) came to speak the Word and lend encouragement.

From the beginning the Mission Friends who lived in Northeast Minneapolis received the blessing of the "mother church" across the river. The reason for the Monroe Street meeting was practicality as much as knowledge and enlightenment. The trek across the river to what was later known as the Swedish Tabernacle was a long distance by foot, especially in bad weather. Even when the one-horse "bob-tail" streetcar came to Northeast a year later, the nearly one-hour trip and the nickel ride became a hardship in terms of both time and money in going to Sunday morning and evening services.

After the death of Pastor Tornquist in the spring of 1882, a young preacher, Eric August Skogsberg was called to become pastor of the Swedish Mission Church. He was rather frail and short in stature, but he preached with a fiery passion. He also designed the Swedish Tabernacle. A so-called religious entrepreneur, he organized just about everything, including a Swedish newspaper and a school, which later became North Park College (now in Chicago).

Efforts among the Northeast mission friends to join together with Swedish Baptists and Methodists succeeded for a while but then failed, due largely to differences in belief and practice. A year after Skogsberg's arrival, the church on the other side of the river floated a loan for the Mission Friends to build their own place of worship at 17th Avenue and Jefferson Street. It would soon be known as "the church next to the casket factory." They purchased one lot for $500. An unknown benefactor donated the second lot. The church was constructed two and a half years before the congregation was officially organized.

The Mission Friends of Northeast organized their first meeting on December 17, 1888. On that day they named their church Swedish Evangelical Mission Church of Northeast Minneapolis and thirteen people signed the charter. They were John L. Blomqvist, Adolf Ekstam, A. Gust Ericksson, Erick Ericksson, Per Hagqvist, John Hokansson, Nils Gustaf Johnsson, John Jungberg, Karl Johan Karlsson, Ludwig Lindberg, Andrew Perman, Charles L. Pearson, and John Olsson.

With the help of volunteer laborers from the community, the 36x48 feet building was completed at a cost of $1200. The first sermon was preached by a pioneer pastor, August Bryngelson in the spring of 1886 and a week later the church was dedicated. The church was described as "simple and plain" but a colorful border along the ceiling gave a touch of beauty or perhaps a wistful memory of beautiful old churches left behind in the old country. There were still dirt streets during this time and wooden sidewalks. In the backyard of the church was a pump for the water supply, and the necessary outhouse.

In 1896 and 1900 there were special meetings held to discuss the problem of slow but steady growth, both

*Ornate sanctuary and choir loft inside Central Avenue Tabernacle, 1963*

in membership and in ministry to children. The options were to move the existing structure and put a basement under it, or build a new meeting house. A vote was taken and most were in favor of building a new church. Two lots on 18½ Avenue and Central were purchased for $1500, with an existing house on the property that sold for $365. The cost of the building was $16,784.79 and the goal of the congregation was to dedicate the new building without debt.

The tabernacle was described as "plain and roomy" and the final plans were a brick building that could accommodate 900 people. It was patterned after the popular design of churches that were common in Sweden representing "The Skogsbergh Influence." Pastor Skosbergh recalled for the builder the type of structure he remembered from Sweden. Built with wide sweeping balconies, which almost surrounded the pulpit on either side, the massive organ pipes were directly behind. An unusual selection of opera seats was a debatable feature. The kids enjoyed the wire rack for the men's hats located just under the seat. Aaron Carlson was very instrumental in directing the interior décor of the sanctuary. All of the mahogany, the delicately carved spindles in the railings surrounding the balconies and the choir seating area, the window assemblies, and many other beautiful features were works of art. Many memories and stories still cluster around the choir loft surrounding the preacher. Many remember the long stairway up to the sanctuary and the Sunday school room called the "beehive."

Then in the 1960s the choice had to be made whether to repair the Central Avenue Tabernacle or build a new church elsewhere. The 1960s were a time of change. The congregation had not grown the way they expected and the surrounding neighborhood was becoming more transient. Many church members were moving to the suburbs and the space and parking had become a problem.

In 1964 the church purchased nine acres west of Silver Lake Road in New Brighton. Although they were planning to move, there still was some uncertainty. In June of 1967 a severe storm damaged the steeple. The steeple was twisted by the wind and some of the bricks loosened and came crashing down to the sidewalk. This was perceived as a message. [Does it take falling bricks to move us?]

Ground was broken for the new church in New Brighton that could seat 504 with a 47-person choir loft, offices and education facilities at a cost of $146,000. The Minneapolis Housing and Redevelopment Authority bought the Central Avenue building and used the land for the Parker Skyview high-rise. Even though the church building is in the suburbs they are still very much an urban church. According to Pastor Wiberg, it's evident that the church maintains very close ties to Northeast.

In the 1920s the church's transition from Swedish services to English was very traumatic. A conflict arose largely among the older members, who wanted to keep the Swedish language, and younger members who knew it would be difficult to attract new members. The community was rapidly becoming Americanized. The older members were afraid if they gave in to English, they might forget their roots.

The first step of the transition was to use English on alternating Sunday mornings and the evening services. Then in 1938 the congregation voted to have all Sunday morning services conducted in English. They conducted Swedish services in the lower auditorium and for festivals for several years.

Julotta was an early Christmas morning service in the church, about 5:00 or 6:00 AM, brought over from Sweden. It was the highlight of the church calendar, a time of rejoicing at the celebration of the birth of Christ. Fewer of the modern generation have kept this observance. Good memories remain of the Swedish language and the hymns with significant wording in the melodic style. Today there are a few churches in the Twin Cities who still observe this memorable service.

Salem has conducted Smorgasbord, which is a spread of delicious food and entertainment even before the move to New Brighton. It was somewhat resurrected in the church on Central Avenue in the 1950s and picked up again in the early years of the 1970s in New Brighton. This event, always held on the first Saturday of December has proven very popular and historical. As many as 1500 people have been served delicious Swedish Sausage (Potato Korv), meatballs, brown beans (Bruna Bunner), fruit soup (Fruit Suppa), rice pudding, limpa, with a few American touches such as Jell-O salads, cottage cheese, and potato salad. The Salem String Band usually provides entertainment. It consistently is an all-male ensemble, singing country gospel melodies. Another performance appearing in the event is the Swedish Singers who are supplemented usually by a Children's Choir. These entertainers are typically dressed in Swedish costumes.

## ST. MICHAEL'S UKRAINIAN ORTHODOX
*505 Fourth Street NE*

*St. Michael's, 1999*

In 1956, the formation of the Uniate Church was attempting to denationalize the Ukrainian people. Poland in agreement with the Vatican, established the Uniate branch of the Catholic Church. Their hope was to catholicize the entire Ukrainian nation. The Greek Catholic church was progressively Latinized with the neglect of the cultural and national traditions, which created much dissatisfaction among the people.

The early immigration to Minnesota came in the late 1870s from Western Ukraine, bringing with it the Uniate faith. Although the Ruthenian Catholic Church Parish was established in Minneapolis, it was continued in Latin, which deprived the people of their own Ukrainian name. This led to protests and the search for a solution. The majority of families of the parish represented all Ukrainian ethnic territories from the Carpathian Mountains to the Caspian Sea.

By 1923 there was a sizable group of Ukrainians living in the Twin Cities. To help them to adjust to conditions of their new home and to meet their need for a social life, a Ukrainian National Home was established. The first meeting was held on August 6, 1925 in regards to their spiritual needs and guidance. This came following an inspirational visit by the Most Reverend Archbishop John Theodorovich.

This group decided to form St. Michael's Ukrainian Orthodox Church and the first officers were elected. Among them were Sylvester Rychley, Mykola Grubryn, John Romanchuk, and William Melnik. On September 6th of the same year, the first service was

*St. Michael's young peoples' choir in 1927*

held in St. George Greek Orthodox Church in Southeast Minneapolis and conducted by Reverend Michael Zaparyniuk. Two weeks later they purchased a lot and contractors for the building were selected and the church became a reality. The first services were held on Easter Sunday, April 25, 1926, although the church was unfinished.

Through the activities of various groups a deeper appreciation of the rich cultural heritage of the people had reawakened pride in Ukrainian national history. It was decided in 1929 to share this culture with the general public. Accordingly, the choral group under the leadership of its pastor made many successful appearances in various churches and private homes. The richly embroidered national costume of the choristers, the characteristic beauty of the Ukrainian songs, and the quality of voices charmed the American public. Under the baton of the Reverend Kornilius Kirstiuk the group continued to make public appearances. The inspired direction of the Very Reverend Paul Korsunivsky brought the music of the Ukrainian National Chorus of the Twin Cities to greater public acclaim.

Ukrainians have always encouraged their youth to greater achievements and leadership, providing for this suitable facilities and opportunities to learn language, national crafts, dances and music. The spirited folk dancing with intricate steps is fascinating and is a public attraction. The life of the parish is dynamic and varied. Both the youth and adults spend two or three evenings a week at various activities. One evening is devoted to folk dancing, another for choir rehearsal, and on Saturdays a half-day is given to study and language, Ukrainian history, culture and traditions, while Saturday and Sunday evenings are usually devoted to some concert program, public lectures or occasional movies.

A school of the Ukrainian Folk Ballet was organized in the fall of 1933, under the general direction of Palletmaster Vasil Avramenko. Roman Fenchynsky, an instructor of the Avramenko National School, conducted the classes, which attracted the young people of the parish, provided an outlet for their energy and stimulated appreciation for the folklore of their people. The Ukrainian Folk Ballet of the Twin Cities has attracted a great deal of attention and admiration of the public throughout the state.

The debut of the Ukrainian Folk Ballet took place March 4, 1934, in the Shubert Theater in Minneapolis. Since then they have presented 400 public performances before a total audience of over 400,000 people.

St. Michael's Parish is truly a unique and beautiful little church, built and decorated according to the Ukrainian style, and maintains quite a few very interesting traditions. The first embroideries hand made by Grandmother Anna Dymanyk, are still frequently used in the church. It has a very excellent A Cappella church choir. The lower level under the church was the center of its unbelievably complete cultural program for its youth and adults, men and women. Now it has a satisfactory separate cultural building with an excellently furnished kitchen and an adequately furnished recreation hall for various church and community activities.

Various activities of members of the parish include a continuous series of programs in public libraries, the Art Institute, the University of Minnesota, the State Fair, in large department stores and the Festival of Nations. These exhibits feature Ukrainian handiwork, woodwork, embroidery and Easter eggs called pysanky. Many serve Ukrainian foods.

Few remember that seventy-three years ago, in this same spot, stood an ice storage house filled with blocks of ice, carved out of nearby lakes and rivers, packed in sawdust to preserve the easily melting ice for summer time use. Now here stands this "House of God" kept sacred by the devotion of its members.

In the Ukrainian church the service of a cantor—diak—is essential. In the past this service was performed by Sylvester Rychley, Onufrey Kuzyk, Dr. Mykola Haydak and now by Mrs. Tatianna Jankovsky.

Some of the church's special organizations are the Ukrainian Folk Ballet, A Capella Choir, Organization for Rebirth of Ukraine, Senior and Junior Orthodox League, Men's Club, Sunday School Classes and Ukrainian Orthodox School.

The sisterhood of St. Michael's is a vital and important organization. From its earliest inception to the present day, the Sisterhood has been the backbone of all church activities. Maria Procai and Mary (Kost) Rychley had been instrumental in organizing a Sisterhood in Minneapolis but it was in 1923 that the nucleus was formed for St. Michael's Sisterhood. This group, which met at the Germain Hall at 949 Main

Street Northeast, sponsored concerts, bazaars, dinners, performed at plays—anything to raise money for the newly planned church to be built. Although the name has changed several times, the women of the parish still continue to be an unfailing source of strength in their faithful and devoted work. The Sisterhood is presently known as St. Olga Sisterhood of St. Michael's Ukrainian Orthodox Church.

At the end of World War II, when the Allied Armies liberated millions of displaced persons in Western Europe, members of the parish began to receive heartbreaking letters from Ukrainians stranded in displaced person camps and pleading for help. St. Michael's parish responded wholeheartedly to these pleas from their kinsmen who could not return to their homeland for fear of being persecuted because of their religious and democratic beliefs, opposing Communist ideology. Return to their homeland certainly meant death or exile to Siberia to hard labor in concentration camps.

As soon as these contacts had been established, St. Michael's established a relief committee. From 1945 to 1948 they sent packages of food, clothing and accessories to various individuals in displaced person camps. About $3,000 was raised for these packages and over 624 packages were sent, plus nine huge boxes of clothing. In addition to the church committee, more than 600 packages were sent privately to Europe in order to relieve the needs of the unfortunate Ukrainian kinsmen.

Later, when the Federal law was passed to admit 205,000 displaced persons into the United States, the parish responded wholeheartedly to provide assurance for housing and placement. They welcomed the new arrivals, finding immediate housing and work, providing clothing and cash as needed. Private cars were pressed into service for moving large luggage, numerous details were attended to such as health problems, soliciting and creating harmonious relations between sponsors and newcomers, and employers with employees. Nearly 5,000 Ukrainian displaced persons have been resettled in Minnesota.

*Original St. Hedwig's destroyed by fire, 1919*

## CHURCH OF ST. HEDWIG
*129–29<sup>th</sup> Avenue NE*

The roots of St. Hedwig trace back to its mother church of Holy Cross, which started in 1886. Holy Cross was the original Polish Catholic Church in Minneapolis, which began three years after the establishment of the first Polish parish in the United States of San Antonio, Texas. The seed was planted when the influx of new members into Holy Cross grew steadily in proportion and created problems. In 1912, the immigration of Polish families to Minneapolis reached its peak and began to overflow their capacity causing serious overcrowding in the parish school. Also the people who lived north of Lowry Avenue and into Columbia Heights had problems attending Polish masses at Holy Cross and the children had problems getting to Polish School especially in the winter. The idea began under the direction of Reverend Henry Jazdzewski who was pastor of Holy Cross. Meetings for organizing a new parish were held among parishioners who lived in the north end of the First Ward of the city. Many Catholic families settled in this residential peninsula bounded by lumberyards, sawmills, flour-mills, and by the Mississippi River on the west. A group of people met at the home of Andrzej Majka on 2723 Grand St. NE. They chose a council and Izydor Job was chosen to go to Father Jazdzewski and tell him about the plans.

With the consent of Archbishop John Ireland, the organizers purchased ten lots in the North Town Addition block six for the sum of twelve hundred dollars. On March 6, 1914 the church was incorporated and Reverend Ambrose Kryjewski, Leon Jedlinski, and Izodor Job signed the articles. For the forty-eight families that comprised the nucleus of the newly formed parish, the first mass was offered in the Holy Cross school hall on Sunday, September 14, 1914. But within a month, St. Hedwig parishioners began the plan for a church building. They collected money going from house to house and they organized dance parties. Because of the financial problems of the times, economy was needed. A frame building formerly occupied by St. Clement Catholic Church at Quincy Street and Lowry Avenue was purchased for $500 and moved to the new parish property. And on Christmas Day, 1914 the first parish Mass was offered.

Some of the founding families were Izydor Job, Leon Jedlinski, Jan Sledz, Franciszek Zontek, Wojciech Grabski, Eugenia Hofstede, John Rosemeyer, Mary Cox, Michal Frankowski, Jan Wisnewski, Stanislaw Cison, Tomasz Kudik, Jan Koniar, Blazej Zawislak, Jakub Swiatek, Piotr Zawislak, Teresa Swiatek, Maryanna Kubiak, Anna Swiatek, Jozefa Zawislak, Leonora Spiczka, Karolina Cison, Kanty Mantuszczak, Marcin Trymucha, Jozef Duda, Jozef Walus, Wojack, Bialka, Krznarich, Kaczor, Dziedzic, Murlowski and Miskowiec families.

A few months later they welcomed Father Maximilian Klesmit as the first appointed pastor on May 27, 1915. A rented house served as lodging for the pastor through the first years until 1918 when the parish built a comfortable rectory adjoining the church. But in July of 1919 tragedy struck and a fire destroyed the greater part of the church. For several months after the disaster the parishioners gathered for mass within the charred ruins of their first church. Within six months of the fire the present church-school building was erected and once again on Dec.25, 1919 the first mass in the new church was celebrated.

It was in this new church building that St. Hedwig Parochial School opened in 1920. The Sisters of St. Francis of Sylvania, Ohio that had been coming weekly from Holy Cross to teach catechism became the school staff. Later in 1925 a parish convent was built for the Franciscan Sisters. At the time of their jubilee anniversary there were five sisters with an enrollment of one hundred and eighteen pupils. There were a total of 160 families in 1964. Lack of space became an increasing problem and they were in need of a bigger church and parish hall.

*Graduation class of St. Hedwig's grade school, 1925. Stanley Kuduk, John Zurek, Louis Kramascz, Joseph Pendzimas. William Job, Catherine Kubik, Mary Eskierka, Josephine Pierog, Manuel Sczech. Margaret Frenzel, Victoria Koniar, Sister M. Estella, Bernice Zawislak, and Eugenia Wryk.*

The Rosary Society is the oldest organization in St. Hedwig Parish, in existence since 1931. Some of the other important organizations are the Young Ladies Sodality of Our Lady, the Sacred Heart Society for Young Boys, the Usher's Club, the Good Will and Holy Name Society. These groups helped to support the church with bake sales, socials, parish luncheons, altar linen, funeral luncheons, and the Summer Bazaar and Summer Picnic. Other groups throughout the years were the St. Hedwig's Alumni Club, P.T.A. Association, Baseball Club, Girls Volleyball Club of St. Hedwig's, Altar Boys and ChoirGirls.

In 1920 a permanent church-school building was erected and the foundation of a Catholic education began. The elementary school with grades one through eight was organized with the help of the Sisters of St. Francis of Sylvania, Ohio. Sister Estella, Sister Ethelreda and Sister Gertrude became the first teachers in the new parochial school. Besides their school duties they were responsible for the care of the sanctuary, the altar linens, the liturgical needs including the supervision of the altar boys, the organ music and the children's choir. The school was closed in 1969.

Father Klesmitt retired in 1968 and Father Frank Kittock took over as pastor. Later Father Ted Guminga became pastor and although he is retired he still serves mass and resides at St. Hedwig's. The church was added onto in 1989. A yearly carnival is held the first week of June, to raise funds for the church. This is a favorite event for former church members to drop by. Pierogi sales are held twice a year where the ladies from the parish get together to make pierogi. The Rosary Society holds an annual craft sale and also takes care of parish funerals.

Some of the traditions that started many years ago were the Santa Visit, where Santa Claus made a visit at the annual Christmas party. All of the kids from the neighborhood were invited and received a sack full of ribbon candy and nuts. Sometimes a toy was in the bag too. This became a favorite event. During Christmas time the St. Hedwig's Girl's Choir went caroling from house to house. They sang a combination of American and Polish Christmas carols and were rewarded with food and drink, usually hot chocolate and candy or Christmas cookies.

Forty Hours Devotion is a religious practice observed in many Catholic Parishes both in Poland and America. The origin of this deep devotion is rooted in the rites of Holy Week. According to St. Augustine, "From the moment of Christ's death to the morning of His Resurrection it is forty hours." This was the practice of the Polish Catholics, although it was not officially introduced into the Roman Catholic Church. Instead, this Devotion which grew out of this ancient forty-hour's wake, was separated from its original place and officially observed at other times of the year.

Midnight Mass and the blessing of Oplatki are also favorite Polish Christmas traditions. One of the most important rituals observed in Polish-American homes is the preparation of the "Swieconka." In former times, the parish priest would visit the homes of the faithful on Holy Saturday to bless specially prepared Easter foods. Today a large wicker basket is filled with symbolic Easterfare that has been decreed by tradition for centuries. The foods included in the basket are: smoked fresh sausage (kielbasa), ham (synka), colored eggs (pisanki and kraszanki), horseradish (chrzan), breads (chleb and babka), a lamb of butter or sugar (baranek), salt (sol), and pepper (pieprz). Some include wine, vinegar, bacon, cheese, sweet Easter cheese, fruit, and a variety of pastries including cheesecake, poppyseed rolls and layered cakes. The basket itself is decorated with pussy willows, greenery, flowers, colored ribbons and is covered with a white linen embroidered cloth, then taken to church to be blessed on Holy Saturday afternoon. As the priest enters the sanctuary, everyone uncovers his basket, secretly peeking at each other's baskets to determine which basket is most elaborate. After a short blessing service, the baskets are taken home to be shared as part of the Easter Sunday breakfast.

*The original Mt. Carmel Church built in 1927*

## MOUNT CARMEL LUTHERAN CHURCH
*1701 St. Anthony Parkway*

Mount Carmel Lutheran Church was the first to be established in the Waite Park community. When the earliest families moved into the homes on the rolling red clay hills in the most northeastern corner of the city there were no churches. In 1926 seven Scandinavian families who had been worshipping on Sundays in the home of Ellen Larsen, 3134 Ulysses Street, decided to organize a congregation and build a church.

The economy was booming. An ideal location, a vacant lot on the northeast corner of St. Anthony Boulevard and Ulysses was available. And they had a local sponsor, the faculty of the seminary of the United Lutheran Church located on 19th Avenue and Taylor Street Northeast.

The area was slowly growing and contained scattered single family homes, dirt streets, and many gardens and chicken coops. The people were generally of moderate means: building tradesmen, railroad workers, and factory employees. Reverend Gerberding and his family traveled by streetcar up Johnson Street to Northeast Minneapolis each Sunday to meet and lead the dozen or so families in worship. Mount Carmel Lutheran Church was chartered on March 28, 1926 with 45 members and a council of six. The Ladies Aid soon followed—collecting dues and dividing into subgroups (the "'sick committee" and the "sewing circle"). The congregation dedicated their new church building and joined the Northwest Synod of the English Evangelical Lutheran Church.

Soon a familiar sight cruising the area in his blue Buick was the first pastor, Reverend Herman Schmid. He preached his first sermon in April of 1927 and was installed June 12. The "Old Mount Carmel" with its neo-Gothic design, high arched windows, and location on the top of the hill was a place to look up to, a landmark.

The ecumenical nature of Mount Carmel was especially evident in the youth group, the Luther League. During the 1930s and 1940s when the fifteen or twenty teens gathered in the church basement on Sunday evenings, almost always there was a Methodist or two, one or more Presbyterians and even an occasional

*Mt. Carmel Confirmation class, 1928*

Catholic present. Discussing the Bible, singing hymns and praying were essential ingredients but just as important was the fellowship derived from eating together, playing games and chitchatting.

Reverend Schmid took great pride in this new church and even hand-crafted the altar, pulpit, and lectern. The Schmid family lived above the sanctuary and on many a Sunday the odor of Sunday dinner being prepared drifted down to the people sitting in the pews.

Attendance increased during the Depression but church funds dwindled. Pastor Schmid as well as two other "ministerial" families; the Reeds and the Dresslers helped with preaching and teaching. The tradition of delivering holiday food baskets began about that time with Bert Reed as one of the early deliverers. When Pastor Schmid accepted a call to return to his native Pennsylvania, he left a congregation that had tripled in membership and was firmly rooted in the community.

Reverend Carl Almer was called and began his work at Mount Carmel on August 1, 1940. With America's entrance into World War II, Pastor Almer found that he was spending much of his time counseling and consoling the families of Mount Carmel and their sons who were entering military service or who had been wounded or killed in action. He resigned his ministry on December 31, 1943 to become a military chaplain. The war raged on with no end in sight and the congregation needed a permanent pastor.

Pastor Paul Waldschmidt with his wife Helen, who directed the choirs and helped teach the children, led the church through the boom years following World War II. The membership grew from 534 in 1946 to more than 1,000 in 1953 and the membership changed in composition—embracing a more diverse congregation including more business and professional people and reaching out into the nearby suburbs.

The sanctuary was jam-packed and the church school classrooms overcrowded. Membership in women's organizations grew from 85 to 190 between 1946 and 1951. Many "smorgasbords" were prepared in the kitchen of and eaten in the basement of the church and the Boy Scouts held an annual bean feed. Ice cream socials and picnics were held on the lawn of the church in the summer. Children from the church and the neighborhood watched movies in the sanctuary on Friday nights enjoying the horses galloping backwards during the rewinding of the films as much as the original run. The church was the center of the community.

At the annual meeting in 1948, the congregation voted to support the expenditure of $56,000 for the basement of the new church (referred to as the "First Unit"). The Building Committee began a campaign to raise funds for the new building. The congregation experienced the project in stages. In February 1950, worship began in the "First Unit" with tile floor, folding chairs, and a huge heavy firedoor separating the new sanctuary from the old "Sunday School building."

Work continued. One member remembered two young boys getting into a bit of mischief around the construction site and hearing a booming voice from the tower (the soon to-be pastor's office) suggesting they desist. At the time they thought it was the voice of God.

On May 9, 1954 the new sanctuary was dedicated. Behind the altar against a brick wall stood the beautiful statue of Christ carved by St. Paul artist Chris Steiner. The choir sang from their special area behind vertical wooden slats. The congregation sat in new pews. "The Waffle Stand" at the state fair was a late summer event—a time to get together and work and earn money. Many parishioners baked waffles and served the public at the stand across from the Old Mill ride.

Pastor Bertram Reed (seminary student during the very early years of Mount Carmel) was ready to return to the Midwest from Washington State. He accepted the call and preached his first sermon at Mount Carmel on June 1, 1955. He immediately saw the need for additional staff and a full-time parish worker and a part-time youth director were employed. He spearheaded the financing and construction of the new parish hall, blending architecturally with the church on the site of the original church building. Then, in 1960, his untimely death left the congregation without a pastor and missing his relaxed informality and ready humor.

There was no longer room for the annual picnics on the church lawn and they moved to city parks such as Columbia and Waite Park. A potluck and games followed Sunday worship. But the Minneapolis Health Department, because of a hepatitis scare, prohibited serving homecooked meats to the public so church smorgasbords, picnics, and potlucks ceased and, for a time, the church lost a popular activity.

The "Carmelite Capers," organized when Pastor Reed commented that there certainly were a lot of "'hams" in the choir, provided many a laugh and great entertainment. Performers and audience alike enjoyed the "Andrew Sisters" (Dan Ready, Bill Kirberger, Sam Hanna) and "Minnegasco" (Grace Jaster)—a few of the many acts.

Pastor Henry Kleinert was installed on July 1, 1961. He and his wife and two teenage children soon became active in the community, as well as the church. Mount Carmel was on the march and Reverend Walter Leitze was called as Associate Pastor in 1964. Pastor A. O. Frank became Associate Pastor in 1965 and served until 1978. Pastor John Palmquist followed as spiritual leader in 1969. Youth night with swim and gym began. Pastor Kenneth Manfolk joined as Associate Pastor in 1971 and in 1977 Pastor Ken Puccio became the Associate Pastor.

The remodeling of the sanctuary was completed and the new Schantz Pipe Organ installed on April 12, 1973. No longer was the choir cut off from the congregation and wood and fabric hid the organ pipes (and the brick wall) on either side of the statue of Christ.

Pastor Dennis Hagstrom was called in 1981 as Associate Pastor and under Pastor Ringham's guidance, Mount Carmel's first woman pastor, Carolyn Keller, was called as Associate Pastor in July 1985.

In order to make Mount Carmel not only welcome but also accessible to all, an elevator was installed to make the church handicapp accessible on May 12, 1985. Mount Carmel Childcare opened in September 1989 with Lisa Alm (Plaziak) as director. Pastor Wally and Lorraine Setterlund stayed on as very active members after his retirement. Pastor Wally had a permanent post at one door or the other after worship every Sunday... greeting friends and visitors with a firm handshake and winning smile.

Differences regarding the direction of Mount Carmel were causing some members to leave at this time. Under the gentle care and guidance of interim pastor Larry Lystig, the congregation began the healing process.

Christmas programs continued featuring "The Golden Strings" Christmas concert which has become a tradition, Vacation Bible School, Wednesday night soup and sandwich, hymn sing, and Lenten dialogue, Bible studies, book discussions . . . the list goes on and on.

The present pastor, George Cruys was installed on February 17, 1991. Originally a Minneapolis boy, Pastor Cruys received total congregational acceptance and still brings enthusiasm to Mount Carmel. Pastor William Hyllengren was hired as Visitation Pastor after his interim at Mount Carmel. How we love his caring ways and his "Scandinavian" jokes.

Adapting to change, the church has sponsored non-denominational neighborhood services and an Alcoholics Anonymous group. It has involved itself in such community activities as NEED (North East Emergency Depot), the Northeast Senior Citizen Resource Center, and Sharing and Caring Hands.

The challenges of Mount Carmel are to build the membership of the church in a changing community and changing time, and to nurture a congregation of many elderly long-standing members while creating a vital ministry for the youth. And also to share and cooperate with other churches in the area, and to continue to support missions.

*New location of Salvation Army, 1999*

# SALVATION ARMY
*2727 Central Avenue NE*

The first Salvation Army Corps Hall was at 1900 Central Ave. NE on the second floor. It was dedicated as the Minneapolis No. 3 Corps in February 1914, with Captain Olofson and Lt. David Westergren officers in charge. Mrs. Corinne Ohlson and Axel Carlson were in the first soldier's enrollment. Activities included a Band of Love, VP Legion, and a brass band of six members. Mr. Axel Carlson was one of the bandsmen.

The Corps changed halls six times during the first two years, but during the time of Captain and Mrs. Joseph Anderson, the Corps moved to 2414 Central Avenue NE where it remained for twelve years.

In 1927, the building at 2524–26 Central Avenue NE was purchased. Capt. Carl Eklund and Lt. Oscar Anderson were the officers in charge at the time of the dedication. During the appointment of Major and Mrs. Alvin Nelson, the building at 2526 Central Ave. was sold, a lot purchased at 2625 Central Ave., and a new Corps building erected there. In July 1951 the Corps moved into its new place of worship and had the dedication, with Lt. Col. H. Rostett officiating.

On June 18, 1972, the new chapel and remodeled building was dedicated. This remodeling and addition took place under the leadership of Major Orville Butts, Corps Officer. Major and Mrs. Leslie C. Sundell succeeded Captain and Mrs. Herbert Lodge in February 1974 and are presently the Corps officers.

In 1997, the Salvation Corps Central relocated into the former VFW building on 2727 Central Avenue Northeast. The old building is still in use. Worship and Bible classes are held every Sunday. Also a youth program for girls and boys with music, choir and band lessons and Bible study for teens are held during the week. They have taken over the NEED foodshelf, a program to help Northeast families.

*Waite Park Church, 1999*

# WAITE PARK WESLEYAN METHODIST CHURCH
### 1510–33rd Avenue NE

In the fall of 1928, a small group of Christians, largely made up of young people, began meeting in the home for prayer meetings. Later they rented a vacant store on 33rd and Johnson Street where meetings continued under the name of the Northeast Christian Mission. They eventually evolved into a larger group that met regularly for prayer meetings and testimony time. They not only stayed in the little mission, but also spent Sunday afternoons calling in the neighborhood and inviting people into their church. Street meetings plus services in the jails and nursing homes were also held.

As the numbers grew and their vision became larger, in 1931 some vacant lots were secured on 33rd and Lincoln. A tabernacle was built and the name was changed to the Northeast Gospel Tabernacle. Since there were no funds to build it, these young people dedicated themselves to the task of erecting this building. Mr. Louis Christen, who had just demolished a large barn and gave the timber for the erection of the tabernacle, gave the large beams. Other lumber and materials were purchased and salvaged from various sources. The basement was dug by pick and shovel, which contained the furnace room and rest rooms. The total price for the tabernacle was something less than $3,000. A mortgage of $1,700.00 was secured at a payment of $14.00 per month. Some of these young people were willing to work all week and to give their entire check for the support of this work, which they felt God had given to them. Among some of the young people at that time were those who are still leaders in the church today. Among them are George Walquist, Mildred Walquist, Fred Odell, Frances Odell, and Don Gearhart.

In 1936, Reverend D. C. Elmer became the first pastor of the Tabernacle, which they named the First Wesleyan Methodist Church of Minneapolis. The following year they became part of the Iowa Conference. The church was organized with 38 charter members which are as follows: George Walquist, Mildred Walquist, Fred Odell, Frances Odell, Mr. and Mrs. H. W. Sperry, Hazel Sperry Paul, Vera Sperry Jackson, Florence Sperry Feyo, Mr. and Mrs. Clare Gerhard, Ed Sullivan, Mr. and Mrs. E. G. Gearheart, Mr. and Mrs. Harold Dunnell, Daryl Dunnell Corgard, Wayne Dunnell, Mr. and Mrs. Charles Gearhart, Mr. and Mrs. Donald Gearhart, Mary Gait McNamara, Cora Tollefson, Mr. and Mrs. Arvid Carlson, Luverne Carlson, Neal Devendorf, Mr. and Mrs. John Douglas, Georg Gearhart, John Gearhart, Lowell Gearhart, Irene Mahan, Roy Odell, Mr. and Mrs. Charles Pitcher and Mrs. Leonard Scott.

The tabernacle was used as a parsonage until in 1943 a new parsonage was built. Then in the year 1949, the church started to build beside its present location on the corner lot of 33ed Avenue and Lincoln Street. With the sum of $2,000.00 on hand for a building fund, they started digging the basement for a 40 by 70 foot structure. After the basement hole was dug with the help of many of the men from the church, their $2,000.00 building fund was completely depleted. "Shall we go on or shall we stop?" was the great question in the minds of the pastor and people. With an undaunted faith they continued on, even though there was no money. After a great deal of prayer and soliciting the building began and in January of 1954, the new superstructure was completed at a cost of $87,000.

In 1950, Irene Archer, now Irene Zobrist was sent to Africa to be the first missionary to be sent out from the First Wesleyan Methodist Church of Minneapolis. Then in 1960 a beautiful home was dedicated as a new parsonage. With the increased number of members, the old tabernacle, now being used as a Sunday School, became inadequate. So in 1965 a plan for enlarging the sanctuary and a new three story school building would be erected.

After a couple of month's construction, it became necessary to knock out the back end of the present sanctuary so that the new building could be attached. This of course, became a very inconvenient time for worship and for Sunday school. Later the Tabernacle was demolished. Sunday school classes were held in the parsonage basement and in the home of Lucille Asp. This went on for one year. And then in 1966, the work was finally complete and the new enlarged sanctuary has a seating capacity of 425 people. The basement floor of the new building now has a fellowship hall in which 250 guests can be served banquet style and a modern kitchen. The years have been enriched by the presence of God's blessings.

*Elmwood, 1999*

## ELMWOOD EVANGELICAL FREE CHURCH
*3615 Chelmsford Road*

Petri Lutheran Free Church on 14th Avenue and Madison Street started a Sunday school and services to accommodate the new community east of Johnson Street. The people met in a home at 2552 Ulysses Street NE. A congregation was formed and Pastor H. O. Helseth served. Some of the first families were the Solsbergs, the J. Mikkelsons, the Thor Mikklesons, E. Steens, T. Egelands, A. Jackson, H. Nordland, A. Hermundslie. This group was incorporated under the name of Elmwood Lutheran Free Church on December 23, 1924. Pastor Helseth from First Lutheran in Columbia Heights was their pastor. They were joined by people from Immanuel Lutheran Church and bought a small white church building on the corner of 26th and McKinley Street NE. In 1931 they enlarged the church and united the two congregations. Pastor Helseth continued ministry.

One of the early pastors was Pastor Julius Hermanslie. Then Pastor Dahle served Elmwood for many years and under his guidance there was a spiritual revival. There were all-night prayer meetings and quite a few people from this small congregation were inspired to go to the mission field. One of our current members, Mildred Bolstad, was one of those who left home and friends and went to Tanzania. She went to Africa in 1946 and returned here in 1957 because of her husband Ray's poor health. After his death in 1970, Mildred returned alone to Tanzania for six years (1972–1978). Thelma Alfsen, who also went about that time is still doing her work from her home base at Macau (Hong Kong). She has written a booklet "The Way to Heaven" that has been translated into many languages. Supporting and encouraging missionaries has always been very important to the people of Elmwood.

The property at 26th and McKinley was sold in 1965 and the new church at 3615 Chelmsford Road in St. Anthony was built and dedicated in November 1965. Pastor Paul Gunderson served from 1970 to early 1980. Pastor Joe Valtinson served from November 1980 to 1995. Pastor Dale Swan served along with Pastor Valtinson from September 1985 to 1991.

On October 3, 1978, an article of amendment resolved that the name of Evangelical Lutheran Free Church be changed to Elmwood Lutheran Church. A congregational meeting was held in 1983. It was resolved that Elmwood Lutheran Church leave the American Lutheran Church Synod. Ninety days later, the resolution was ratified. As a result, Elmwood Lutheran Church operated as an independent Lutheran Church for eleven years. Elmwood's new church sanctuary was started in the fall of 1986. Led by Pastor Valtinson, the majority of the work was done by the men of the congregation and the move into the beautiful new sanctuary was completed in August, 1987.

The church applied for membership in the Evangelical Free Church, stating the desire to fellowship with like-minded churches, and was accepted in April 6, 1994. On August 7, 1994, the congregation voted to change the church name to Elmwood Evangelical Free Church.

Upon Pastor Joe Valtinson's retirement, the church family extended a call to Pastor Randy Andersen. He is a graduate of Trinity Evangelical Divinity School and has served two Evangelical Free Churches prior to coming to Elmwood Church. Pastor Andersen has served since March 1, 1996.

*Holy Triune, 1999*

# HOLY TRIUNE LUTHERAN CHURCH
*1114–22ⁿᵈ Avenue NE*

In 1964, Holy Triune Lutheran Church began its ministry to the community. This church was a merger of Concordia, St. Petri and Immanuel Lutheran churches. Concordia Evangelical was located on 22ⁿᵈ and Fillmore NE and ran from 1910 to 1948. St. Petri was located on 15ᵗʰ and Madison NE and operated from 1888 to 1946. Immanuel was located on 15ᵗʰ and Monroe and ran from 1893 to 1963. At the tenth anniversary celebration in 1974, the cornerstone was opened and contents of the cornerstones of each of the three churches placed in a new cornerstone. Holy Triune congregation now is caretaker of the remembrances of the three historic congregations. Pastor Orrin H. Eittreim serves the church.

87

*Gustavus Adolphus, 1999*

## GUSTAVUS ADOLPHUS LUTHERAN CHURCH
*1509–27th Avenue NE*

The early 1900's were marked by a heavy immigration of Northern Europeans into the Minneapolis area. The immigrant population was growing and expanding "up the hill." With the rapid growth of the city, the need for another Lutheran Church in Northeast Minneapolis became apparent. In 1911, under the direction of Pastor O. A. Elmquist of Emanuel Lutheran, steps were taken to establish a new congregation.

A building at 27th Avenue and Lincoln St. NE was rented and a Sunday School started. The organization of a Ladies' Aid was accomplished in 1912 and in 1913, the Brotherhood men's group was established.

*The Little White Church on the Hill at Lowry Avenue and 3rd Street, 1936*

As the result of the activities of these groups, Gustaf Adolph Swedish Evangelical Lutheran Church began in September 22, 1914 with a membership of 37 and 34 children. Emanuel transferred the property at 27th and Lincoln to the new congregation. The original structure was a small white building.

In the beginning, financial assistance was received from the Minnesota Conference of the Augustana Synod. Property indebtedness, transferred along with the building in 1914, was paid off in 1919 and in 1921 the congregation became self-supporting. The growing congregation added a kitchen and a Sunday School room to the Chapel structure in 1921. Then in 1926 a lot was purchased at 33rd and Pierce St. NE as a site for the North Branch Sunday School. This was used for over 20 years as a neighborhood extension of the Church. By the end of 1928, the Building Fund had reached $590.

The membership in 1930 reached 309 communicants and 39 children under the Pastorate of Paul Gustafson. It was also during this time that a major change took place in the life of Gustaf Adolph Swedish Evangelical Lutheran Church. Swedish was dropped and English was introduced as the language of the congregational worship.

The present church structure was erected in 1937, and an educational and office wing was completed in 1954. Baptized membership now exceeded 2,000. In 1958, a Moeller pipe organ was installed. Joining the Augustana Home Corporation of Total Retirement Living took place the same year. While already a twenty-year member of Luther Park Camp Corporation in Danbury, Wisconsin, in 1982 the people of Gustavus joined Plymouth Christian Youth Center, a mission to the inner city of Minneapolis.

The merger of three Lutheran church bodies (Lutheran Church in America, American Lutheran Church and the Association of Evangelical Lutheran Churches) in 1988 formed the new Evangelical Lutheran Church of America.

On September 24, 1989, Gustavus celebrated its 75th anniversary. Property for parking was purchased in 1991. The church completed a renovation project and made the church structure handicapp accessible in 1992. The church has over 700 baptized members.

Pastors who have served Gustavus are Reverends Einar Renahl, Ernest J. Sakrison, Paul J. A. Gustafson, Adolph W. Dickhart, Reuben H. Ford, Einar J. Oberg, Thomas J. Kelk, Roger D. Schwartz, Timothy J. Schurler, Paul W. Setterholm, and Mark Ditmanson. Others are J. G. Hultkrans, August Samuelson, J. E. Shipp, Gustaf S. Olson, Carl Everett, William Seigel, Clifford Marshall, Thomas Jacobson, James Nelson, and Robert O. Hall.

Gustavus has its own monthly newsletter called the G. A. Gazette. Some of the social opportunities at the church are an annual Ice Cream and Pie Social, a Mother-Daughter Banquet, a Men's Breakfast and the Christmas Pageant potluck. There are five organized woman's circles and four adult social groups. The Senior Choir, Bell Choir and Contemporary Choir always welcome the musically inclined. And the Quilters meet once a month and have donated over 1,000 quilts.

Several special events are part of Sunday School: a Christmas Pageant and potluck dinner, the Bible Village, visits to Bethany Covenant Home, presentation of Bibles to third graders and the Pet Fair. Teens Need Teens (TNT) has the opportunity to plan and organize an Easter Sunrise service and pancake breakfast. They also spend a week in Chicago donating time at Cabrini Green. Ski trips to Duluth and canoe trips down the St. Croix are also planned.

Service to the community is an important part of the mission of Gustavus Adolphus. A great deal of time and money goes to Augustana Home, Luther Park, Northeast Dinner Bell, Lutheran Social Service, Our Savior's Shelter, and the Northeast Emergency Depot.

*House of Faith, 1999*

# HOUSE OF FAITH PRESBYTERIAN
*668 Broadway Street NE*

House of Faith Presbyterian Church, 668 Broadway St. NE, was organized Oct. 19, 1887, with 18 charter members. Representatives of Presbyterians who assisted were the Reverend Peter Stryker, Capt. J. C. Whitney and B. F. Knerr. The first two elders were John Pitbiado and Norman Mattice. Reverend Norman McCloud was the first pastor.

The present building was erected and dedicated Nov. 17, 1889. Several additions were built throughout the years. For years it was called "The Lighthouse on the Corner." A few members still remember some early pastors such as Reverend D. E. Evans and M. B. Irvine.

The Ladies Aid and Missionary Societies were organized in 1889. Some members of the Ladies Aid, now called Priscilla Circle, have been members for 49 years.

House of Faith still ministers to the neighborhood. Pastor Walter Clark leads Sunday worship and the communicant's class and ministers to the spiritual needs of the congregation and others.

*Gloria Dei, 1999*

## GLORIA DEI LUTHERAN CHURCH
*30th & McKinley Street NE*

The congregation of Gloria Dei Lutheran Church was organized on February 23 1951, beginning with seven communicant members. The following April, the congregation first met in worship at the Hollywood Theater, thus consummating several years of prayerful planning and work on the part of both clergy and laymen.

Mr. Robert Walther first recognized the opportunity for mission work as far back as 1947. He called it to the attention of his brother-in-law, Reverend Alvin G. Fehner, who at that time was serving on the Mission Board of the Minnesota District of the Lutheran Church, Missouri Synod.

In the spring of 1950, five pastors of the Synodical Conference canvassed the area near 30th and McKinley N. E. and found it encouraging for the establishment of a new mission. The Mission Board appointed Rev. Ralph Radtke of Columbia Heights to serve as Counselor in the organization of this new congregation.

On February 22, 1951 the present site was purchased and in August, ground was broken for the first unit. This building was dedicated on November 9, 1952.

Many of the people of this parish are of German descent. Some early members came from St. Matthews of Columbia Heights. On April 15, 1951 Reverend Luther Anderson of Reedsburg, Wisconsin was installed as our first pastor and served until 1954. The pastors of Gloria Dei are Reverend Brinkman and before him there was Reverend Sestak, then Reverend James R. Fehner in 1962.

Special events of the church include the Annual Salad Luncheon and Craft/ Bake Sale. It's always the first Wednesday in October and the proceeds go to a shared community charity. Members are asked to bring a dish to share but a favorite that is served each year is the German potato salad.

Special services are held on Christmas Eve and Christmas Day with singing of carols. Each year the Easter Sunrise Service is held at Sunset Memorial Cemetery. Afterwards breakfast is served back at the church. Outside services at 9:00 are enjoyed from June through Labor Day every year at Demming Park on St. Anthony Boulevard and Fillmore.

The present parsonage was dedicated in 1956. The Sunday School and worship facilities became inadequate. So the church was added on to in 1956. Membership in 1962 was 350 communicant members and over 600 souls. Mrs. Orris Briley is the organist and choir director.

Gloria Dei is very much a mission church. Early members were D. Agather, J. Anderson, L. Archer, D. Archer, A. Bahr, V. Baggenstoss, R. Boyer, A. Baken, G. Busse, O. Briley, R. Dunklau, C. Egleland, L. Eckhardt, B. Harris, G. Havrilla. W. Hasse, A. Johnson, W. Klein, D. Kersten, J. Norback, F. Kersten. S. Kvalheim, C. Kohner, W. Krischuk, H. Lausche, R. Luhmann, D. L. Milliren, W. Milliren, G. Pagels, B. Podas, R. Robinson, G. Schoenhals, R. Schindler, K. Swedeen, J. Swedeen, M. Heryer, E. Anderson, S. Tarman, R. Wanzong, R. Walther, P. Wieman,

*St. Charles Borromeo, 1999*

# ST. CHARLES BORROMEO
*2420 St. Anthony Boulevard*

The parish of St. Charles Borromeo was established in the fall of 1938. Archbishop John Gregory Murray assigned to Father Charles F. Doran the task of organizing a parish within an area bounded by Broadway and Johnson Street on the south and west, and by the Anoka and Ramsey County lines on the north and east. The area included what had formerly been part of St. Clement's Parish.

Father Doran celebrated the first mass Dec. 8, 1932. It was attended by about 50 parishioners in the Roy F. Miller home on 2223 Benjamin Street NE. For the following nine months, Sunday masses were offered in the auditorium of Pillsbury School, 2255 Hayes St. Northeast.

The problem of finding a good site for a church and school was solved when the Armour Company offered to sell the parish a six-acre site at the southeast corner of Stinson and St. Anthony Boulevards.

Groundbreaking ceremonies for a church–school were April 19, 1939. The building was ready for occupancy by fall. The parochial school opened Sept. 15 with about 180 pupils. Father Doran said the first mass in the new church Oct. 26th, and the building was formally dedicated Nov. 12.

In 1947, the parish included 950 families; by 1951, the total had risen to 1,150. St. Charles was rapidly outgrowing its facilities. A convent, now developed into a parish center on 2739 Stinson Blvd. NE was added in 1946, and in 1952 two wings were added to the church - school. By 1954, however, it was plain that a new parish church must be built. Ground was broken for the new structure June 10, 1957. The church was dedicated July 9, 1959.

St. Charles maintained a parish school (kindergarten through 8th grade), with an enrollment in 1976 of about 520. The parish has religious education programs at preschool, elementary, junior high and senior high and adult levels. The parish staff is also active in several areas of pastoral ministry, with visitations to the sick, the elderly and the bereaved. A parish organization of recent vintage is a club for senior citizens, the VIP Club.

*Grace, 1999*

# GRACE UNITED METHODIST CHURCH
*Lowry at Cleveland Street NE*

The first members of what is now Grace United Methodist Church organized in the "old" Pierce School at 636 Fillmore Street Northeast on April 8, 1905. Reverend Shull gave guidance to those first meetings. It appears that the congregation was an outgrowth of a community Sunday School which had been meeting in that area since 1890.

In 1910, the cornerstone was laid for a new building at Fillmore and Summer Streets. Times were extremely difficult and the construction had to be delayed for a number of years. It was resumed and completed with assistance from the Central Avenue business community in 1914. One of the older members recalls receiving "missionary barrels" which contained clothing and other help for members of the congregation. As a mission congregation it also received financial help from the national United Brethren in Christ Church.

In the late '30s, plans were laid to move to a new location, which was Lowry and Cleveland Streets. Worship was in Pillsbury School for nearly a year between the sale of the former building to Our Lady of Mt. Carmel congregation and the completion of the new structure. The new church home was dedicated in January of 1939. In 1962, the addition was completed.

Currently Grace Church, along with two other United Methodist congregations, is sponsoring a Vietnamese family. Grace has four choirs, a three-year confirmation program, and a camping program. Grace Church has a buying club called "Care and Share," which enables members to buy groceries cooperatively and use the savings to assist in the relief of world hunger.

## ST. JOHN'S EVANGELICAL LUTHERAN CHURCH
*610 Broadway Street NE*

*The Main Street Church on 6th and Main Street, 1869*

It was on the 13th of October 1867 that Pastor Fachmann organized Evangelische Lutheranische St. Johannes Kirche of St. Anthony. At first, services were held in the home of Mrs. Helen Malchow. Because of the small quarters, a schoolhouse near 14th Avenue and Main Street was rented soon after. Two years later the congregation bought the quarter acre lot between Sixth and Seventh Avenue on Main Street. A church seating about 165 was immediately built. The cost of this structure was $1075. At the same time a one-story schoolhouse was erected. Later this building was torn down and replaced with a two-story structure.

The lower floor of the schoolhouse was used for summer school. The upper floor served as a meeting place for the Ladies Aid and Young People's Society. Social and business meetings were held there. There were no modern conveniences in those days, no furnaces, only stove heated rooms. Kerosene lamps furnished the light. Wood and water had to be carried up the outside back stairway.

In 1899 the church was remodeled. A sanctuary was added to the church and a vestibule, belfry and steeple to the other end. A bell was purchased and placed in the belfry tower. That same bell is now hanging in the present church tower.

The organ in our old church on Main Street was a reed organ. With two pedals and had to be pumped with the feet. It was quite a task to play and pump at the same time. That is probably the reason why the first organist, Mrs. Freda Behrend was so strong and healthy on her feet. She played the reed organ until the move into the first new church. At the start she received the tremendous sum of fifty cents a Sunday for playing the reed organ.

The first parsonage was built in 1869. It was located at 625 Main Street NE. Behind the parsonage was a vacated quarry hole infested with rats. Some of these creatures occasionally managed to find their way into the small cellar of the parsonage. The parochial school opened in 1876. This house together with the church and schoolhouse was sold in 1910.

The first resident pastor was the Reverend Frey. His successors were the Pastors Herzer, Achilles, Kogler, Quehl, Dowidat, Kehrberg, and Grummert. Pastor Quehl served 23 years, pastor Dowidat 58 years, and the others covered the remaining years.

In January of 1904 there was still a small membership of only 35 people. But after missionary endeavors, more and more new members were added. English services were introduced and before long there was insufficient room for all the worshippers in that little church.

In 1907 an attempt was made to reach each parishioner by mail monthly for encouragement and greater interest in the church. That was accomplished through St. John's monthly *Messenger*. At the time of its inception, the German language only was used in preaching and in conducting meetings. So for a number of years the greater portion of the parish paper was printed in the German language. Gradually, there was less German and more English. In 1924 German was omitted entirely.

St. John's *Messenger* was first called *Der St. Johannes Bote*, edited by Pastor Dowidat from 1907 to 1962. Since then the Pastors Kehrberg and Grummert continued to edit the *Messenger*. Some of the advertisers of the *Messenger* are still the same, namely Eklund Clothing Co., the Aid Assoc. for Lutherans, and Washburn-McReavy. German School opened in 1908. English services began on the second Sunday evening and the last Sunday of each month.

It was decided to build a larger and more spacious church. The old church school and parsonage were sold to Archbishop John Ireland for the modest sum of $5,500. New church grounds were bought at Broadway and Washington Streets Northeast in 1909. The owner was renting the property to the Crown Sidewalk Company. Chute Brothers owned the land and offered it for sale. By some fortunate misunderstanding in our favor we obtained the property for the price of the mortgage which was a trifle over $1300. Work on a stone church began early in 1910. The cornerstone was laid June 12th and by Feb. 12, 1911 the church was dedicated.

The property at 625 Main Street was sold to Our Lady of Mt. Carmel, the Italian church. The first pipe organ was purchased after moving to the new church. It was a Moeller organ. Adeline Zell had the distinction of being our first pipe organist. When she got married to Will Kramer, Elfrieda Struss succeeded her for the next 5 years. Winifred Reichmuth took organ lessons from Miss Struss and so when Elfrieda married Herbert Meyer, Winifred became our organist and served for the next 25 years. The Ladies' Aid Society was saving money to pay for the pipe organ. They had about $1300 saved but that wasn't enough. We had heard about Andrew Carnegie who had a pipe organ fund to supply poor and needy congregations with money. We

*Confirmation class, 1906*

wrote a letter and six weeks later we received a reply saying that Andrew Carnegie would be pleased to give one thousand dollars toward our new pipe organ. The ladies were surprised and overjoyed. The organ lasted for twenty-seven years.

The congregation then rented the upper floor of a duplex at 1327 6th Street NE for their pastor. After two years the congregation bought a lot on Adams Street and built a parsonage there. That was the first really up to date parsonage.

As time went on, the congregation grew and prospered. Large adult classes were instructed and confirmed. Adult confirmation classes ran into the thirties, forties and more. The largest class was in 1921 numbering sixty-three. Thirty-two of these had to be baptized before they could be confirmed.

These adults, together with twenty-nine from the children's class, added 92 communicant members to St. John's congregation that Palm Sunday in 1921. Joseph Robert Jones, 92 years old, was in the 1930 adult class. He was baptized, confirmed, had his first communion on Easter Sunday, and died three days later. The Minneapolis chief of police (Frank Brunskill) was in one class, and the chief of the fire department (Earl Traeger) in another. In one class seven different nationalities were represented.

A ladies missionary auxiliary was established in Minneapolis as well as in St. Paul to give financial assistance to the cause and an economy store was established in each city. One half of the profits support these missions. The other half is sent to the Bethesda Home in Watertown, Wisconsin.

In 1922, when the services became overcrowded, a daughter congregation was organized in South Minneapolis. A vacated church building was bought at 39th and Grand Avenue South. They named it the Pilgrim Church.

The congregation of St. John's grew until a second morning service became necessary. And when that second service became overcrowded something had to be done, either enlarge the church or build a larger one elsewhere. There was no suitable site nearby so the congregation bought four lots on the corner of Fifth Street and Second Avenue SE. The congregation planned to build a new church there. Then came the Depression. Construction came to a standstill. The congregation had to wait a few years for better times.

In the meantime the city deeded the land on the Sixth Street side of the church. So they decided to stay and enlarge the church. The Southeast property was sold for the sum of $8,000. So the work for the enlarged and remodeled church began. For the next nine months church services were conducted in the Sheridan Junior High School, just three blocks west of the church. They bought a Hammond electric organ and took it along to the Sheridan School. When finally the organ loft was ready, the new and larger pipe organ was installed. For 29 years this instrument gave entire satisfaction and required very little upkeep expense. Thus St. John's congregation had three different organs throughout the past one hundred years.

After several delays the building was finally ready for occupancy and was dedicated December 11, 1938. It now had a seating capacity for 876. At one time St. John's congregation had a little over a thousand communicant members. Its membership has since decreased. Many moved to the outskirts of the city. The adult classes became smaller and smaller because by that time too many other demands were made on the pastor's time.

Some of the organists who have served St. John's congregation were Otto Froehlich, Bartlett Butler, James Albrecht, Mrs. Paul Malnau and Marion Hutchinson. Not to be out done in the music department, the choir directors were Ted Kobs, Hazel Tkach and Paul Comnick.

In 1954 the congregation celebrated with Reverend Dowidat his 50th year in the ministry. A recognition service was held at which time Reverend Dowidat was presented a check and the keys to a new automobile. A reception and dinner followed the service. The third parsonage was built at 1435 Adams Street costing $24,000.

Pastor Dowidat announced his retirement after fifty-eight years of continuous service in St. John's from January 1, 1904 to January 1, 1962. As a token of appreciation, he was given a sizable check, a monthly pension, free telephone service, and last but not least, a framed portrait of himself which is now hanging, electrically lighted, on the back wall of the church auditorium.

In 1959 a need was seen for a church to serve the people in the northern suburb of Brooklyn Park. Pastor Willard Kehrberg and the trustees of St. John's, together with Reverend Roman Palmer and a committee from Pilgrim, selected a site at 69th Avenue and Osseo Road in Brooklyn Park. St. John's purchased the property and built a small chapel. The chapel was planned so that it could be converted to a parsonage when the need would arise. Today the small chapel is a parsonage, and a church has been erected to replace it. Brooklyn Lutheran Church is served by Reverend Dorn and is a flourishing congregation.

Some of the organizations are St. John's Men's Club, St. John's Choir, St. John's Bowling Club, Martha Mary Guild, Priscilla Group, Altar Guild, Christian Guild, and St. John's OWLS. In 1967 St. John's observed its Centennial Anniversary. The Christian Guild established the St. John's Library in 1971. The church Exterior Restoration Project began in 1973 and the sandblasting of the Colfax stone is completed. A year long celebration is observed for the 125th Anniversary in 1992.

*Pierre Bottineau in his later years, 1880s*

# 4 Immigrants, Steamers, Trolleys and a French Explorer

## *Who Is Pierre Bottineau?*
## *And Why Is His Name All Over Northeast?*

**By Karen Boros**

Reprinted from the *Minneapolis Argus,* March 14, 1973

Pierre Bottineau was not an early settler of St. Anthony Falls. He did move to the area in 1845 and he did build a house for his family but he didn't settle. One thing that seems to keep popping up in Bottineau's story is his tendency to move on to new areas and new people as soon as the place he was living started taking on what the neighbors probably referred to as a civilized look.

Ironically, whenever he moved away from civilization it would only be a matter of time before people would find out where he was and followed him. When Bottineau moved from Pig's Eye to St. Anthony Falls he found a town of nearly 50 people living in sod or elm-bark huts along the eastern banks of the Mississippi.

His house, built of wooden shingles, was across from the northern tip of Nicollet Island, which at that time was covered by a forest of ancient maple and elm trees. The western side of the Mississippi was inhabited by small groups of Indians and used as grazing land for the Fort Snelling cattle.

Bottineau was the son of a French fur trader, Joseph, and his Chippewa Indian wife, the Clear Sky Woman. He was born in Dakota Territory at a place called "Rat's Point" during the winter of 1817 while Clear Sky was on a buffalo hunt. When his father died, Bottineau, in his early teens, went to live as an apprentice guide with Antoine Le Count who was lame.

In 1830 Bottineau was hired to carry messages for a fur company between the settlement at Selkirk, Manitoba, and Prairie Du Chien, Wisconsin. The story is told that during one of these trips he ventured out onto the ice covered Red River accompanied by Le Count and another companion. The ice broke and dumped the three into the water. As his companions floundered and were unable to swim or climb to safety on the thin ice, Bottineau swam for shore breaking his way ahead and dragging his friends behind him. Some years later in 1837, a young adventurer named Martin McLeod engaged Bottineau to guide him from Fort Garry (now Winnipeg) to Fort Snelling. His friends Richard Hay, an Irishman, and Captain J. Pays, a Pole accompanied McLeod. The group was carrying a message to the commander of Fort Snelling from "General" James

*G.A. Brackett and Pierre Bottineau left Minneapolis in 1869 to chart the new Northern Pacific Railroad.*
*Picture was taken on the second day out on the expedition westward.*
*(Brackett with gun and heavy beard in forefront, Bottineau is left of Brackett with gun and heavy beard)*

Dickson who was planning on being crowned king of a vast Indian kingdom he visualized in California. McLeod kept a diary of their trip and described Bottineau, then in his seventies, as tall, well built with dark eyes and a frequent smile. His hair was black and straight. He spoke most of the Indian languages used in the northwest, plus French and English.

The little band set out from Fort Garry on December 20th and traveled until mid March when they became lost during a storm. The storm cleared, the next day dawned mild and pleasant and the little group was on its way again. They had not marched long when Bottineau came across fresh deer tracks and took off across the countryside after the animal while the other three continued on.

All were apparently oblivious to the second storm moving in rapidly from the north, which McLeod noted in his diary as something "no pen can describe." During that storm the Irishman wandered off and was never seen again. The Pole was found alive the next morning with his arms and legs frozen. McLeod had burrowed into a snowbank with a buffalo robe and survived. Bottineau was able to build a fire during the storm and passed the night without noticeable discomfort. McLeod and Bottineau moved the Pole to an abandoned Indian hut, gave him all but two of the blankets, cups for melting snow, fire wood, all of the remaining food and told him they would be back. They then continued the march, killing their dog for meat.

McLeod's diary notes that "dog meat makes excellent eating."

Twenty-six days later the pair arrived at the trading post after marching five days without food. They immediately returned to the Indian hut on horseback and discovered the Pole had died shortly before their arrival. Not long after the McLeod trip Bottineau and his first wife, Genevieve LaRance moved from Fort Garry to the French settlement near Fort Snelling. They lived there until 1840 when the Army forced the settlers to move. The Bottineau's moved to Pig's Eye (now St. Paul), where they purchased a piece of land known as Baptist Hill. Their home was located where 7th Street and Jackson Street meet today in downtown St. Paul.

In 1845 Bottineau sold his St. Paul land for $300 and purchased property in St. Anthony Falls for $150. Bottineau's Addition, as the tract of land was known, extended along the river from about Central Avenue (probably by East Hennepin) to Plymouth and five blocks east. The only area settler with a claim as extensive as Bottineau's was Franklin Steele who had been a provisioner at Fort Snelling. Steele had ridden from Fort Snelling under cover of darkness to stake out his claim before the arrival of the town site promoters. He and Bottineau had the only wooden shingled houses in St. Anthony. The forest on Nicollet Island where area residents had established sugaring operations using the giant Maples was ultimately Steele's victim. Looking around at the sod houses of his neighbors, Steele apparently decided that the area needed a sawmill. He sought and was promised financial backing in this venture by a group of Boston businessmen and in the fall of 1846, groups went up the Mississippi to harvest timber to use in building the mill.

That winter, described by one journalist as so harsh that "men were forced to work as cooks and housekeepers," the logs became frozen in. They were lost in the spring thaw. Not wanting to fall behind in his schedule, Steele promptly harvested the trees on Nicollet Island and built the mill. In 1849, Bottineau donated the land now occupied by St. Anthony of Padua. The original church was to have been constructed of native limestone but it proved to be more expensive than planned so a wooden structure was substituted. Apparently Bottineau had earlier tried to donate the same land to the church when property was being bought at what is now the St. Paul Cathedral. He was turned down.

In 1853, General Isaac S. Stevens, Governor of Washington Territory, hired Bottineau as a chief guide for the Pacific Railroad Expedition across North Dakota to Fort Union at the meeting of the Missouri and Yellowstone Rivers. Stevens breakfasted with the Bottineau family and wrote to his wife telling about the event. It was attended by Bottineau's mother, four children by his first wife, his second wife Martha Gervais and a baby, his sister, a brother and the brother's wife and the wife of a brother who was away. The meal was described by Stevens as consisting of "two roast suckling pigs, eggs, beefsteak and etc."

During the time he lived in St. Anthony Falls, shortened to "St. Anthony" by Steele, Bottineau earned his living as a guide, selling real estate he advertised as "cheap for cash" and piloting a river boat across the Mississippi for a fur company. He lost his money gambling and is said to have amused himself by skipping silver dollars across the water.

In 1855, Bottineau decided the time had come to move on. He left St. Anthony and marched north through thick woods until he came to a grassy area. He announced, "This is Paradise" and immediately was at home. "Paradise" is known today as Osseo. The next year Bottineau was hired by the Army to lead an expedition from Fort Snelling, seeking new sites for military posts. In 1862, he was hired for $100 a month by James Fisk to follow the Stevens route to

Fort Union. Bottineau reported for duty accompanied by Daniel, his teenage son.

Bottineau continued to guide expeditions for Fisk for four years. His last expedition was in 1869 when he took a group, including the Governors of Vermont and Minnesota and their ladies along the old route to Fort Union. He retired to a farm at Red Lake Falls in 1876 where he built a brick house near a bend in the river. In 1879, a petition signed by a number of Minnesotans urged the United States Congress to grant Bottineau a pension of $50 a month. Ten years later the old guide wrote to a member of Congress asking for $50 a month saying that the $25 he was receiving was not enough on which to live. There is no record on an increase being granted.

Bottineau died July 27, 1895, after fathering nine children by his first wife and 18 by his second. Ten of his children were alive at the time of his death. He is buried in Red Lake Falls.

In 1863 a preliminary survey of the N. P. railroad to the Pacific coast was made by Pierre Bottineau, William R. Marshall, governor of Minnesota, and George A. Brackett (seated, left to right), together with three officials from Jay Cooke Company, Philadelphia bankers.
Photo from Al P. Hechtman of Osseo.

# Immigrants

Most European immigrants made the two-week trip in third class quarters or steerage, the cheapest and most crowded spaces below deck. They were huddled together much like cattle, sleeping in tiered bunks of three. As the ship heaved and turned, people became sea sick, dishes fell, babies cried and women screamed.

The cost of steerage was about $18 and accommodations were almost unbearable. The agent who arranged the trip from point of departure to point of destination, charged anywhere from $45-$60. Everything was dirty, sticky and disagreeable to the touch. Many lives were lost on the trip over. Courteous officials examined first and second class immigrants briefly. But those in steerage were sent to the holding center for a full physical and mental examination. They felt that if one had the money for an expensive ticket, he or she would be unlikely to become a public charge, one of the main reasons for the inspection process at Ellis Island. The fear and language barrier must have been overwhelming. The facilities at Ellis Island between 1905 and 1914 processed more than 10,000 immigrants each day.

Traveling steerage was an experience most were anxious to forget. Many had saved for years to be able to afford the tickets for an entire family. Minimal facilities and horrible food made the immigrants wish they had never left home. Oftentimes, steerage class passengers were allowed on deck for only a brief time each day.

*Hilma Swenson Anderson, her brother and friend Alma posed for a picture in August of 1910 in Sweden just before they were ready to sail to U.S.*

MINNESOTA!

CURE FOR THE PANIC

## Emigrate to Minnesota!

Where no Banks exist ; a supension is unknown.
Land and Water of best kind. No Ague and
Fever there. CLAIMS can be made by rich and
poor.

## THE MAN OF SMALL MEANS

CAN SOON REACH COMPETENCY.

Climate dry and healthy. The rich respect and
assist the poor—all labor together. The finest
Lands are open to pre-emption.

### Saint Paul is the great stopping place,

From there you can go to any point, as emigrant
settlers start daily to the various Land Offices and
Districts.

## T. B. W.

Thos. E. Sutton, Printer, 142 Fulton Street, New York.

*Advertisement urging people to move
to Minnesota in 1857*

## Reasons for Leaving the Homeland

Most newcomers between 1880 and 1914 came from eastern and southern Europe. Many had left their homelands to escape ethnic, religious and political persecution. Others were peasants chased out by overpopulation and poverty. Some came to avoid conscription into the army. Their countries were dominated by foreign powers that mistreated their people. Contractors that were sent by American corporations to hire cheap labor for their mines and mills lured many people to the United States. In 1883, a labor paper reported how these contractors recruited European workers from "some of the most wretched districts of Hungary, Italy, or Denmark," with stories of fabulous wages in America. The contractors bamboozled the poor creatures, roped them in and made contracts with them for payment of passage that many immigrants could not understand. When they reached their destinations they found their golden dreams turned into nightmares, as they were put to work in mines, factories, or on the railroads.

They had no money to buy farms. It was important for them to live close to friends and relatives as they had in the "old country." For this reason, they were willing to take jobs in mines and factories and endure crowded quarters. Very few spoke English, and some could not read or write any language. Of the thousands who came most were young men. Within two decades relatives in America encouraged an even larger exodus from Europe. New arrivals spread out to take work in the Chicago garment shops and meat packing plant, the steel mills of Pittsburgh, Detroit, and Cleveland.

*The Marino family: George Donatelle,
Jennie Donatelle, Mary Marino (Richie)
and her brother Herman Richie about 1911*

Newspapers pictured these newcomers as 'greenhorns' who knew nothing. Sometimes they were portrayed as dangerous aliens. They were caricatured as unable or unwilling to adjust to life in America or to assimilate easily. This was soon proved false. Only one third of those who came were illiterate and most of those who couldn't speak English learned to do so within ten years after they arrived. Many settled in Pennsylvania coal-mining towns but some chose to live in large cities like Boston, New York, and Baltimore. Their stamina helped build America into a strong industrial and economic power.

These new Americans also dutifully wrote letters to their families across the sea, and these letters invariably described a wondrous land of abundance. The arrival of cash and letters had an enormous impact on emigration. By 1914, millions of immigrants arrived in the United States; most of them joined relatives already here.

### Life in Eastern Cities and why they moved on

By 1865, the Lower East Side of New York had 15,000 tenements, and 480,000 people crowded into them. Some 3,000 people lived in one block. There was no plumbing or heat in these two room dwellings. An average of eight people shared an apartment. Few of these rooms had windows and the hallways had water puddles and were often filled with filth and stench. To help pay the rent, many families took in boarders who slept on fire escapes or on rows of mattresses on the floor or on the roof. People remained crowded in firetrap buildings. Tenements for the poor made up a third of New York City's housing. More than half the city's fires were in tenements.

By 1910, millions of immigrants and their children worked in poorly lighted and unsafe mines and mills. Half of the children in New York City aged 5 to 18 could not attend school because they held jobs. Some labored in sweatshops. Others delivered messages, ran errands, shined shoes, or sold matches. These conditions existed in other eastern cities also. They became so polluted and overcrowded that the immigrants did their best to move on to other parts of the country.

*Grandpa Koniar brought this trunk from Poland in 1904*

*Immigrants waiting at the
Milwaukee Railroad sheds in 1910*

## Immigrant Room Reflections

They arrived in Minneapolis with numbers on their caps. They had been processed at the New York port of entry, then shipped onward by boat or railroad car, bound for a new life, a fresh beginning in Minnesota.

They were the pioneers of the early 1900's, the strong and stalwart men and women of Europe who brought their skills, their heritage, and their dreams to America. Thousands of new immigrants arrived at the Great Northern and Old Milwaukee Depot in Minneapolis, to be sent into a dark, crowded holding room. There they sat on hard wooden benches, waiting for someone to "claim" them and get them started in the land of opportunity: friends or family, strangers from assistance agencies, foremen representing their future employers.

Sometimes they waited for days, rationing what little food they had left, keeping a watchful eye on their "America" trunks. On the outside of the trunks were steamship labels and directions to their new homes; on the inside, their most precious possessions: family heirlooms, kitchen utensils, warm clothing, a feather tick, or a clod of dirt from the homeland.

While they waited in the unheated, brick-lined room, they shared a single toilet and shower with all the other immigrants. They re-read tattered newspapers from home, filled with advertisements promising the good life in America. The ads told of free homesteads, three dollars for a day's work, and a robust and healthy climate.

Thousands read those advertisements and came to settle this land, to work in mines and lumber camps, to raise families. Many passed through the doors and into a new life, full of hope and promise, hard indeed but rewarding.

## Arrival in Minneapolis

Some immigrants could not tell time and had to be told when to go to work. They came to established communities where friends and relatives helped them find employment. They also provided lodging, advice and encouragement. Boarding houses sprang up all over the East Side in that period to provide for the newcomers. At times they housed as many as fifteen roomers. In the late 90's a roomer paid twelve dollars a month for room and board and washing.

Soon after their arrival, some immigrants began to take courses at Sheridan School to prepare for the examination antecedent to citizenship in the United States. Among the subjects taught were American History, the American Presidents, civil government, reading and writing.

As wives arrived from Europe, communities stabilized. Old ways were preserved by families and celebrated in holiday picnics and feast days with traditional foods, and songs and dances in bright native costumes.

The immigrants also made strong efforts to retain their ancient customs. They built their own churches and named them after saints. They also subscribed to their native newspapers. Newspapers were a way to preserve the language, hear about the old country, and learn the ways of America. The ethnic press was also a force to promote charitable projects in the ancestral homeland. By reading poetry and classics from their native country, this kept their culture alive from one generation to the next.

*Moved from Pioneer Square in downtown Minneapolis during the gateway renewal in the late 1960s. It now stands on Fifth and Marshall Street NE, near a small section along the river that was rebuilt with single-family homes.*

# When a Steamer Sailed Five Miles Through Minneapolis Loop and Didn't Get Stuck

Reprinted from the *Minneapolis Journal,* March 4, 1927.

The Good Ship Enterprise sailed first to Sauk Rapids, and then right down the Street in the Old St. Anthony Loop, which now is Main Street, Minneapolis. Today, they plan for loaded barges, landing at the Minneapolis terminal. A plan is urged for a lock to bring barges right into the Minneapolis loop. Service up and down the river will start with the coming of spring.

But 65 years ago, a steamboat towed two barges majestically right down the main street of the town, right through what corresponded to the Minneapolis loop of today, never pausing, splashing mud all over the pedestrians and on horse and buggy rigs tied up at hitching posts, bounding over the muddy Main for five miles, then sliding gracefully back into the Mississippi River. And that beats anything riverboats or barges ever have done since, or ever will do again. Yet it really happened.

It happened back in 1862 when roaring steamboats plied busily over the waves of Minnetonka, when there was a daily pilgrimage of citizens to Chalybeate Springs, down under the bank near where the Tenth Avenue bridge is now. They came to drink supposedly medicinal waters; only two years after Franklin Steele, then owner of Fort Snelling, had given the abandoned military post to the State Agricultural Society for the first exclusive State Fair. A time when the Sioux outbreak was sweeping Minnesota, and Minnesota's men were in the south, helping to win the

*The steamer Enterprise making portage above St. Anthony Falls on Main Street in 1863. Navigation here was difficult. Later Captains W. F. and P. S. Davidson ran her as a freight boat between St. Paul and La Crosse and it sank in 1866.*

Civil War. The village of Minneapolis was very young and St. Anthony Falls was a metropolis.

That very year, the St. Paul and Pacific Railway reached

St. Anthony Falls, as the first railroad into the city, and built a station on Main street near Central avenue. Work on the first railroad track in Minnesota had started only a year before. The steamer Alhambra had arrived at St. Paul only a few months before, towing a barge carrying the famous locomotive William Crooks, three platform cars, a tender and a passenger coach. The first Tonka steamboat, a stern-wheeler, had been put on the lake in 1855 by Reverend Charles Gilpin who built the boat. The first propeller boat didn't reach "Tonka" until 1868.

And 11 years before that epic event, the good ship Enterprise had started regular runs to Sauk Rapids on the upper river. The Enterprise was the second boat on the upper Mississippi. Captain John Rollins built the Governor Ramsey, a sternwheeler, in 1850, as the first boat on the upper river. Then Z. E. B. Nash of St. Anthony Falls built the Enterprise, the first and only steamboat in history to sail through the Minneapolis loop and get away with it.

There wasn't much at Sauk Rapids when the Enterprise began its trips. But the town developed rapidly. For in the early '70s the flourmill and machine shop on Main Street were flourishing, as the city's leading industries. The Russell House was busy. The school, up on the hill among the trees, had a good attendance. There were two churches. Trains pulled into the depot. Logs were coming down. Business was good. Pictures made at the time show that trees surrounded the W. H. Fletcher residence, "Sunny-side," and the home of George Goodhue. George W. Benedict lived in a fine two-story home with a picket fence all around. L. Robinson, Sr. had a stone house with a bay window alongside a granite quarry.

Every home boasted lightning rods. Many boasted orna-

**STEAMER**

**GOV. RAMSEY,**
**John Rollins, Master.**

THE light draught Steamer GOV. RAMSEY, will hereafter ply regularly between Saint Anthony and Sauk Rapids, leaving St. Anthony every Monday and Thursday, at 1 o'clock, P. M., and Sauk Rapids every Wednesday and Saturday, at 8 o'clock, A. M.

☞ For freight or passage apply on board.
June 24, 1850.

mental ironwork and scrolls, highly popular at the time. For Sauk Rapids was young, then. And so was Minneapolis. It was July 2, 1857, records show when the Enterprise started on its first trip to Sauk Rapids. Business wasn't good at all though the boat operated for quite awhile. At last, the owners gave up and James McMullen contracted to move the Enterprise from the upper to the lower Mississippi. There were a few things, such as the falls and the apron and the bridges and the rapids and the big log booms in the way. But that didn't stop Mr. McMullen.

He loaded steamboat and barges on trestles, yanked them out of the river, and marched them through the mud and slush on Main Street, clear from the upper levee to the vicinity of the infant University of Minnesota. Then he slid them back in the river. It was a feat of engineering and steamboating never rivaled here.

And that is the Odyssey of the only boat that ever sailed through the Minneapolis Loop. Of course there was no loop for there were no streetcars to loop. But Main Street corresponded to today's loop, at that.

# MAP OF MINNEAPOLIS

...ACCOMPANYING...

## HUDSON'S DICTIONARY OF MINNEAPOLIS

### EDITION OF 1900.

---

*STREET RAILWAYS* Indicated by **NARROW** Green Lines.

*PARK WAYS*  "  "  **BROAD**  "  "

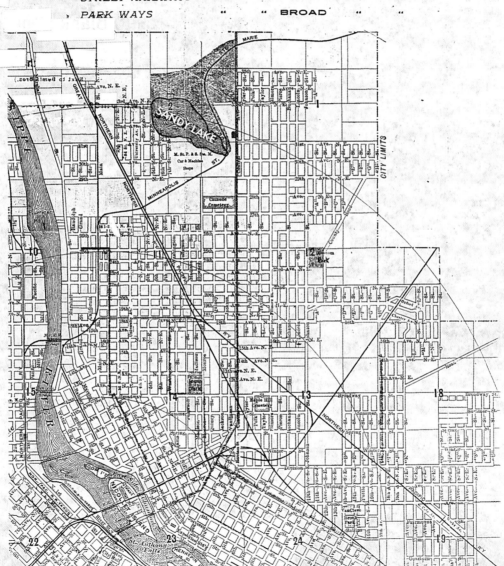

# The Disappearance of Lake Sandy

Once upon a time, around the turn of the century, Northeast Minneapolis had a lake of its own. It was not a large or a distinguished lake. But it was there and it belonged to Northeast.

Lake Sandy was located west of Central Avenue, on both sides of the present St. Anthony Parkway. Part of it was under the land now occupied by the Soo Line Railroad yards and the remainder of it was the forty acres on park property to which Theodore Wirth refers to in his book called *Minneapolis Park System 1883–1944*. Early planners also visualized lakeside housing. A 1914 public plat of lands for parks and public parkways shows a Sandy Lake Addition, platted for homes which never materialized on NE Fifth and Sixth Streets from 31st Avenue to 33rd.

Lake Sandy ceased to exist somewhere around 1919. Exact information about the lake's parameters, such as depth and volume, is unavailable. The area of the former lake had been a wetland periodically and in it's final demise it was graded, drained and maintained as a municipal golf course. There is little doubt that Lake Sandy was a popular recreation area in the late 1880s and early 1900s. According to park board minutes it was popular and served as Northeast's most used recreation area. It was a favorite hunting and fishing area and at one point, was the only City Park with an ice rink, warming house and concession stand, according to park board records.

In the early 1900s, something happened to the lake. Historians, among them Marion Shutter and Isaac Atwater, say the lake was fed by underground springs which dried up. Wirth, in his last reference to Sandy Lake called it a "large area of swamp land." Almost eighty years after the lake mysteriously disappeared there are not many clues as to what happened. Nothing is documented in Minneapolis Park Board proceedings or in Wirth's book.

Several theories have been advanced about the drying up of Lake Sandy. These include drainage, change and diversion of surface runoff due to urbanization, lakebed destruction and infilling. Park officials in the late nineteenth century were mainly interested in draining the lake and installing athletic fields or enlarging the golf course which was considered more beneficial than a shallow lake. Soon after acquisition of Columbia Park, drain tiles were laid (in 1892) and connections to existing sewer systems were sought to accelerate drainage.

In October, 1893, the park board bought a 183-acre site that became Columbia Park. The land included Sandy Lake, which measured 40-acres. The park was named Columbia because of its proximity to Columbia Heights and because the land was purchased during what was known as the "Columbian Year." The Minneapolis Improvement Company, which included Thomas Lowry and other prominent business leaders, sold the land for $208,376.50 and donated $20,000 for "immediate improvement of the park" in 1893.

At the same time Columbia Park was bought and improved, the park board also made plans for a dredging program which eventually "affected every lake in the city," according to Wright. As early as 1914 problems of athletic field use are connected with drainage of "the meadow" (no lake then). In 1918 the park drainage system was connected with the Soo Line drainage system and the meadow was considered dry enough for athletic activities. Not until 1925 are problems of wetness mentioned again in the park board's annual reports. Then, the problem of surface water disposal reappears. There is evidence that suggests Sandy Lake may have been filled with material dredged from Lake of the Isles from 1907 to 1911 when improvements were made that connected it to Lake Calhoun. In the years 1905, 1910, and 1912 Sandy Lake shrinks on park board maps and then in 1918 it is not listed at all. During this time, Lake of the Isles gets progressively larger.

Ever since the golf course was built there have been at least three attempts to restore Sandy Lake, in 1927, 1928 and 1933, and the citizens requested the installation of swimming facilities. Instead the meadow was plowed and seeded in 1937 and fairways installed in 1940. The project was included in long range capital improvement plans for the city in the early 1980s.

After a six-year campaign that has as much to do with neighborhood pride as rediscovering an old lake, city officials authorized a feasibility study to determine whether a 40-acre lake in northeast Minneapolis that dried up shortly after the turn of the century can be restored. Ever since the disappearance of Lake Sandy encouragement of its restoration has been strong. In the 1980s some feasibility studies were done to rehabilitate the lake. The "Lake Sandy Restoration Committee" and the "Northeast Planning Council" along with other citizen groups have generated a significant amount of interest.

In an effort to learn more about Lake Sandy, officials printed announcements in Northeast Minneapolis to try to find people who remember the shallow lake. Only a few, now in their 70s and 80s came forward. Most recall the lake in its later stages, just before it ceased to exist, when it was mostly marsh. Some of the old settlers recalled a one-time creek, which ran down hill into the lake, in the vicinity of St. Anthony Parkway.

"It was like a big swamp with a lot of cattails sticking out," said John Barno, 74, recalling what was left of the lake in 1918. "It was just swampy. There were parts of it clear but the part that was clear was about as wide as a street and a half-block long. It just dried up, that's all." Florabelle Runyan, 81, a lifelong northeast Minneapolis resident, recalled: "I remember the lake more or less as a mud hole; I don't remember it having a shore, I was small then."

Miss Mildred Fisk lived on Johnson Street until her death two years ago. In her retirement years she was known for her collection of Northeast history and appeared on KTCA-TV to document an earlier time. Her old pictures included a cow pasture at the present intersection of Lowry and Johnson, next to a slender walking trail. She recalled childhood picnics on the shores of Lake Sandy, far from the bustle of early downtown Minneapolis, and carrying home small pink shells to commemorate those occasions.

The symbolic future for northeast Minneapolis—a vision of loons, jogging paths and expensive homes overlooking the water—lies in an unfinished feasibility study. The reality, for the moment, consists of a dry lakebed, a public golf course that floods and 70-year old memories.

For years, Lake Sandy has been an occasional joke at City Hall; even its supporters could not resist the fun. Walt Dziedzic, First Ward City Council member, once planted a plastic fish in the lake bed and later stopped a tour bus to point out the former lake and the fish to sightseers. Mayor Don Fraser, at one point, reportedly agreed to sit on the golf course in a canoe when heavy rains flooded part of the lakebed, but then backed out, saying he feared his suit would get dirty.

It's difficult to rediscover Lake Sandy. The only re-minders are a few old plat maps at the Park Board and the Minneapolis Public Works Department plus one small reference in the worn Wirth book in the library. It is most alive in the minds of the senior citizens calling to share their pleasant memories while the restoration was under discussion.

# Gerber Baths

*Gerber Baths on the Mississippi River in 1910*

*Play area of Gerber Baths*

In its heydey, the Gerber recreation area drew children and their families from all over Northeast Minneapolis. It was a swimming area in the river guarded by lifeguards in boats. Admission was just five cents to those who could afford it. Most couldn't. The most profitable day brought in about 30 cents. Gerber Baths, located on Hall's Island was also a favorite place for band concerts, a great playground and later started showing silent movies. It was named after Michael Gerber, who owned a successful book binding business. He was a big-hearted man and paid for the bath house and playground equipment. He was the alderman of the

Eastside at the time. The island was located just north of the Plymouth Avenue Bridge at Eighth Avenue and across from Boom Island. You could get to the island two ways, by going over the Plymouth Avenue bridge or by the foot bridge on the Ninth Avenue side.

In the early 1900s Hall's Island was formed because of the accumulation of sand and debris along the boom piers near Boom Landing. Over time the detached land pieces connected in a continuous island that was separated from the mainland by a shallow channel. In 1906, Dr. P. M. Hall, city health inspector deeded the island to the city for municipal purposes only. With the provision that the city made it into a public park and the shallow east side channel into a swimming and skating park for children.

Swimming in the river became a great attraction on hot summer afternoons. Before Gerber Baths opened young boys would go to the nearest bridge and swim in the river. But this could be risky. As word of the drownings spread, more of the youngsters felt safer at Gerber

*Michael P. Gerber, founder of the bathhouse stands at left. Swimmers in regular street clothes or modest bathing suits of the day take a dip in 1910. Note the Grain Belt Brewery in the background across the river.*

Baths where lifeguards kept a close watch. Chet Remarcik, a long time Northeast Minneapolis resident responded with a casual "no place" when his mother asked where he was headed those summer afternoons. "None of the parents wanted their kids to go too far, especially to the river" he said. During the early years swimming suits were rare. You could rent a bathing suit but most of the boys swam in their overalls and undershirts. Swimming suits were awkward and resembled long underwear.

With its great appeal to children Gerber Baths became a family center on Sunday afternoons and band concerts drew large crowds to Hall's Island on early Sunday evenings. Later, silent movies were shown on an outdoor screen. At first, the movie projector continually broke down, interrupting practically every movie at some point. As the novelty of this new invention wore off and its technology improved, the films ran more smoothly. These were the forerunners of today's outdoor movies.

The iron crowbars of a wrecking crew were intended for the old bathhouse in 1929. But fate had different plans. Its history made it seem appropriate that the abandoned building should say goodbye to the world in a mass of flames on the fourth of July. When the firemen arrived they found a skyrocket sticking in the roof. With the flames roaring, they could not save the building and perhaps it was not intended that they should. While spectators watched, the old structure made its last bid for public recognition, and then collapsed.

*View of Gerber Baths showing trolley tracks and footbridge leading to the island*

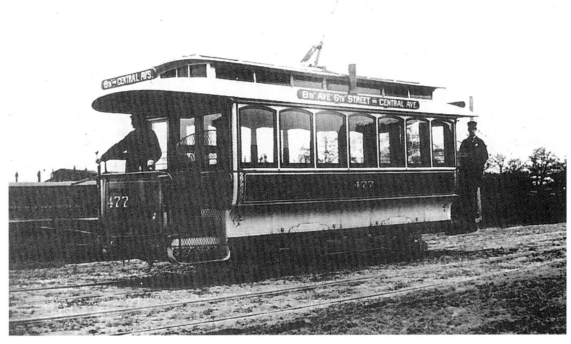

*Minneapolis Street Railway car on Central Avenue in 1890*

# The Polish Flyer, Monroe Express and Other Street Cars

Thomas Lowry was a lawyer and a real estate speculator. He built up Northeast Minneapolis, Columbia Heights and Lowry Hill. His vision was to create a simple transportation system that would help him sell lots at the edge of town. If in case his customers would build homes he would also need to provide a way to take them back and forth to work. So he bankrolled the city's streetcar system in 1875 and for the next twenty-four years. As a reliable means of transportation the streetcar system turned the Twin Cities into a growing metropolis. Where streetcar tracks were laid, people built homes and businesses. Each night they patiently waited at the corners where every hour on the hour they could ride the trolley for work or pleasure.

First came the horse drawn omnibuses. Horse drawn streetcars that traveled on rails soon replaced these. They could hold more people and were easier to pull. Separate horsecar companies were founded in St. Paul and Minneapolis. The first streetcars seated only fourteen passengers and were dragged on tracks through unpaved streets by horses and mules. When mud was not a problem, snow

*At Broadway and Monroe Streets one of the first horse cars operated in the state of Minnesota 1888*

routinely caused havoc and the layer of straw spread on the streetcar floor wasn't much help in keeping riders warm.

Primitive cars were ten feet in length with two long seats. Some passengers were reminded to pay their fare by the ringing of a bell. The driver stood on a platform protected by a sheet iron dash, which came slightly above his knees. He was required to drive the horse, keep a sharp look out for passengers, take their fare and make change. After dark, the car was illuminated with an oil lamp that was usually dim and gave off a bad odor. In winter, a small sheet iron stove in the middle of the car supplied heat. No car was permitted to run faster than six miles per hour. Drivers worked twelve to sixteen hour days with only a twenty-minute dinner break. They were also required to wash their car at the beginning or end of their shift. Plus the pay for all of this effort was just $35 per month.

The horses cost from $135 to $150 each and required six horses for each car operated. A bell on the horse's collar signaled the car's approach. Horses were a problem. Up to seven were required to keep a single car in service all day. They produced epic quantities of manure. They were slow, couldn't handle steep hills and were subject to disease.

Lowry's Twin City Rapid Transit Company took a giant step on Christmas Eve 1889 when it launched an electric-powered streetcar down Minneapolis' South Fourth Avenue. Within two years, the last horse was sent to pasture, and local travelers made the trip from one downtown to the other in just a short while via University Avenue.

In 1891 St. Paul and Minneapolis merged and formed the Twin City Rapid Transit Company. The streetcar companies were often unstable financially, especially during the 1890s, when money was scarce and the bicycle craze provided stiff competition. It wasn't until the late 1890s that the trolley caught on and business thrived. Lowry died in 1909.

When the era of the 1920s ended there were 523 miles of track carrying 1,021 "banana yellow" cars. So entered the golden age of streetcars.

According to headlines in the Minneapolis newspapers of 1907, the company instituted its first "pay as you enter" streetcars, and this promptly became known as the "pay gate" issue. Some women's organizations fought the innovation, claiming the gates were not wide enough for the women's hat styles of that year.

Northeast got its first trolley in 1882 when tracks were laid along Hennepin Avenue. At Central Avenue, the track split continuing along Hennepin.

The Central Avenue portion of the line traveled north and turned onto Monroe Street near the present-day Bank's store. From there it continued north on Monroe to 18th Avenue then turned east to Central and north to Lowry Avenue. Major additions to the streetcar system were built in 1891 with a double-track line on Second Street NE from 17th Avenue to Lowry and a single-track line along Central between Monroe and 18th. In 1893 the Central Avenue route was expanded to 40th Avenue in Columbia Heights. The Second Street Line was fondly referred to as the "Polish Flyer."

On November 8th 1911, track was laid on 18th Avenue between Central and Johnson Street and on Johnson from 18th to 28th Avenues. The East Minneapolis station with 26 inside storage tracks was on East Hennepin Avenue between Second Street NE and Fourth Street. It opened in

*Small boys jammed stones into a switch and the car took out the front of a grocery store on 33rd and Johnson Street*

*East Side Station at First Avenue between University and Fourth Street in 1901.*

1891 and closed June 19, 1954, the last car station to operate in the Twin Cities. The building is now the Superior Plating Company.

Streetcar service exclusively for employees of Northern Pump Company began in 1943 when two trolleys, painted red, white and blue ran between the plant near Fridley and the intersection of Marshall and 30th Avenues NE, over the line of the Minneapolis, Anoka & Cuyana Range Railway. The line was acquired by Northern Pump. Identification badges served as fare.

An abbreviated fare history appears below:

| | |
|---|---|
| 1875–1921 | 5 cents |
| 1921–1925 | 8 cents |
| 1925–1948 | 10 cents |
| 1948 | 11 cents |
| 1949 | 12 cents |
| 1950 | 15 cents |
| 1953 | 20 cents |

For 46 years the fare remained at 5 cents, and for 23 years it remained at 10 cents.

The Grand-Monroe line nicknamed the Monroe Express was abandoned in 1952. The Monroe end was then combined with the Nicollet-Second Street line.

The Soo Line freight interchange was on the west side of Central Avenue, just north of 36th Avenue NE. From that point the new line crossed the short single-track stretch of track used by Twin City Rapid Transit's Columbia Heights cars on Central Avenue NE, then turned north and ran parallel to the TCRT line, now double track, to 37th Avenue NE and Reservoir Boulevard. So from 36th to 37th Avenue there were three tracks along Central Avenue NE, two of them for TCRT streetcars on the Columbia Heights line and one used in both directions by the waterworks line.

*East Side Station showing cars on tracks, 1954*

*Car # 2 at 13th and Second Street in front of 13th Avenue State Bank, the forerunner of Northeast State Bank, 1950*

Getting past De La Salle on Nicollet Island before 3 PM when school let out was a challenge. The students liked to get in the car and pull a rope that disconnected the streetcar from the trolley line, which supplied electricity to the car. It was done in fun but could cause problems. If they pulled hard enough and broke the rope, the conductor had to crawl out on top of the car and fix it.

During the 1940s, the last decade of growth that coordinated with the public transportation system, the two downtowns dominated shopping, employment and institutions. Retail clusters sprang up at major streetcar transfer points. Even though streetcar ridership dropped after World War II, 165 million passengers were carried in the Twin Cities in 1949.

The last streetcar lines were converted to bus routes in 1953.

*Great Northern Depot , 2 Hennepin Avenue opened in 1914 and closed in 1978*

# *Great Northern Depot Was a Link to Adventure*

**By Stanley L. Baker**

It is a sad commentary on today's railroads to see the Great Northern Railroad depot (later the Burlington Northern depot), a long-time landmark of this city, being torn down. I went there the other day to have another look at the old structure and I was filled with nostalgic moments.

As a boy, I spent many a summer day watching the passenger trains arrive and depart from the depot. It was located within walking distance of my home in northeast Minneapolis. I had a favorite spot to watch the trains coming and going behind the north end of the depot, a two-foot wide limestone ledge running along the wall of a six-story red brick warehouse. It was opposite the depot and a bridge spanning the tracks on First Street and it was an ideal spot for train watching. Here I had a panoramic view of all the tracks leading into the depot, a box seat, so to speak, in this theater of train movements.

Mornings were the best time to watch all of the activity, as this was when most of the passenger trains arrived and departed. Perched on my ledge, I could hear the whistling of a passenger train a long way off approaching the grade crossings, the whistling growing louder and louder as the train got closer and closer. When it finally reached the yard junction, the engineer would highball with two long blasts, acknowledging the switch tender's "all-clear" signal to proceed to the depot.

The engine and string of cars would roll close by me while I eagerly scrutinized the passengers sitting at the coach windows and listened to the sound of the wheels going clickety-clack over the maze of switches and crossings leading into the various track stalls. To me, the arrival of each passenger train was a link with faraway places, creating a feeling of mystery and adventure.

Watching the train leaving the depot was a spectacle just as exciting. As soon as the conductor shouted "all aboard" and waved to the engineer, the giant locomotive came alive. There would be a hiss of steam and smoke starting to erupt from the stack. As the iron monster prepared to ease out of the stall, it would sound off with a short exhaust bark, followed by several louder blasts. The huge driving wheels would slip in an effort to gain traction on the shiny steel rails and the train slowly would begin to roll out of the depot. As the noise of the engine's exhaust increased, great clouds of smoke would belch from the stack. When the locomotive got close to where I sat, the thundering blasts of the exhaust would be deafening, echoing off the walls of the nearby-buildings.

As the train picked up speed and the demand for steam pressure lessened, the sound of the exhaust would diminish and the billowing smoke plume would level off, trailing over the entire length of the train and gradually dissipating above the last car. As the observation coach disappeared around the bend, I would be left with an empty and lonesome feeling.

Many times I would go inside the depot to see all that was going on—people standing in line at the ticket and baggage counters, rows of benches filled with occupants in the waiting area, passengers milling around at the track gates ready to board the trains, travelers arriving from incoming trains being greeted by friends and relatives, redcaps soliciting tourists' luggage, the loudspeaker announcing the arrival and departure time of the trains. It was a noisy and busy place, much like the airport terminal today.

I would spin around on a pedestal stool at the long marble soda fountain, wishing I had enough money to order a sundae or a strawberry soda; gaze at the mural along the wall depicting a scene of the Blackfoot Indians at Glacier National Park; browse around the souvenir concession; select a free timetable from the rack, imagining that I was one of the lucky ones going somewhere by train.

To be part of all the hubbub going on inside the depot was an exciting experience for a youngster. Outside, the sidewalks were crowded with people, taxis were lined up at the curb, picking up and unloading passengers, streetcars rumbled by, filled to capacity—all a familiar everyday occurrence back in the days when travel by train was the way to go.

But times changed as the years went by. Railroads shifted from steam to diesel, passenger business declined, and before long, there were only a few remaining trains using the depot, eventually taken over by the Amtrak. The last passenger train left the depot on March 1, 1978. It was the death of this 65 year-old structure, ending an era. This magnificent landmark will soon be gone, only a memory. How the mighty hath fallen!

*Stanley L. Baker is a long-time collector of railroad memorabilia and has written a book on the subject His article appeared in the "Readers Write Saturday" Neighbors Section of the Minneapolis Tribune, July 1, 1978, 5B and is reprinted with permission of the author.*

*Ambassador Sausage Company celebrated 50th anniversary in 1982. All of the employees and their spouses came out for wieners, brats and all the fixings', old time Polish music and tours of the plant for family members. In front row Jim Koch, owner Ethel Arnold, her daughter Shirley Severson, Matthew and Delores Balafas.*

# 5 Connections – The Places We Remember

## AMBASSADOR SAUSAGE COMPANY

427 Harrison Street. At the age of 73 Ethel Arnold was named Small Businessperson of the Year by the Minneapolis Chamber of Commerce. She took a small floundering sausage company and restored it to making a profit after the death of her husband in 1958. The firm was in debt and within $1^1/2$ years she turned the company around. After making a few changes, sales were still flat and they needed an effective promotion to increase product awareness. Her marketing tool was an oversized Scotsman dressed in a kilt. She sponsored a contest among her distributors to submit a new name for the mannequin. The suggestion of "Ambassador Man" won out. Ethel liked the idea and changed the Scotsman to a hot-dog dressed in a top hat, tails and carrying a cane. Not only did the company survive but went on to do over a million dollars a year in profit. "They're all done in the old-fashioned way," Ethel said. "We have an old fashioned smokehouse, and we're here because we've emphasized quality all those years." She celebrated 50 years at Ambassador in 1986, where she started stuffing wieners and packing sausages on her 21st birthday in 1936. Because her hometown of Bowlus, Minnesota didn't have a high school, 15 year-old Ethel Arnold hitched a ride on a creamery truck in 1931. She was headed for Minneapolis where her grandmother lived near Edison High School. She spent her last nickel taking a streetcar to the superintendent's office to seek permission to enter Edison. Later she found out she couldn't afford the fee the school district required for accepting a nonresident. With only an eighth grade education she raised two children and rescued a tiny sausage company that was a week away from bankruptcy. The sign on her desk read, "A woman has to do twice as much as a man to be considered half as good." Wimmers Meat Products bought the company in 1996. Even though they are located in Nebraska, the Ambassador products are sold only in Minnesota.

## AMBLE'S CONFECTIONERY

758 Monroe Street NE. In 1930, John Amble came home with an ice cream machine, and Amble's Confectionery became the first store this side of Chicago to serve home made ice cream. A favorite stopping place when band concerts at Logan Park were packed with kids from all over. Young store clerks in starched white uniforms served cones, malts, sodas, cokes, root beer and all kinds of concoctions to a hungry crowd on hot summer nights. They'd roll out the popcorn machine and park it on the corner. They were also the first around to introduce soft serve malts that came in a small cup for five and ten cents each. Amble's had a refrigerated soda fountain and cigar

*Amble's Confectionery about 1931. Notice the brick streets and old streetcar tracks*

*John Amble, Sr.*

counter. They packaged their own ice cream in pints and quarts that sold for 35 cents and 59 cents and kept it cold using block ice that was delivered by a horse pulled wagon. The entire family worked at the store. All six children came in after school. The mother worked during the day and the father came in after he got home from his job on the railroad. They were open seven days a week until 10 or 11 at night. There was no age limit for employment in the early days so many well-known Northeasters had their first job at Amble's. Carol Amble worked after school when she was about eleven. It was her job to sell candy that was kept in a glass counter with penny candy in dishes on top. Some of the popular candies were chocolate soldiers, Mary Jane's, green leafs and long sticks of black and red licorice. All of these were a penny. Candy bars sold for five cents, like Milky Way, Mr. Goodbar and Snickers. Nut Goodies were ten cents. You could get a Holloway sucker for just a nickel that lasted all day. John Amble first took over the candy store in 1929. There was also a dry goods store in the same building. Nathan Darowitz owned the tailor shop. After a while they bought out the tailor shop and expanded into groceries and added a restaurant. The restaurant did well at the noon hour. There were eight booths along the Broadway wall and tables too. They served hot dinners with two kinds of meat; mashed potatoes, a vegetable and dessert-like bread or rice pudding. Mrs. Amble made the dinners at home and they would carry the food over in a basket and put it on a steam table. The family lived across the street on Broadway and also owned a filling station called Amble's Standard Oil across from the store on Broadway and Monroe.

*Andy and his wife Anna celebrated
their 50th anniversary*

## ANDREW MANSHAK
## SHOE REPAIR SHOP

206–13th Avenue NE. Andy's shop was a small wooden structure with crooked wooden steps leading to a narrow, worn out screened door. A sign above read "Shoe Repairing." Inside was an old pedal-driven sewing machine, workbench and piles of shoes. An ancient stove gave off the smoky aroma of burning wood mixed with the smell of leather. Known as the Mayor of 13th Avenue, for over sixty years he worked in the shoe shop every day from 7 in the morning to 7 at night. Andy was very well loved. A small man, he wore a leather apron and spoke broken English. He learned the shoe trade in his native country of Slovakia and came to the U.S. in 1907. His little frame building was built in 1918. He loved to chitchat with the customers. Some of which would tease him about being the oldest merchant on 13th Avenue and how he should run for mayor. He would go home for lunch, which was two blocks away and if he had to use the bathroom he'd have to hike his way home, even if there were customers in the shop. He never took a vacation except when his daughter got married he closed up shop. Every Sunday he sang in the St. Cyril's choir and then hopped on the streetcar after church to visit his boy's grave in the cemetery. His shop was a busy place where he did general shoe repair and skate sharpening. Andy devised a special inner soul for George Mikan. So the whole Minneapolis Laker team were regular customers and so was the Minneapolis Fire Department. He was very proud of the signed photos that lined his wall; pictures of important people that came into his shop. He was such a good dancer and a very colorful character. He always took time to say hello. Andy was known and loved for his stories. He often told about the time he made insoles for President Eisenhower. Not knowing his size, he looked at a picture of the President and guessed at size 11. Actually, the President wore 10½. Andy sent the insoles to the Governor of Minnesota, who gave them to the Presi-

dent. It wasn't long before a letter came from the White House with a note of thanks and it was displayed on Andy's wall. No one is sure how Andy got the title of Mayor of 13th Avenue. It may have started when a local bank held a celebration for Andy and his wife on their 50th Anniversary. No one doubted the nickname was accurate and well deserved. He was the last member of the original Northeast Business Association. He worked continuously until the day he died in 1975 at 86 years old.

## DADY'S DRUGSTORE

1226 NE Second Street. John Dady remembered looking in the window of the Graben Brothers Drugstore as a child. He was fascinated by the flashing neon lights of the pinball machine and the colorful drugs in the window. He never dreamed he would one day be the owner of his own drugstore. Dady bought the drug-store in 1945 from Bill Debolak who also owned Rolig Drug. Dady's income for the first month was $1200. He accounts this to being open every day from 8 AM to 10 PM. Art Erkel was the very first owner of Dady's or Second Street Pharmacy as it was later called. He also owned a drugstore located on 13th and Main Street. Dady's became a popular gathering place, complete with pinball machine, a soda fountain in the front of which they sold ice cream and pop, and four booths and the pharmacy in back. Dady owned one of the last Hires Root Beer Barrel dispensers. He says he has never seen another one like it. Kids from neighboring schools, Sheridan, St. Anthony and St. Cyril made Dady's their hang out. Dady was known for his friendly service and ran a running charge account for his customers. He didn't send out bills for the first 15 years in business. Customers paid whenever they wanted, usually once a year. As an added service, Dady's Drug sold stamps, money orders and paid utility bills for customers. So many regulars over the years refused to get their prescriptions anywhere else. He knew his customers by name and could give personal care. Some even called in the middle of the night. As the chain drugstores increased, the smaller neighborhood druggists suffered. The fountain was removed in 1965 and replaced by a greeting card display. In later years he did good business selling Polish rosaries, flags, plaques and religious greeting cards. Then after forty years on 13th and Second Street, Dady sold the drugstore to Harlow Strike in 1984. He and his wife, Margaret retired. And it closed in 1997 and became a retail store for eyeglasses. According to Dady there were once seventeen drugstores in Northeast Minneapolis, now there are only two left in the whole Northeast area. He has fond memories of mixing drugs by hand, and advising people on anything from medicine to personal problems at home. He bought more than one wedding or engagement ring of customers who had broken up. Dady's was located on the flood plain and many times the store was completely under water. He also remembers watching for "the Polish Flyer," a fond nickname for the Second Street Trolley. Almost like the loss of a family member, the closing of Dady's Drug signifies the end of an era.

## DUSTY'S

1319 NE Marshall Street. For 50 years, Dusty Stebe has poured beer and served dago burgers and pizzelle to his Northeast neighbors. The former iron ranger and his wife Pat purchased the bar from the Brewery in 1951. The history of the bar goes back to the beginnings of the city. The first name on the land deed is Minnesota's first governor, Henry H. Sibley. Information about the owners from then until 1891, when city water was hooked up, is unavailable. But sometime in those years, Grain Belt purchased the land, built the existing building and began serving its beer. The bar, sitting in the shadows of the Brewery, prospered for many years until liquor was outlawed. During the bootlegging period of the 1930s, booze was stored in the small apartment upstairs. When the intentionally limited bar supplies ran out, workers lowered more on a haul line that ran through a fake ceiling. The covered tiles doubled as a rack to hold the booze. Today, the fake ceiling is still there, however, unneeded. When prohibition was repealed, Dusty's prospered

again. The Brewery hired more than 400 people, many of who watered at Dusty's after work and on the weekends. But the prosperity sagged when the Brewery closed in 1976. People still come in from all over the city and suburbs to reacquaint with their Northeast roots.

*Inside Eklund's Clothing in 1912.*
*Nels is standing on far right.*

## EKLUNDS CLOTHING

403 East Hennepin Avenue. Nineteen year old Nels P. Eklund left his native Sweden in 1880 to seek his fortune in America. His first job was in Burlington, Iowa where he worked as an errand boy in a clothing store. He worked his way up to buyer in two years. After moving to Minneapolis, he became a partner with Peter Nelson in the firm Nelson and Eklund. In 1894 Nels took over the firm when his partner died. Located on East Hennepin on the corner where Central Avenue and Fifth Street meet, it began as a store catering to the working man, the blue-collar worker. In 1910, Mr. Eklund changed location and leased the corner store across East Hennepin on Fourth Street. This was against the wisdom of his friends. They commented that nobody had made a success in that location which became a challenge to Mr. Eklund. Six months prior to moving, he instructed his helper to save all their good-looking stock boxes that the merchandise came in. One Sunday his closest friend, Emanuel Carlson helped him move his entire stock to the new location on an express wagon as used by children. The empty boxes were placed above the shelves holding the merchandise. When the new store opened on Monday morning, customers came in and congratulated Mr. Eklund on the large stock. He proudly pointed to the empty boxes and acknowledged the

*Nels Eklund handing his daily deposit*
*to a bank teller in the 1920s*

large stock of merchandise. Mr. Eklund's pet and most trusty slogan over the years had been, "Better values—location does it." Through the many changes in merchandising, he remodeled his store and expanded Eklund's to become one of the leading men's clothing stores in Minneapolis. He continued to work at the store into his nineties. The sons Alan, Arnold and Neil maintained the fair honest merchandising policy that won lasting friends and customers of fourth and fifth generations. Even with the improvements of East Hennepin and the creation of the one-way streets, Eklund's continued to flourish although not in the rapid pace the company enjoyed in prior years. In the late 1970s and the early 1980s, businesses in the immediate shopping area began to move out of the area. People were beginning to shop in the neighborhood malls as many of them were moving out into the suburbs. For this reason, the business began to slide and by the summer of 1984, Eklund's decided they would have to close their doors for good. This was a very difficult decision for Dick Eklund especially because he was the only member of the family still in the business. Paul Eklund and Jim Wiberg had retired earlier. So this left Dick and Jim's wife Ellie to finalize the closing. Thus the end of an era came to a close after 91 years of serving the many friends in Minneapolis' Eastside and all of the metropolitan Twin Cities.

## FRANCES' FAIRY DOLL HOSPITAL AND GIFT SHOP

105–107 East Hennepin. Frances Rodengen opened a doll hospital in 1952, and it became the largest doll repair shop this side of Chicago. People from all across the country would bring in or send their dolls to be fixed. The Baby Bilo doll for example, had moveable eyes and an odd shaped head. The eyes were made of glass and even came in different colors. They would close and turn depending on which way the doll was facing. There were lead weights inside the plaster of Paris doll head that controlled the eye mechanism. These weights made of Duco cement would always dry

up causing the eyes to sink back into the head. So the wig and the top of the head had to be removed in order to get at the weights for replacement. The replacement of doll body parts was one of the most common repairs. Sometimes a dog would get ahold of a doll and chew off an arm. Frances would go out scouting for old dolls to use for parts. The Salvation Army Thrift Store was a good place to buy old dolls. In the upstairs of the doll factory there were piles of shoeboxes that contained body parts, a doll mortuary of shoes, eyes, legs, heads and even boxes of wigs. Some were really old and made of kid leather. Frances would wash the hair; comb, curl and even replace it. Frances' sister Anna made doll clothes for the shop. She was an accomplished seamstress, and made the clothes according to customer specifications. Wedding dresses or baby clothes were common requests. It was left to Mr. Rodengen and his son Roger to restring the dolls if the arm mechanism came undone. This was not an easy job. Using elastic string and hooks, a great deal of pressure and strength was needed to pull it tight enough. There was also a toyshop but this took too much time away from the flourishing doll repair business. Also a part of the service was a paintshop for the dolls that needed repainting. The eyebrows, eyelashes, skin color, finger tips and toes would wear away and a new facial expression was put on the porcelain dolls when they left the hospital. Frances was also a collector of dolls. Shirley Temple dolls and Kupie dolls were popular in the 1950s. Some of the dolls that were worked on dated back to the early part of the nineteenth century. The owners of the Gluek Brewery would collect dolls from different countries. It was always exciting to see the different ones that they would bring in from their travels. In the early 60's the building was condemned, demolished and replaced by the Riverplace complex. The doll hospital was sold and Frances retired.

## FREDERIC JANDA STORE— POPPYSEED MAN

2201 NE Second Street. At seventeen, Frederic came to Minneapolis in 1911, from Nowy Targ, Poland. After World War II he joined two Polish men in a grocery market on Fourth Street and Twenty-second Avenue. They called it the Polish Provision Company, Meats and Groceries. During the late 1920s they separated and each started their own store. Peter Biernat operated his on Lowry and Third Street. The third man opened his store in Columbia Heights. Janda moved a few times and then when Masley, a grocer on twenty-second and Second Street died, he decided to take over this store. Masley was a seller of poppyseed and Janda decided to take over his lucrative business; he developed the business and became known as "Poppyseed Man." He purchased poppyseed from a distributor in the Netherlands in large quantities and sold it all over the city. This became his main source of income. He married in his late 40's. His wife was a poet. He retired from his store at the age of 90 or so and was relatively wealthy. He died shortly after his 100th birthday.

## GRUMPY'S BAR

2200 NE Fourth Street. Grumpy's was formerly known as Zurbeys. With its high ceilings and as home to community celebrations and charities, Zurbeys has seen everything from Slovak dancing to Russian New Year festivities and Polish meat raffles to support East Side Neighborhood Services. In his time, previous owner Andy Zurbey could be seen playing a polka on his concertina. Other great concertina players also visited Zurbeys, including Ray Ardnt, Ed Schney and Donny Robak, whose dad made and repaired the accordion-like instrument. Zurbey recalls different languages among the ethnic groups limited communication away from Northeast's bars. "Everyone intermingled in the pubs. Nobody but your own ethnic group understood your language. That didn't matter. Somehow,

the public houses interpreted everyone's feelings and we communicated about everything from religion to politics to neighborhood problems." The tavern with its sociable atmosphere and touch of Chicago style has been serving the neighborhood since Prohibition ended. Current owner, Pat Dwyer, a native of Chicago's Irish pubs and now long-time resident of Northeast, purchased the bar after a distinguished career as a record producer. As a member of the community, he wants Grumpies to be the mixing place of generations. A place to continue the past traditions of festivities and public association.

*Fr. John Memorich and his wife with Andy Zurbey playing his Concertina at the bar in about 1991*

*On McKinley Street behind the greenhouse. The house in the center is*
*the family home. Hans Rosacker stands to the right of employees*

## HANS ROSACKER COMPANY

1850 Stinson Boulevard NE. The Hans Rosacker Company began in 1902. Hans and Amalia moved from a farm near Morgan, Minnesota and started the business with a great deal of determination and not much money. They first started delivering flowers with horses. Hans, Jr. as a kid delivered to downtown Minneapolis and East Hennepin by hopping on a streetcar. Their children Henry, Robert, Hans, Jr. and Arthur helped out when they were of age. And soon the business turned into the largest florist on the East Side of town. As a wholesaler they also sold to retail florists from all over the Twin Cities. Husband and wife teams were not common in those early days and that could account for some of their success. She was the mainstay of the retail part and he was the grower. She went to the flower shop every day, arranged flowers in the morning, and went out in the afternoon with bouquets in hand and delivered them to her sick and shut in friends. She was a very kind woman. Everyone called her Grandma Rosacker. Adjacent to Hillside Cemetery, the entire block was filled with greenhouses. Their main business consisted of bedding plants with

*Storefront of Rosacker Florist Shop. Second from right is Amalia Rosacker, co-founder of the business 1930s.*

booming sales of poinsettias and lilies for special occasions. Roses have always been their specialty and Rose Acres or Acres of Roses became the trademark in the 1950's. Grandma Rosacker was an active member of St. Paul's Lutheran Church and donated the largest stain glass window in the front of the church. She drove a big Buick and bowled regularly, even in her later years. The family sold off the business in 1971, half ownership to Hans Jr., and Donald Rosacker and the other half to Marv Saline, who had been office manager since 1941. Marv Saline sold his half to Hans Jr. and Donald in 1991. The fourth generation now owns and runs the business. The greenhouses have recently been torn down, and the company will now operate strictly as a retail flower shop when the new strip mall called Stinson Market Place is finished. On the same block the Rose Court Townhomes will be erected, to honor the memory of a landmark family business that graced the corner of 18th and Stinson Boulevard for 96 years.

*Art delivering parts in his motorcycle.*

## ISLAND CYCLE SUPPLY

21 East Hennepin. The brothers, Art and George Johnson were in the bike business for 50 years on Nicollet Island following in their father's footsteps. They were the second owners of the company. Nels Swandberg and John Anderson first owned it. They sold bikes and auto parts when they established the business in 1898. George Johnson bought the Island Cycle Shop in 1922, after he returned from World War I. His brother Art joined him in the business shortly after. Art once made deliveries in a sidecar motorcycle. They moved two doors down in the 1930s because the business had grown so quickly. George was blinded in the 1930s by some metal splinters but his is a success story as a bike repairman. Many customers remembered watching him. Although there were thousands of bike parts in the shop, he knew just exactly where the part that he needed was stored and could go right to it. He was also a wealth of information and knew every manufacturer. Theirs was a strong family business. Art, his wife Helen and brother, Ed operated the sales end. Art's son Tom worked there too, along with granddaughter, Debbie. Terry Osell was the head mechanic. The business was their life. They used to play Santa and deliver bikes and trikes while kids were gone. Art's father had built the first car to actually operate in Minneapolis. A one-cylinder stationery engine took it up to speeds of 40 miles an hour. Mechanical tinkering was also part of Art's childhood. He took apart an alarm clock at a young age, made a cart out of it and wheeled toast across the table to his father. Other accomplishments include writing what one president of General Motors called, "The most comprehensive bike catalog he'd ever seen." The 1938 catalog featured a "Doodlebug Racer," a version of the early scooter and other innovative bicycles. You can still purchase a reprint of this early catalog. The Johnson family had been waiting for the bike boom in the early 1970s for fifty years.

*Helen, George and Art Johnson, 1972*

Sales went up drastically. Art attributed it to pollution, conservation and increase in health consciousness. Both Helen and Art were active in the business well into their senior citizen days. Art used to ride in the winter, rigging his wheels by wrapping them in rope. In 1970 urban renewal began on Nicollet Island and the cycle shop moved to its present location at 425 Washington Avenue North. The company recently celebrated their 100th anniversary in the bike business as a wholesale distributor. George died in 1986 and Art in 1988. But Helen continued to work 40 hours a week until her illness when she was in her eighties. When asked about retirement, she simply stated that she would be too bored. She died in 1994. The business is still owned by family members.

## JACOB'S 101

101 NE Broadway Street. The Jacob family came to the United States in 1950. Michael and Albert came first. The following year Ramez and their mother joined them. They opened a family grocery in downtown Minneapolis. By 1971, they had saved enough to purchase what was then the 101 Bar, owned by John Sosnieki. In the beginning an elaborate Lebanese dinner was served one night a week, and later expanded to three nights—Friday, Saturday and Sunday. They expanded the business in 1983. Truly a family business, Albert, his wife Elaine and Michael's wife, Therese, cook in the tiny kitchen. Everyone else, including the nine children in the family helps out by tending bar, busing tables, mopping, cleaning, washing dishes and cooking. The Jacob's family has closeness, common among the Lebanese that ties cousin to cousin and brother to brother. A fourth Jacob brother

died in Lebanon and Ramez has raised his brother's son as his own. A sister still lives in Lebanon. Michael and Albert met their wives while on vacation in their homeland. Food has a special place in Lebanese culture. It is a way of giving guests and family something very personal. In the old country, serving abundant courses of food is equated with showing love. Families there have been known to throw out everything in their possession, just to serve a beautiful meal for special guests. They want to go beyond their limitations, but if you turn them down, they feel hurt. Lebanese food preparations are often complex and exacting. Vegetables are delicately sautéed; meat is meticulously trimmed of fat and seasoned with blends of herbs and spices. Vegetables are cored, stuffed, sautéed and used as wraps for other mixtures of vegetables and meat. Fine pastries are rolled thin and filled with nuts and honey. Some of the specialties are tabouli salad, lamb shiskabob, cabbage rolls, humus with Lebanese flatbread, and home made Baklava.

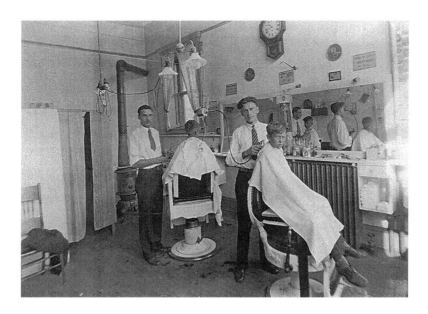

*Joe's Barbershop in the 1930s. Roman Boike is on left and Joe on right.*

## JOE'S BARBERSHOP

1306-Fourth Street NE. Joe Kolodjski at age 97 is known as the oldest barber in Northeast Minneapolis. According to Joe, he got out of school, got his license, and worked the rounds. He was on East Hennepin, on Lake Street, out in Wayzata, Rogers, and then he got in with the lodge of the Polish National Alliance (PNA). The barber they had in there was into the sauce and wasn't always paying the rent, so they threw him out and put Joe in there. He learned the barbering trade at Twin City Barber School in downtown Minneapolis where he met Roman Boike. The shop was first Boike and Kolodjski, barbers. Later Roman Boike bought the shop that now belongs to his son Art Boike at 1308 Second Street. In the early days Joe remembers giving scalp treatments for balding men and lots of facials. They used ultraviolet light and special ointments. Women first started coming into the barbershop when the wind blown style or shingle cut became popular in the 1930s. Joe was a jack of all trades. He was a jeweler, watchmaker and also fixed electric shavers on the side. Joe played the saxophone and violin and performed in a Concertina Band with Frank Buchinski. He also marched in the American Legion Gopher Band for the Aquatennial. Other barbers that worked in the shop were Paul and later Joe's son Kenny. Joe calls his house the Polish Mansion because of its history. It is over a hundred years old and was built by a man named Preziski. When Joe moved in it had a tennis court and had all bedrooms in the house. The family that lived there had ten kids. The second owner was the Wisnewski family that opened the quarry in this area and one of the sisters owned Wines Department Store at 1701 Fourth Street NE. Joe's claim to fame was that he starred in a Levi Jeans commercial that ran on television for two years. In the commercial Joe was filmed in the shop and walking down by the railroad tracks on Third Avenue and Washington. The shop closed in 1995.

*We want a bath! Dozens of children tried to storm closed doors of Ryan Baths when the temperature rose to 85 degrees. The doors were closed because of an argument over financing involving the Minneapolis Park Board and the city council. Meanwhile, the kids were caught in the middle as the days grew longer and hotter 1954.*

## JOHN RYAN PUBLIC BATHS

28 NE Second Street. John Ryan Baths was a place where immigrants could take a bath with only a five-cent charge for a towel, or they could bring their own.

Very few people had bathing facilities in their homes. A public celebration marked the opening of the bathhouse on May 1, 1923. Music was provided by the Fireman's band for a concert and dancing. There was also a swimming contest in the new pool with a silver cup offered as the prize. At a cost of about $125,000 the building was named by the city council in honor of John Ryan, veteran First Ward alderman and chief sponsor of the new baths. The bathhouse contained a swimming pool, showers and lockers. The building was divided in half with one side for men and one for women. It was a family pool that was open every day. Several political feuds resulted over the bathhouse. In 1925, Alderman Richard Dunleavy chiseled the name of John Ryan off the stone facade during an incumbent race for Alderman. He claimed that Mr. Ryan didn't contribute any more than any other taxpayer. In 1932, a great controversy arose when the mayor recommended closing the John Ryan Bathhouse for six months a year in order to save money in city service. The St. Anthony fraternal order of Eagles and the mothers of children attending Holmes School protested against the closing. They declared that the bathhouse was an important part of the community. And they were afraid that the children would seek out recreation in the unguarded Mississippi River where drowning might occur. After a great deal of debate the 44-year-old city-owned building was leased by the Crystal Pool Health Club and later the East Side Athletic Club. Finally in 1964, when the building was badly in need of repair, it was sold to the Ukrainian American Youth Association for $46,000 and was used as a youth center. Later the building was torn down and condominiums were built during urban renewal. The Ukrainian Center moved to 301 NE Main Street.

## JOHNSON STREET MARKET

3258 Johnson Street NE. Many area residents remember stopping for candy, soft drinks, cigarettes, or a few groceries when it was "Red's," or even earlier when William and Louise Sexton operated "Sexton's Grocery." The Sexton family originated in the Howard Lake, Winsted area of Minnesota. Brothers, William and Clarence Sexton each operated small grocery stores in Minneapolis as early as the 1920's. William ran the Johnson Street store and Clarence ran a market on Emerson Avenue North. Few of the current residents can remember the senior Sextons. Catherine Ochu, her sister Margaret, and brother William (Bud) Sexton grew up in the house attached to the store. Catherine started working there in 1929, when she was fifteen. At that time, there was a forty-acre farm one block away and fishing pond nearby. After the untimely death of her husband, Margaret returned to her parent's home and assisted in the grocery store. For a time the Sextons rented out the back room, which opened onto 33rd Avenue to a local barber. When the barber vacated the room, it was converted into a mini-gym where neighborhood lads took boxing lessons. Johnson Street and 33rd Avenue was the end of the streetcar line and the cars were reversed by hand. Occasionally, the trolley car became disengaged from the cable, sometimes by accident and sometimes by the devilment of the local pranksters. The conductor then had to reconnect the car to the power line. Daniel Sexton, Catherine's cousin, insisted he had nothing to do with such an activity. His son Pat remembered hearing that a streetcar had once jumped the track and crashed into the store. When the senior Sextons retired in the late forties, Margaret and Catherine continued operating the store. In 1953, Catherine and her husband, Morris (Red) Ochu took over the business. Red had a full time job at Dispatch Oven in southeast Minneapolis so Catherine was the primary storekeeper. Older residents, who were kids in the fifties and sixties, have warm memories of what they considered an extensive "penny candy" section. Pat Sexton, who worked in the store when he was in high school said, "A nickel bought a lot of candy, a big bag full, when I was a little guy." In June of 1987 after Red's death, Catherine at age 73, closed the store. She retired after 58 years in business. She wanted to stay in the neighborhood where she grew up, but she found out she couldn't manage her garden and the house. Now in her mid-eighties, she lives in Hopkins at a health care facility. She is very much remembered and missed by former candy buyers and all her neighbors.

## LAURA'S 1029 BAR

1029 Marshall Street NE. The "1029" Bar began as a place for Polish immigrants to gather. Starting out as a boarding house, the abstract of the property dates back to the mid–1800s but the construction date of the building is uncertain. The business was a speakeasy during prohibition. An Irish immigrant stonemason named Thomas Garrigan owned the building around the turn of the century. Laura Hutera's grandmother operated the boarding house. They served three meals a day and had a little store in the front where Grandma sold plug tobacco and miscellaneous things. Thomas Garrigan and his sons also built the Carr Cullen Company across the street, a sash and door business that once stood where Graco is today. Grandfather Hutera sold the boarding house in the early 1900's to the Northern Pacific Railway. They suspected the rail line would go through there. Stan Wojack bought the building in 1949. At that time the railroad still had rights for a telegraph wire in the backyard. Jim and Laura Purcelm bought "Laura's 1029 Bar" in 1972 from Frank Gozda and Red Wozniak, both first generation Poles. They moved into the small apartment in the back and began running the bar. Under the name, "Frank and Red's 1029 Bar" the tradition continued, serving food from a crock-pot behind the bar, stuffed with Polish sausages. Once the brewery closed, Laura's began drawing its clientele from all over the city. No longer was it an almost exclusively Polish public house. The Purcelms added a full kitchen. During remodeling they discovered the walls were eighteen inches thick with three courses of brick laid at right angles. A fortress built for protection against the Indian raids during the Sioux Uprising. Laura and Jim also removed a false recessed ceiling and discovered one of the bar's original features: the old fashioned tin circular designed ceiling. Following a tip from his friend Tony Jaros, Purcelm moved the bar from the traditional wall style to a center design. Now more patrons can gather around the bartender and share stories about the old days.

bands of trumpet, drums and accordion kept the place hoppin' on Friday and Saturday nights. More recently the bar was taken over by new owner Dan Hendricks and is now called Tubby's. But the décor is still the same, the back bar is the original with half inch thick mirror that covers the whole wall of almost 40 feet. *Claim to Fame*—One of the Mary Tyler Moore Shows, based in Minneapolis, with Lou Grant, Mary Richards and the gang was filmed in the *Last Chance Bar*.

## LAST CHANCE BAR

2500 NE Fourth Street. This bar is at the corner of Northeast's old liquor patrol area, which goes back to 1884. As you approached the west, the sign read "Last Chance Bar." If you were coming from the east, it read, "First Chance Bar." It's the only bar for miles if you're traveling eastward on Lowry Avenue and the first if you're going west. In the 1940s it was called Joe's Bar, owned by Joe Worwa. Marty Kubik and James Bautch purchased the bar in 1995 from Richard Cady and his mother Helen who owned the bar for thirteen years. They served Coney Islands, baked beans, and home made soup of the day. They also started pull-tabs with donations to local schools including Sheridan, Holy Cross-and St. Hedwig's. Old time polka bands were regulars. Gary Kent, Chuck All-sion and the Konca Brothers with their three-piece

*Last Chance Bar before remodeling inside and out in 1967. They tore down the Diamond DX gas station across the street to make a parking lot for bar customers.*

## LINDA'S HAIR AFAIR
## AND AL'S BARBERSHOP

1606–1608–22nd Avenue NE. The building dates back to 1905 when Mr. and Mrs. Ryerson owned it when it was Johnson Street Beauty Shop. She ran the beauty shop and he had the barber shop next door. They shared lunches together and talked back and forth through the side door that adjoined the two shops. The land north of Broadway Avenue in the early 1900s was solid farmland except for the shop and one house. Alberta Johnson owned the shop in the 1950s. Alberta had a quilting frame in the corner and resumed her quilting in between customers. Since Linda Petroske took over the shop she has claimed it with her own style. Linda got her start back in Dinkytown where she used to do Mama D's hair. Then she began her beauty career working on the same corner of 22nd and Johnson Street since 1972. First at the Feminine Lady and then at the Career Girl, both on the other side of

Johnson. Linda was encouraged to buy her own shop when she received the first raise in ten years. The lady who influenced her the most was Lucille Kaedden. "You can do it!" she said and even helped her to find a place. She has been there ever since. She continued to do the former owner's hair until she went into a nursing home. Two of Linda's regular customers, Mary Rolek and Alis Ottoson have been coming to the shop for over thirty years. Linda's shop is filled with lush green plants from the front bay window to the back door. There is a story behind these plants and they all have special meaning. The first two African Violets were given to her the day she opened the shop in 1985. The lady, who gave them to her said, "Anything will grow in Linda's Shop because of all the hot air that flies around." Many of her plants have been gifts from the families of her customers who have died. The first came from a man who came to the shop. "Would you like a gift from mother. Something to remember her by." And since then others have done the same. Some of her customers have been coming to her for so long that they are more like family to her. Another customer wanted Linda to have part of her wedding bouquet. And the plants just keep growing. And the memories live on too. Linda loves to reminisce about the old methods of styling hair. Old-fashioned curling irons, antique boot hooks, and neck clippers are displayed in one corner of her shop. "These belonged to my mother. Can you imagine? These curling irons were heated on the back of a wood stove or chimney lamp," she says. Some of her older clients still ask for the cold wave perms that were harsh, tight, frizzy and would take all day. "My grandmother used to curl my hair in rags. Then there were finger waves, bobby pin curls, clamps, clippies, and the figure eight bun in the fifties. Remember sponge rollers and spoolies. My aunt had decorative ivory hairpins. The sixties were wild. Girls did everything to straighten their hair. They used to iron their hair and even used orange juice cans and "Dippidy Do" for setting."

*Ludwig Home Bakery run by Edith and Carl Ludwig in 1980. Vienna Twist Bread in the window 26 cents a loaf in 1966.*

## LUDWIG'S BAKERY

354–13th Avenue NE. A walk down Thirteenth Avenue once provided Northeasters with an opportunity to treat their tastebuds to something really special. Such delights as fresh baked apple turnovers, cinnamon bread, or fresh peanut brittle. A master baker, Carl Ludwig baked for over 28 years on Thirteenth Avenue. Carl was born in a house two blocks from the bakery. His grandparents came from Luxembourg right after the Civil War. Before purchasing the bakery he created pastries and made candy at Charlie's Café Exceptional in downtown Minneapolis for over four years. He learned his baking techniques at the Dunwoody Institute and graduated in 1937. He also brought back some baking tricks from far away places. In 1942, he was baking for the Navy in the Aleutian Islands. There were no ovens and it was so cold the yeast would freeze. So he began using sourdough kept warm in a pouch that he wore around his neck. He says they called his bakers the sourdoughs. It takes a lot of love, and pride to make a small business work. His reputation was built on the unusual, things that you couldn't find in other bakeries and ethnic specialties, some he couldn't even pronounce. He was thrilled to see people's faces when they bit into one of his special treats. Twelve to eighteen-hour days and a seventy to eighty hour workweek were common around the holidays. Carl Ludwig's crew, including Larry Gladhill and Ethel McCabe, made for a warm atmosphere. In December of 1980, Tom and Sandra McDonald bought the bakery. Carl continued to work there and taught them the business. He also accepted an offer to work part-time for the rest of his life. They ran the business for a few years until it closed in 1983.

*Mary and Ralph Marino 1942*

## MARINO'S

2205 Central Avenue NE and the Deli at 1946 Johnson Street. Ralph Marino was born in Italy in 1896. Although he passed away long before Marino's Restaurant was even thought about, he was the one who taught his wife, Mary Marino, much of what she knows about food and cooking. Mary, affectionately known as "NaNa," by most, established her reputation over the past 60 years while cooking in various well-known Minneapolis restaurants. In March of 1969, her sons Jim and Louis opened Marino's Cafe so that she had a place of her own to serve her delicious home made recipes. NaNa's daughter Vicki and her husband Ed Matthes purchased the restaurant in August 1971. Ed and Vicki doubled the size of the restaurant in 1977. The business expanded again in 1985 by adding the Deli at 22nd and Johnson, run by Ralph, Vicki and Ed's son. Another son, Eddie, expanded the restaurant again in 1995, with a popular banquet room. Now up to four generations work at Marino's Restaurant and Deli, from NaNa to Eddie's daughter Andrea and assorted cousins. It's been twenty-nine years for the restaurant and thirteen years for the deli. In 1998, they celebrated a special anniversary because it has now also been ten years since the third generation purchased the operations. Eddie bought the restaurant and Ralph the Deli. Some of the specialties are "SOS", which is a creamed ground beef concoction that Ed Matthes brought home from the Marine Corps. People come in wanting their "SOS" served in their special way— with eggs, over potatoes, or with melted cheese. Special desserts include pizzelle, an Italian cookie and scartzelle, an Italian cheesecake. The menu at the deli features fourteen sandwiches with the SubMarino heading the list.

*Mary Marino celebrated her 63rd birthday with her daughter-in-law, Marie and Denny Bennett in 1970*

*Opening of the 13th Avenue State Bank, 1948*

## NORTHEAST STATE BANK

77-NE Broadway Street. Just after World War II when a former Third Northwestern Bank moved its branch to Midway in St. Paul, the people in this area were left without a bank. Five men: a banker, an attorney a butcher, a manufacturer, and a dentist got together and applied for a charter. Ray Julkowski, Ray Mikolajczyk, Walter Larson, Walter Kostick and Walter Warpeha formed the Thirteenth Avenue State Bank that opened its doors in 1948. Frank Pecchia became one of the bank's greatest assets. He was well liked and the perfect ambassador for the bank. If you had a problem, you could call on Frank Pecchia. But the driving force behind the major growth of the bank was Walter Rasmussen, who hitchhiked down from Pelican Rapids and worked his way up from a teller at Columbia Heights State Bank. In 1958, he took control of the bank. He moved it to the corner of Broadway and Marshall and renamed it Northeast State Bank. After the construction of the new building in 1963, Rasmussen commissioned a sculpture with nineteen flags representing the mix of nationalities in the community, bold and bright above the bank's front door. In 1973, the bank built a playground where kids were invited to play after banking hours. That same year the bank sponsored its first Northeast Tea and Arm Wrestling Tournament, which grew in the succeeding four years attracting contenders from across the country. Sven Ivan O'Myron Wisnewski, the champ of the Northeast side and Walter Rasmussen's pride and joy, became the bank's mascot. For decades pierogis, Polish sausage, mariachi bands and polka dancing have been regular parts of the annual picnic held at the bank. In 1974, a contest was held to design a flag for Northeast Minneapolis. The winning flag, still flying over the bank today, has stripes reflective of the many neighborhoods of NE Minneapolis, a band showing the solidarity of the community and stars representing the ethnic groups within the neighborhood. Part of the success of the bank is its eagerness to promote small business, which helped it to grow along with the community. And in September of 1997, the Walter C. Rasmussen Community Center opened, giving customers and business owners a place to meet—for free. The bank adopted Holland Elementary School and Northdale School, providing tutoring and playground equipment. 10,000 flowers are planted annually to provide a wonderful place for the community and its events. Belva Rasmussen, one of the first female banking CEOs in the state took over after her husband's death in 1991. A native of Aruba and three generations of bankers, it was because of her that the bank went from a very automated structure to a more community driven bank. Belva changed the decision-making process to include all middle managers and was determined to spoil customers with superb service.

## OLSON HOSPITAL

1828 Central Avenue NE. Thousands of patients flocked to Northeast between 1913 and the mid–1930's to receive a special treatment at Olson Hospital. Dr. John Olson founded a treatment that was considered a medical oddity at the time. His "Capsular Treatment" could cure many diseases including gall-stones, paralysis, cystitis, dropsy, St. Vitus Dance, ulcers, skin disorders, female diseases, gastritis, dementia and numerous other diseases caused from impure blood. The treatment consisted of a series of vegetable powders (laxatives) administered twice daily for three days, followed by a capsule. This forced the blood throughout the body and purified the blood and other tissues. Many doctors scoffed at the idea and eventually the treatments were stopped. Olson sold the facility and it became Nash Hospital, which was known for a porch stretching the width of the building and across four large pillars that faced Central Avenue. The arrangement of rooms provided access to sunlight and fresh air. In 1956, Sidney Shields purchased the building and changed the exterior. It became known as Central Hospital and operated as a long-term care facility with a bed capacity for 63 patients with 38 employees. In 1961, Shields purchased the Albinson-Peterson Mortuary next door, which was torn down and a new wing

*Olson Hospital, now Central Avenue Care Center, 1999*

was added. The capacity expanded to149 residents. A courtyard was added between the wings and the distinctive columns disappeared. During the construction phase, bats from the tower across the street kept getting into the building. Hazel Wilcox, a long time employee of 36 years, told a story of one night. "I turned on the light and there was a bat sitting on this lady's chest. Fortunately, they were both asleep, but it was a real shocker." Hazel worked as a nurse's aid and later became a LPN. Another major change was the installation of the elevator. Before then, moving residents was a difficult process. If a person was going up and down the stairs, they'd sit in a chair and they were carried. Eventually the building was renamed Central Care Center and currently employs 140 people. It is owned by Beverly Enterprises and was remodeled in 1985.

*Polish Palace 1997*

## POLISH PALACE

2124 Marshall Street NE. Monica and Larry Cichy purchased the bar in 1974. They changed the name from Cos and Steve's to Pulaski's Bar. A cornerstone on the building dates back to 1893 and the name M.H. Theis is carved beneath the building's roofline. During the remodeling, a turn of the century prescription bottle was unearthed. The label dated 8–29–09 from Kampff-Warneke Company at 2426 Second Street was prescribed by Dr. Wright. The Cichy's gutted the upstairs. They added a game room and decorated it in the turn of the century motif. Monica refinished the original mahogany bar and they removed the side door. She said, "Women weren't allowed in bars many years ago and they'd stand at that side door if they wanted something, but they couldn't come in. "When they pulled down the ceiling they marveled at their discovery of thirty-foot single span joists of untrimmed white pine. Another bricked up doorway in the basement could have been a tunnel that led to the Gluek mansion or out back to the river. After all it was a Speakeasy during prohibition.

## RABATIN'S

337–13th Avenue NE. Rabatin's was once an institution in Northeast Minneapolis; a favorite gathering place for several generations. During World War II it was a place where soldiers would meet up with their old friends and shared a malt with their best girl. And their parents went there too; to meet up with their friends and neighbors and find out the news about what was going on overseas and in the rest of the country. Then a new generation in the sixties made it their special dwelling. Kids from Sheridan, St.Anthony and De La Salle Schools mobbed the place on dance nights. "Don't carve your initials in the booth," somebody would yell. But they did. George loves Joanne, at least on Friday nights over a fudge sundae. The soda fountain was never remodeled or changed in any way.

It was so picture perfect that it was used as a setting for the movie "Little Big League." The jukebox was installed in the 1950s, but the stainless steel soda fountain, the wood booths, and the stools, chairs and tables all date back to the big-band era. Nothing phony or fancy; banana splits, sundaes, malts and shakes, all made with Northland ice cream. An honest to goodness old ice cream parlor: the counter, the cash register, the small thick glassed window panels, the green walls, the miniature Coke bottles, the home-cooked daily special, and an owner that greeted customers by name. Stephen and Mary Rabatin's family ran the place for 50 years. Mary Rabatin personified the immigrant idealism that was so much a part of Northeast Minneapolis. She'd go to church every day,

*Ann Cisek, Margaret Olejar and her granddaughter and Mary Rabatin, 1990*

work twelve hours a day in a café kitchen and make afghan blankets for the grandchildren at night. No part of the day was ever wasted. A big booth in the back was where the family ate all their meals. It was also where the Rabatin kids did their homework at night. Mary and her husband Steve met in the Slovak village of Kalava, and got reacquainted after they immigrated separately to the United States in 1922. Steve was an entrepreneur. He started with an upholstery business and bought a bar at thirteen and University. He sold the bar and built Rabatin's Café in 1941. When Stephen died in 1948, leaving six children from age three to eighteen years old, five waitresses and the family ran the place and worked seven days a week until the 1970s. Mary did all of the cooking. She was famous for her hot roast beef sandwiches with mashed potatoes and gravy, and chicken soup. Home made American fries and Chili were also the mainstays. Workers from the Grain Belt plant would stop by for lunch and Rabatin's became the center for mingling of language and song. Joe Kapala and Father Joe Balent would come into the kitchen looking for Holubki; old-fashioned "pigs in the blanket" made the Slovak way. Rabatin's was part of a two-block long business community on Thirteenth Avenue. They closed in the evenings when the Ritz theater closed, later they served only breakfast and lunch. Jim Grell and his wife Patty took over the restaurant in 1994, and re-named it the Modern Café. The Grells have tried to preserve the look and feel of the Old Rabatin's, a classic neighborhood café.

*Warren and Jack Ready 1946*

## READY MEATS

3550 Johnson Street NE. Ready Meat's is a bustling, successful landmark business in the Waite Park community. Dan and Warren Ready joined their brother Jack and purchased Larson's Meats at 22nd and Johnson when they returned from military service during World War II. Dave Carlson bought into the business in 1978, Dale Carlson and John Shimshock in 1981. They moved to the new location in 1980, when they purchased a 7–11 Store located at 3550 Johnson Street. The building was completely refurbished with new fixtures, showcases, and refrigeration system. It can certainly be described as a fully modern "old fashioned" market where each customer is served individually by knowledgeable meat cutters. Their products are truly international. The Swedish sausage and meatballs were first prepared in quantity for local churches. Customers soon began requesting it over the counter, and although the recipe has changed a bit, it is essentially the same as that served at many church dinners. All of their meat is choice quality; their many varieties of sausages are homemade. Their spaghetti-pizza sauce, developed by Jack and Helen Ready back in the fifties, is excellent. During the holiday season, a ton of lutefisk and 500 plump turkeys pass over the counter of Ready Meats each year. Poetry was always a part of the counter display. Ernie Ready, until the mid–80's, had prepared a new poem weekly for display. Health problems forced him to give this up.

*Ethel Sundly serves a cup of coffee at*
*Rolig Drug in the 1960s*

## ROLIG DRUG

359–13th Avenue NE. Soda fountains at the corner drugstore are part of a bygone era. Gleaming counters of stainless steel, ornate mirrors with soda fountain dispensers and cozy booths became an essential part of the modern drugstore in the early 1930's. Rolig Drug was one of the most popular hangouts on the Eastside. Workers from the brewery, the Board of Education and other neighborhood businesses came in at noon during the week. Then after school, they were bombarded with teenagers from Sheridan School. Of course on the weekends, the Ritz Theater crowd stopped in before and after the movies. Before long, it became a regular stopping place on Sunday after church. Consequently they were busy all the time. All the businesses on 13th Avenue were booming. Marjorie Szykulski started working there in about 1943, and that's where she met her husband. She worked in the pharmacy and sold cosmetics. She was also in charge of ordering and took over when the lunch counter got too busy. She had a way of keeping the school kids in line. Everyone used to call her "the boss." They served cold sandwiches, sweet rolls from Ludwig Bakery, malts and huge ice cream cones made with Bridgeman's Ice Cream, a rare delight. In the fifties and sixties flavored cokes and fizzes were all the rage. Served in Coke glasses with a straw the cokes or charged water were then flavored with lemon, lime, chocolate, or vanilla. This was the origin of "the cherry coke". Root Beer floats and sundaes were also popular items. In the early years Joe Magiera and later, Bill Debolak owned Rolig Drug. This was before Dean Rolig took over the place. Everyone liked Dean. He was good to the employees and the teenagers liked him too. He also gave special attention to the seniors who came in to the pharmacy. Later owners were Ken Vertheim, and Charles Thang. Lorraine Niziol came in to work the lunch rush from 11:00 to 1:00 during the week. She worked there for ten years while her kids were in school. Some of the other regular employees were Ethel Sundly, Jake the delivery guy, Judy Niziol, Teresa Fabian, Rosemary Charboneau, Elva and Joyce Hafner. The waitresses wore white uniforms; white shoes and always had to wear hairnets. Later they wore blue jackets. Rolig's closed its doors in the early 1980's, about the time when the bakery and the Ritz Theater closed.

## SCHWERDFEGER MEATS

358 Monroe Street NE. August Schwerdfeger was born in Siefershausen, Hanover in 1864. He came to America in 1881 and learned the butcher's trade in Muscatine, Iowa. In 1882 he was attracted to Minneapolis, a place for energetic young men and women. For five years he worked for Louis Luetger and Anton Schumacher. In 1891, he engaged in partnership with John Schmidler, a fellow employee at Schumacher's Market and bought out their employer. They had about $2,400.00 between them as capital. After five years, Mr. Schwerdfeger sold his interest to his partner and opened a new place of business for himself on 358 Monroe. He developed the building on the corner block and continued his business there for fourteen years. In the early 1900's they would fill up their horse-drawn wagon with meat and then go door to door selling right off the wagon. The ladies would come out with their platters and bowls. August's brother joined him after the first five years and in 1910 he sold the business to his nephews. Mr. Schwerdfeger invested in realty and became a developer in this locality. He also took an interest in social and fraternal organizations and was an active member of the Elks, the Sons Hermann, and the Turners. Having no children of their own, he and his wife Metta adopted three or four children and some elderly people.

*Greg Kubik, Paul Cisewski, Mary Gerken, Marlene Hiltner, Roxanne Jorgenson, 1999*

## STASIU'S

2500 University Avenue NE. It's hard to imagine a 'Northeaster' who doesn't know that 'Stasiu' is short for Stanley in Polish. Stasiu's brings to life a vivacious vein of Northeast's past. Present owner, Marlene Hiltner, named the pub for her late husband's grandfather, a Polish immigrant who made his way to the Polish sector of Northeast in the early 1900s. The land the pub sits on dates back to the mid-nineteenth century. Since the city doled out its liquor licenses to the breweries of Northeast, Stasiu's has provided a place for locals to talk politics and kindle friendships. Marlene,

a native of the neighborhood, loves the sense of togetherness Northeast has. Long-time bartender, Greg Kubik, remembers when Stasiu's was called Al's, started by Al Grabowski in 1949. It was the center of the Polish community. Although the Poles dominate Stasiu's history, today it attracts folks from all over the city as well as the newest, multi-ethnic members of Northeast, the artists. Stasiu's opened its doors on Ground Hog's Day in 1975. The very first customer was Howie Ulen who worked at NSP. Since then it has been an eatery by day and a pub by night. It draws patrons from all walks of life and has even dived into the popular '90s (that would be the 1990s) culture of take-out food. The sign on the back door reads "Home of the Duzy", a roast beef Au Jus with a touch of garlic and served on a home-made hoagie bun. They also serve the Krakowska, Polish sub and Polish Pizza. Marlene owned the bar with her husband, Hubert Sentyrz, who was killed in a plane crash in 1988. Sentyrz was teaching his friend and soon to be brother in law, to fly when the plane went down in Ham Lake. Employees and customers were devastated when they heard. Everybody loved Hubert, a good-hearted man who is still fondly remembered. Four of Stasiu's employees have worked at the bar for over twenty years. Ironically, Greg Kubik, Paul Cisewski, Roxanne Jorgenson, and Mary Gerken Spensley were all raised in Northeast. Stasiu's is proud of their three original softball teams that have been playing since the opening of the bar.

*Claim to Fame*—Of all things, the Urinals. A pair of antique porcelain urinals were snared from the West Hotel when it was torn down in 1940. They even have a place to rest your beer. According to Roxanne, "We have more women going into the men's bathroom than men. They all want to look at the urinals."

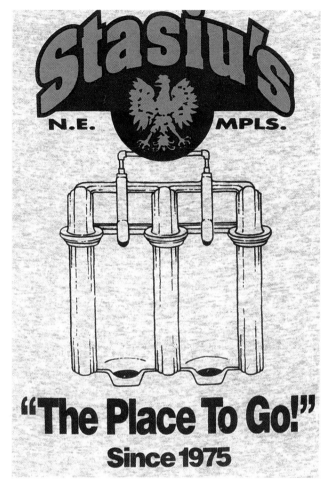

*Logo on front of Stasiu's "T" shirts sold at the bar*

*Ted Gromek, Joseph Gromek, Ann O'Connell*
*and Ed O'Connell in the late 1940s*

## STEVE'S BAR

459 Adams Street NE. Owned by the Gromek family for over 36 years, it was a family bar and a place where customers always felt welcome. Even single women would come in to the bar alone. They could sit at the bar and play cards with the guys. For a short time they weren't allowed to sit at the bar and had to sit in booths. Boy did they get upset. One of the reasons was that you had to sit at the bar to get the special, "buy two drinks and get the third one free." The first owners were Frank and Patty who sold the bar in 1939 to Joseph and Wladyslawa (Gladys) Gromek. So it became Steve's Bar, named after their son who helped his father run the bar. Both Joseph and Wladyslawa came from Poland. Joseph worked at the papermill in St. Paul and worked at the bar when he returned home. Wladyslawa took in seven boarders. She boiled towels and starched aprons in a big copper kettle. There were 24 white shirts with starched collars and cuffs plus aprons to keep clean every week. Laundered the old fashion way without modern soaps and fabric.

Guys from B.F. Nelson would come in for a beer and a shot of whiskey after work. One of the regulars would say, "I have to go home to Mama, she got supper ready." The fellows wore long underwear year round in those days. They were cool and absorbent in the summer. She washed all their underwear. Many times Joseph would get a call late at night from one of the wives, "Can you get my husband out of jail?" Then they'd come to meet him at the bar and he would lend them the $200 bail. There was a party once a year at Coon Lake. And Joseph always took pride in serving a wild game dinner each year for his customers. In 1962 when Joseph died, the name was changed to C & A Bar. His two children, Chester Gromek and Anastasia (Gromek) Audette took over the ownership of the bar. The youngest daughter, Cecilia worked as a waitress. It was torn down along with four other bars: Pete's, Larry's, the Point, and Ted's Bar in 1974 to build the new Webster School.

nights during canning season the trucks would unload their apricots and peaches right on the sidewalk. Sometimes up to 500 crates. Sig had been in the grocery business since he graduated from De La Salle in 1936. Sig's wife Betty, who worked with him in the grocery business for over 32 years, was also employed at Stillman-Schimidler. They later opened the Kersey Food Center in 1961. The Stillmans, George, Norman, Leonard, and Arthur owned seventeen grocery stores in the Twin City area.

*All of the Stillman stores participated in a Hawaiian contest to see which store could decorate the best. One customer won a trip to Hawaii. Clerks and carry out boys at the Central Avenue Store were Pug Faggerly, Dick Parlow, Edith Kayser, Geraldine Wykrent, Betty Wykrent, Sig Wykrent and Dick Manley in 1959.*

## STILLMAN-SCHMIDLER MARKET

2416 Central Avenue NE. In the early 1900s, Schmidler Meat Market would fill up their horse-drawn wagon and then go door-to-door selling meat right off the wagon. The original store of Stillman-Schmidler started in the early 1940s. It was a small mom and pop store located in the middle of the block of 24th and Central. In those early days personalized service, credit, phone orders and delivery were as typical as self service is now. A new super market like store, complete with shopping carts was built inside the old fire barn in 1951. Sigmund (Sig) Wykrent managed the store. They were so busy right from the start that they never even had a grand opening. On Friday

## TONY JAROS' RIVER GARDEN

2500 NE Marshall Street. Formerly called Johnny's River Garden and named for the gardens that were maintained west of the building, Tony Jaros bought the pub in 1961. He renamed it Tony Jaros' River Garden. In 1962, he and his wife Mattie moved in upstairs where they raised three children. The building itself is over a hundred years old. Originally built by the Grain Belt Brewery to sell its beer, it's listed on the National Registry of Historic Buildings. With the famous Laker behind the bar, the River Garden quickly became a mainstay of the neighborhood. The kitchen is known for its pork tenderloin, and the bar serves the famous "greenie" a 1971 invention of Tony's son, Tommy (deceased). People come by the busloads to taste the greenie. Today, Tony's daughter Elizabeth and son Dan who oversees day to day operations own "Jaros". They have tried to maintain the neighborhood atmosphere, attributing Jaros' popularity to their father, the "greenie," and the people who come in.

## WIG AND BOTTLE

2501 NE Marshall. The Wig and Bottle was once a pearl in the Northeast neighborhood. Owners, John and Dorothy Skowronski opened it in 1965. They had owned the Lowry Bar on the same corner for the previous thirteen years. The night manager was Hank Kocinski and the cooks were Karl Sigerson and Harold Picker. The two sisters, Gladys Zembal and Florence Zawadski also worked there. Even though it was Polish owned and managed, the menu was not. The only Polish dish was the Krakowska sandwich, (a Polish luncheon meat) which you were not likely to find elsewhere. Their specialties were roast duck and quail with wild rice, lobster bisque roast and filet of veal. Some of the favorite accompaniments were peas a la francaise and maple baked acorn squash and a simple dessert of strawberries cardinal. A regular feature was the Great Dinners of the Month. The décor was warmly pleasant, with dark wood and heavy beams, red armchairs and decorative gaslight chandeliers. The noon light came through the stained glass windows overlooking the booths at the bar. There was a middle room with a hand-carved fireplace and wine rack, and farther back another large dining area with two levels and a large meeting room downstairs. When Grandpa Wladislaw Wisnewski and his brother Stephan first stepped on American soil and went through customs, their names were changed to Walt Miller and Steve Smith. They were headed for Duluth to seek their fortunes in the timber and brush country. Later, a stubborn streak and a legal problem got their original names back minus a couple of letters. So many people in Northeast have an appreciation of the sound of Polish names and find pleasure in saying them the way they once were said. The Wig and Bottle burned to the ground in 1979, and was never rebuilt because of new building codes.

## 22ᴺᴰ AVENUE STATION

2200 University NE. Even before Johnny Sokol introduced the big poker games to "Sokol's," he'd brought
professional boxing to the bar in the WWI era. Always a
player, Sokol made entertainment synonymous with
the location of the present-day 22ⁿᵈ Avenue Station.
Much of Sokol's initial designs still exists, like the wood
floor in the back that was originally earmarked for
dancing, the front awning that stretches out over the
sidewalk and the big noon meal. Sokol himself was a
prizefighter and refereed many fights in the early
days. Always a place for Polish and Ukrainian immigrants, the corner of 22ⁿᵈ Avenue and University has
alternately been a country music haven, a polka den
and a dance hall. Whatever the form of entertainment,
present owner Glen Peterson says that Sokol's spirit
lives on.

## 331 CLUB

331–13th Avenue NE. Overlooking the interior of the 331 Club like a link to the past, a giant mural spreads across half the wall, inviting patrons to reminisce about times gone by. The mural shows what 13th Avenue NE looked like in the 1940's. Back then, 331 Club was called Andy and Vic's. And prior to Andy and Vic's, during Prohibition, it was a barbershop. The stands from the original barber chairs are still preserved below the present floor. Of course, the Ritz Theater is prominently displayed in the mural, as well as Northeast Radio and TV. Bartender Kelly Jones painted the mural commissioned by owner Steve Benowitz. 331 Club is also known as the location for scenes of "Grumpier Old Men." During shooting, the streets were blocked while actors Jack Lemmon and Sophia Loren recorded their parts.

# 6 Alleluia! Nazdrowie!

## *Why So Many Bars in Northeast Minneapolis?*

In Northeast Minneapolis a great number of bars inter-mingle with the landscape of houses and churches. You won't find this type of geography anywhere else in the city. Northeast Minneapolis has 34 bars, compared to five in all of Minneapolis, south of Lake Street—an area about six times as long. One of the reasons for this was the liquor patrol that dates back to 1884.

In the early days of St. Anthony saloons were "male refuges". Men used saloons as social centers and women visited in each other's homes. This interaction was a vital part of their well being. The majority of the blue-collar workers by the turn of the century worked for the railroad or the breweries. At the end of the workday they headed for the nearest bar. No matter what language was spoken, after a few drinks, the various ethnic groups began to mix.

Saloons became popular and were profitable businesses. In 1876 there were 140 bars in the city of Minneapolis. But not everyone approved. There were those who believed that they were the centers of drunkenness and vice. Drunkenness accounted for more arrests than any other crime in Minneapolis and other cities.

Minneapolis officials tried to solve the problem with "moral geography." They drew boundaries around a portion of the city to contain the saloons. In order to protect their neighborhoods, they decreed in the city charter that liquor could only be sold in two relatively small areas that police could patrol on foot. One was a downtown strip that followed the river along Washington Avenue and stretched for a short distance down Cedar Avenue South. The other was the immigrant neighborhoods across the river; an area roughly bounded by Lowry Avenue Northeast in the north, East Hennepin in the south, and Northeast Fourth Street on the east.

Mayor George Pillsbury, a Republican of the flour milling family was a stern, righteous New England Yankee. He was strongly supported by the city's Scandinavians. Some men cashed their paychecks in saloons but others cashed their paychecks in grocery stores. Although Pillsbury wanted to ban the saloons

*Friendly's Bar New Year's celebration, 1955*

allow them to operate. A 1935 citywide referendum allowed the bars to stay open.

Bar owners and temperance reformers repeatedly attempted to amend the city charter but were always defeated. Only in 1959 was the downtown liquor patrol area modestly expanded to Lyndale Avenue on the west and Franklin Avenue on the south. In the rest of the city, you still could not buy strong liquor although you could purchase 3.2 beer. Finally, voters abolished the patrol areas in 1974. Today it would be virtually impossible to open a bar on a residential street.

Many changes occurred in Northeast during urban renewal in the 1970s when the freeways were built. A whole block of bars on Spring and Adams Street were torn down to make room for the new Webster School, including the Point, Steve's, Larry's Northeast Bar, Mr. Dave's and Guil's. Friendly's Bar and Bowling Alley was torn down along with the B.F. Nelson Company

from the neighborhood all together, he had to settle for a petition of liquor patrol limits, higher license fees and minimum distance restrictions between saloons and schools.

Saloonkeepers appealed but the Minnesota Supreme Court upheld the city rules. Although Mayor Pillsbury wanted to restrict saloons to business areas away from houses, much of the Northeast liquor patrol area included residential neighborhoods, as it does today.

Prohibition changed the picture and the liquor patrol was no longer needed. But after prohibition was repealed in 1933, the liquor patrol limit was reinstated. Officials didn't enforce the limits for two months and 37 bars hopped outside the patrol area. Some wanted to shut the renegade bars down; others wanted to

*Guys from B. F. Nelson came into Friendly's*

and other neighborhood businesses to make room for highway I-94. Artoro's, Merchants and the Huddle Bar were removed during the East Hennepin renovation.

However, the legacy lives on. Northeast streets are still crowded with bars. Five neighborhood bars still stand like sentinels on the quiet residential street that links the Last Chance and Mayslack's on Northeast Fourth Street. The Last Chance Bar got its name from being the first place you could get a drink going into town and the last place going out." There were no more chances to stop for a drink past Lowry Avenue going east.

Although some bars have changed their image to attract customers, many remain the same old-style neighborhood bars that they have been for the last century. They may have new owners but the clientele is the same, drawing crowds half from their own neighborhood and the rest, Northeasters who now live in nearby neighborhoods and suburbs. Many are working people; some are retirees and even the younger crowd. Some claim the only thing that kept them close was the churches and the bars.

*Grand Opening celebration at Friendly's Bar, 1949*

# East Side On-Sale Liquor Dealers' Association (in 1940s)

ARONE'S BAR
501 Central Avenue NE

ANDY & VICK' S
331–13th Avenue NE

AL'S PLACE
2500 University Avenue NE

M.J. BUCKLEY
957 Central Avenue NE

BOB & BILL'S
SQUARE DEAL BAR
224 East Hennepin Avenue

BUCK & JOHN'S
1628 University Avenue NE

CHRISANO'S CAFÉ
402 East Hennepin Avenue

EAST HENNEPIN CAFÉ
501 East Hennepin Avenue

GUS'S PLACE
2200 Fourth Street NE

JIM HEFFERON
112 East Hennepin Avenue

JACK'S PLACE
201 Lowry Avenue NE

JAX BAR
1928 University Avenue NE

JOE'S BAR
2500 Fourth Street NE

JOHN & JULIAN
2500 Marshall Street NE

JOHN'S PLACE
2121 University Avenue NE

JOHN & JOHN'S PLACE
Central Avenue NE

JOHNSON'S PLACE
1428 Fourth Street N

KIERCE'S BAR
456 Adams Street NE

KITT'S BAR
860 Monroe Street NE

MAIN STREET TAVERN
311 Main Street NE

MARSHALL BAR
1319 Marshall Street NE

MERCHANTS BAR
229 East Hennepin Avenue

GILL NORDELL
429 Third Avenue NE

CHRIS OLSON'S
507 East Hennepin Avenue

THE OLD SPOT
617 Marshall Street NE

PINE TAVERN
301 Harrison Street NE

POINT BAR
501 Fourth Avenue NE

RIVER TAVERN
2501 Marshall Street NE

ROCKAWAY BAR
2124 Marshall Street NE

STANLEY'S. BAR
40 East Hennepin Avenue

STEVE'S BAR
459 Adams Street NE

SPORTS INN
729 Marshall Street NE

TERMINAL BUFFET
506 Central Avenue NE

TOM'S BAR
839 Fifth Street NE

TUREK'S PLACE
1032 Third Avenue NE

VALENTINE'S INN
359 Monroe Street NE

WALTER'S BAR
641 Marshall Street NE

WORWA'S BAR
2300 University Avenue NE

1029 BAR
1029 Marshall Street NE

ONE-O-.ONE BAR
101 Broadway Street NE

*E.J. Peterson Drugs 1946 Johnson Street, 1936*

# Just What the Doctor Ordered: Hennepin Country Drugstores

**An abridged version of an earlier article by Tom Clark**

*Early Drugstores*

In the early years of St. Anthony there were twenty drugstores on the East Side. The first three opened in 1859. Thomas, John and Oliver Gray had the longest continuous involvement in Minneapolis drugstores, which lasted until the present day. Thomas Gray once boarded in the Ard Godfrey House when he first arrived in Minneapolis. He started a drugstore opposite of Bridge Square in 1857. The store advertised "drugs, medicines, paints and oils." The wooden structure burned in 1864 and was replaced with a brick building. Other early drugstores were Crawford's on 10th and Main Street and Rose Drug on Second and East Hennepin.

Besides compounding prescriptions the earliest drugstores sold paint, window glass and also served as a general store. Ornate walnut prescription cases resembled a Baroque confessional and fancy bottles filled with brightly colored water were displayed on top. Medicines were mixed by hand on top of these counters. Wild cherry bark was used to relieve bronchitis. Goose grease and turpentine was made into a poultice. Glycerin and rosewater as a lotion was made from actual rose petals and distilled waters and it was made right in the drugstore.

During recess from Mrs. Butterfield's School, the children in early St. Anthony would come into Crawford's Drug on Main Street for crushed sugar soaked in a wintergreen solution. And Frank O'Brien, who worked there, recalled in 1920 that they enjoyed it when he teased them by opening the ammonia jar or the asafetida drawer to give them a whiff. In addition to his other duties, which included cutting window glass and mixing paint, he also had time to attend to the "Bible Depository" which occupied one corner of the store.

As the population of Hennepin County increased, new drugstores continued to open. The city of Minneapolis showed an increase from 62 drugstores in 1890 to 105 in 1904, 148 in 1920, and close to 300 by 1930. Stores were dotted along through-streets every four blocks or so.

Drugstore decor changed dramatically sometime around World War II. The ornate was simplified, the dark colors brightened. Counters became illuminated showcases. Ceiling fans gave way to air conditioners. Schwartz cabinets replaced walnut prescription cases with pull drawers.

Charles Walgreen modernized drugstores by installing mirrors and plate glass windows. He put in more elaborate displays and turned the ancient soda fountain into a bright and popular lunching place.

And prices changed! In 1909, most prescriptions cost between 35 cents and 50 cents. John Dady's first day gross sales in 1945 was $124. In 1989, prescriptions ranged from about $4 to $200, and averaged $15. Though the pharmacists' gross profits have risen with inflation, the percentage of their profits from drugs actually fell between 1960 and 1989.

*Marjorie Szykulski and Jake, at Rolig Drug 1960s*

### The Prescription Counter

The nineteenth century was an era of quackery and of snake oil, medicine shows, proprietary cures, granny medicines, bark-and-root formulas, and Indian cures. All over the Midwest, the salesmen for Watkins Products of Winona sold nostrums, spices and shoelaces from horsedrawn wagons. Doctors prescribed and pharmacists made up whatever remedies were known or thought to heal and comfort in the age before modern drugs.

The last quarter of the 19th century saw a major increase in the number of wholesale drug manufacturers and the College of Pharmacy at the University of Minnesota opened in 1892. But it was not until 1899 that Baeyer's (later Bayer's) aspirin came out in Germany and not until 1910 that diphtheria antioxin was available. This was followed in the 1920s by insulin, in the 1930s by sulfa drugs and in the 1940s by antibiotics. These of course, revolutionized the drug industry.

Behind the frosted-glass partition of the early corner drugstores and under gold letters proclaiming a "Pharmaceutical Chemist" were the tools of hand manufacture. In the 1960s, Erwin Smetana of Hopkins still displayed his pharmacy's medicine-mixing machine whose label read, "Union Churn . . . First Premium Awarded at the Ohio, Indiana, Michigan, Wisconsin, Illinois and New York Fairs . . . 1865, 1866, 1868."

It was a noisy machine, according to Frank O'Brien, whose hand churning of roots and herbs was sometimes done by a husky boy. Examples of the mixtures produced in such machines included snakeroot and pipsissiwa which were used for rheumatism; dandelion root, which was a laxative; and senna leaves, which were popular as a purgative.

The mortar and pestle and the ball mill, which was a large kettle were commonly used for mixing drugs. By steeping powdered roots, stems and leaves of certain herbs in a percolator a liquid was produced. Another early method of preparing a prescription was to a pour a mixed powder into small white papers. The papers were folded and formed into a packet and then placed in a box. Each paper was equal to one dose. In the early days a drugstore was expected to carry a homemade cough syrup. A druggist in the Seven Corners area was selling an old Swedish remedy in 1963 called "Peterson's Lung Balsam," which his father sold by the barrel since 1888.

The pharmacy counter always had a ledger for recording each prescription by hand. A spindle was also used to store individual prescriptions. There was a sink, of course, for drawing water and washing pharmacy utensils.

*Marjorie Szykulski and Lorraine Niziol*
*at Rolig Drug, 1975*

### The Soda Fountain

The development of the soda fountain, carbonated water, and Coca-Cola, all invented in the 19th century transformed drugstores and changed the lifestyles of people throughout Hennepin County and the world. Also drugstores played a major role in popularizing ice cream.

Carbonated water was sold in drugstores as a "restorative" and an "aid to health" in 1803. Soda water was sold in bottles or in glasses dispensed under pressure from a fountain. People still got their medicine at the local drugstores but they also asked for a "Bromo" which was drawn from a hanging blue bottle charged with carbonated water. Or they'd have a cup of coffee while waiting for a prescription. The $195 package for drugstore owners included a counter; 165 pounds of sulfuric acid, a barrel of ground marble (a carbonate) a case of extracts for syrup, and six soda tumblers.

Then in 1838 a Philadelphia shopkeeper added lemon flavoring. And soon came vanilla, strawberry, pineapple, chocolate, orange, ginger, raspberry and sarsaparilla. Frank O' Brien remembered that wild "strawberries were gathered from the prairie on both sides of the river in abundance" for the soda fountain at his St. Anthony drugstore in the 1860s.

Ice Cream was used for the first time in a soda at a Philadelphia Exhibition in 1874. Later the ice cream companies helped druggists to finance the purchase of their stores. Minneapolis companies like Steele DeSota, Kemps and Jersey helped to get locations, furnished electrical signs and even painted up the store. And until around 1968, the ice cream companies gave a rebate on bulk ice cream so that druggists could pay their rent.

A pharmacist from Atlanta experimented with a combination of coca and the kola nut. He aromatized the beverage and added sugared syrup. When carbonation was added, drugstores were the first to reap the benefits of Coca-Cola advertising because it was only available at drugstore counters. Minneapolis druggists kept Coca-Cola syrup in their basements by the barrel or at least bought a barrel jointly with a neighboring druggist.

Early fountains took on a Victorian charm with the marble, mahogany, ebony and decorative glass with polished metal faucet arms. Rows of fancy glasses were stored on top or above the counters. And underneath were lead coils refrigerated at first with crushed ice. The more elaborate fountains had pillars and pilasters, resembling castles and were given proud names such as "The Borealis" or "The Pontiac."

Even in pioneer days, pharmacies had been social centers for the neighborhood or a town's main street. Pot-bellied stoves, cuspidors, pinball machines, straight-back chairs and checkerboards were invitations to lounge. Soda fountains added to the social function of drugstores. A great number of people stopped in on Saturday nights after they went to the dances at the local halls,(the PNA, the Polish White Eagle, and the ODHS). While sipping cokes at the fountain, customers were given the opportunity to impulse buy.

When the glory days of drugstore soda fountains passed and soft drinks became available elsewhere, druggists found it hard to keep fountain employees occupied. The fancy Victorian counters of early days became modern stainless steel and Formica. The new Walgreens on Ninth and Nicollet installed an all metal streamlined soda fountain. Gray's Campus Drug in Dinkytown could boast that Bob Dylan with his guitar, John Berryman with scribbled notes, and Hubert Humphrey and Wendell Anderson had all frequented their fountain.

Rowdy teenagers could be a challenge to the druggist, but a firm, "Do it my way or out the front door," was usually enough to restore calm. Already in the fifties, fountain business had slackened. Dean Saeugling's experience at 36th and Bryant in Minneapolis was typical. When his cooler needed expensive repairs in the late sixties, he re-luctantly closed the fountain and used the space more profitably for toys and pet supplies.

*Soda fountain at Central Pharmacy*
*2300 Central Avenue, 1952*

### A *Varied Merchandise*

The corner drug also sold a variety of items. Perhaps the most popular was tobacco. A ritual of choosing the right cigar from the humidor was popular for decades. A wide variety of cigars were stocked Muriel, Roi Tan, Blackstone, and Antonio y Cleopatra. The drugstore was like the convenience store where you could pick up pop or cigarettes.

Years ago, there seems to have been an occasional blurring between the sale of liquor and the sale of medicine with alcoholic content. Frank O'Brien in the nineteenth century alluded to folding money being left behind liquor bottles by "imbibers of Spirits of Vini Galici" and eventually finding its way into the cash drawer. Brandy, of course, was prescribed for many years as a remedy. During Prohibition, wholesale druggists became major distributors of medicinal liquors. To keep bootleggers out, a 1932 ruling said that a wholesale firm's liquor sales could not be more than 10 percent of its business. In those years, a doctor might prescribe liquor for a cold and in some drugstores this was brought out of a special room. After Prohibition, combined liquor and drug stores were not allowed except for those that had liquor licenses prior to Prohibition. Rolig Drug and Ideal Drug were two of a handful in this category in Minneapolis. A universal drugstore item was sweets. Pioneer druggists knew how to make licorice sticks out of glycyrrhiza roots and they brought back tamarack and spruce gum from the woods each spring. Personal products, like straightedge razors and Brilliantine for the hair, were always popular. A household item prominent in earlier drugstores was the natural sponge. Relatively expensive, the sponges were displayed either in glass jars or in wire containers like wastebaskets. Each one had a tag attached by needle and thread. "You'd pick out one you'd like," recalls David Kersch. "If it was a nice shape and soft, it'd probably cost you a dollar. If you'd get a smaller, odd-shaped one, that'd be only 25 cents. Cameras and Photo developing have continued to be a popular drugstore service of today, as it was a century ago.

A 1906 ad for Newell's Minnetonka Drug Company suggests the wide variety of drugstore merchandise: "Proprietary medicines, toilet preparations, veterinary goods, stock, foods, poultry supplies, household preparations, stationery, sporting goods, drugs, chemicals and drug sundries, a full line of choice confectionery, choice soda water and ice cream."

Territorial disputes arose between grocery stores and drugstores. The State Board of Pharmacy in 1959 tried unsuccessfully to prevent Red Owl Grocery Stores from selling common medical remedies. There were strict rules that pharmacies had to keep aspirin and cough syrup behind the counter. The big argument was that you could go over to the grocery store and pick up such items right on the shelf. And so the drugstores, in order to compete, put in grocery products. But it was hard to contend with cheaper quality brands.

One means of survival was to concentrate on one or two specialties. Some stores became branches of the U.S. Post Office. Some sold flowers, Edison wax-cylinder records, imported perfumes and others became outlets for surgical instruments and home aid stores.

### Decline of the Independent Drugstore

Several issues brought about the decline. One issue was long workweeks in single-pharmacist stores. As early as the 1860s, Frank O'Brien complained that he worked six to ten hours each day and was often roused in the middle of the night. Over the years, one-pharmacist stores were common, and their situation is typified by Frances Roith who described her husband Joseph's career at stores including Richfield's Roith Pharmacy: "He was so busy at the store. He made one trip to Canada for fishing. Other than that, it was 7 days a week at the store, 365 days out of the year."

The larger stores gave the pharmacists a way of splitting shifts and days off. Another way was chain stores. Often a pharmacist would own two or more stores. Examples are the four Gray Brothers stores years ago and the four Merwin stores currently in Minneapolis and the northern suburbs.

One of these chains, Snyder Brothers, started as a single store in Minneapolis in 1928 but went statewide and continues to be a large concern after changes of ownership. A second mushrooming company was Walgreens, which began as a single Chicago store in 1907, but opened its twenty-ninth Twin Cities store in 1987, with 1,300 stores nationwide. Liggetts was a chain that started on the East Coast and had several Minneapolis outlets from about 1918 to the 1940s. Like many independent drugstores, Liggetts had a franchise to handle Rexall products.

Owners retired and neighborhoods declined. But the biggest reason for the decline was the margin of profit was no longer what it used to be. A big impact on the decline of neighborhood drugstores was the spread of discount stores around the 1960s.

When John Dady opened his northeast Minneapolis store in 1944, there were about ten drugstores in the two-square-mile area bounded by Lowry, East Hennepin, Central and the Mississippi River. By 1980, there were only two. In 1987, 21 metro-area pharmacies closed their doors while 24 new stores opened. But the change was that only three of the new stores were independent.

It remains true that the corner drugstore specializes in service: home deliveries and face-to-face contact, as well as updated drug information. But cultural patterns have changed. Many customers are willing to do without this neighborhood service and are willing to drive out of their immediate neighborhood for bargains elsewhere.

The 20th-century full-service pharmacy seems unlikely to go out of existence. Drugstore fountains will remain rare. The discount alternatives may become more prevalent. And customers may have to drive farther to reach a drugstore. But the American public, according to a recent Gallup poll, rates the pharmacist highest for honesty and ethical standards - higher than clergy, teachers or physicians. This confidence suggests that in Hennepin County, as throughout the country, people will continue to want the same pharmacist in an accessible place where they can obtain reliable prescriptions and drug information.

*Lorraine Niziol, Marjorie Szykulski and Ken Vertheim at Rolig Drug, 1975*

Sulfur and molasses was a quick pick-me-up. Wild cherry bark was used to relieve bronchitis. Pumpkinseed for tapeworm was a favorite. One doctor used to say that the pumpkinseeds tickled the worm. Another remedy was goose grease and turpentine for a poultice. Glycerin and rosewater as a lotion was made from actual rose petals and distilled water. We used to make it up right in the drugstore. Sweet spirits of nitre were used for the bladder, and paregoric was used for intestinal troubles. Originally, paregoric was a remedy for teething; mothers rubbed it on the babies' gums.

*The period 1910–1940*
*recalled by Roy Johnson in 1969.*

How plainly, in memory, I can see displayed on the shelves of Crawford's drugstore the "all curing" patent medicines of that date - "Hostetter's Bitters," "Clark's Sherry Wine Bitters," "Hood's Sarsaparilla;" and many another abomination in compound.

The "prescription" case contained hundreds of glass-stopple bottles filled. . . with remedies in powder as well as in liquid form.

I made putty, mixed paints, cut and fitted window glass, charged soda fountains, washed bottles, filled prescriptions, made illuminating fluid, swept the store and then had time to attend to the "Bible Depository" which occupied one corner of the store.

*The period 1860–1900*
*recalled by Frank O'Brien in 1920.*

*Earlier published in* Hennepin County History, *Winter,*
*1989–90, and in* Minnesota Pharmacist, *October, 1990.*

*Humboldt School on the corner of 14th and Main Street, 1882*

# Early Schools

Most early Minneapolis and St. Anthony settlers were from New England and the Middle Atlantic States in which public schools had been inaugurated and tested. The first school in the area was started in June 1849 by Electra Backus in a shanty near Second Street in St. Anthony. Backus was also the area's first Sunday school teacher and taught in the same room in which the day school was taught. In December 1849, the St. Anthony Academy opened. Both St. Anthony schools were private, the patrons paying a tuition fee for each scholar enrolled. St. Anthony quickly outgrew both buildings and two school buildings were built—one on the site of Backus'school and the other at Central Avenue and First Street SE.

In 1850, St. Anthony got its first public school system when city officials divided the town into two districts and decided each district would have its own school, both of which opened in 1851 with Miss Thompson and Miss Mary Schofield as teachers. Thompson's school lasted only a few years. Schofield's, the Second Ward School at University Avenue and Sixth Street NE, later became Everett School, the oldest in the St. Anthony district. The wood-frame building was destroyed by fire in 1887 and rebuilt. The district closed the school in 1932 and sold the site. The building was demolished in 1947.

Also in 1851, St. Anthony added a third School building on land donated by Franklin Steele near University and Central. The building, the Primary Depart-ment of the University of Minnesota, acted as a college preparatory school until destroyed by fire in1864.

Apparently St. Anthony was satisfied with its schools. In the city charter of 1855, no mention is made of schools. Up to that time, they had been man-aged to the satisfaction of the people and no inter-ference was desired from the city government. While the Minneapolis school system struggled financially, St. Anthony encountered other problems. The student population was growing faster than the city could pro-vide schools. By 1861, St. Anthony had 1,302 scholars between the ages of 5 and 21. Male teachers received $30 a month salary; female teachers $20.

East Side directors were possibly too prudent and conservative. From 1865 to March 1867, at least a dozen meetings were held to secure sites for school-houses. But nothing further seems to have resulted from the proceedings.

By 1866, St. Anthony had raised $13,500 in taxes for two schools, but it took the city another year to find suitable locations. Eventually the city built Winthrop and Humboldt Schools. Winthrop opened in 1867. The wood-framed building was demolished in 1899 and rebuilt as East High School. The school later served as the Boys Vocational School.

By 1872, St. Anthony had more than 1,900 stu-dents in four buildings when the city merged with Minneapolis. It was decided to keep the East District of St. Anthony and West District of Minneapolis

*Lunch line of East Side High School, 1900s*

*Graduating class or Glee Club at East Side High, 1920*

schools separate. Both were placed under control of the Minneapolis City Council where it remained until 1967.

The combined district had 99 teachers and 5,215 students, 190 who were in the high school division though there was no separate High School. Despite the shortage of high school space, the first school built after the merger was Webster Elementary.

By 1892, Minneapolis Public Schools had more than 23,000 students, including 1,600 in four high schools (East, North, South and Central), with Charles N. Jordan as the superintendent. Jordan brought many changes, dropping Greek and introducing Norwegian, French and Spanish. Jordan is also credited with starting the PTA and a teacher's pension fund, summer vacations for students and playgrounds.

From 1892 to 1896, the district added eight schools on the East Side: Prescott, Holland, Schiller, Van Cleve, Pierce and Sheridan (all elementary schools), and East High.

Several temporary schools were also opened on the East Side, including Nicollet (1898) on the north end of Nicollet Island, Columbus (1907) at Winter and Hoover, Gersham (1917) at 35th and Second, Cavell (1917) at 35th and Tyler which was later moved to 34th and Fillmore, and Cary (1924) at 33rd and Cleveland. All closed a few years after they opened.

By 1922, Minneapolis Public Schools held buildings valued at more than $15 million, including the district's newest school, Edison, which was built at a cost of more than $766,000, the most expensive school (at the time) in the system.

**Humbolt School**—In 1868, Humboldt school opened on Main Street, between 13th and 14th Avenues NE. Humbolt was originally called the First Ward School. Later it was named in honor of Karl Humbolt, the German statesman or it may have been after Alexander Humbolt, the early explorer. The school was closed and demolished in 1941.

**Holland**—The Josiah G. Holland School, a three-story masonry and wood structure was erected in 1886, with additions constructed in 1905 and 1916. The original building was located at 1707 NE Washington Street, which was demolished in 1968 after the district built the new Holland School on 16th and Fourth Street.

**Van Cleve**—Named after Charlotte Ouisconsin Van Cleve, one of the original civilians who accompanied the first troops to Fort Snelling in 1819. The school began as a portable wooden unit in 1894. A permanent brick building was built in 1896 on the south side of Lowry between Jefferson and Monroe. The school closed in 1942 and the building was torn down in 1953.

*Van Cleve School 1920*

*Pillsbury School, 1907*

*Whitney School, 1945*

**Pierce**—The Franklin Pierce Elementary School was located on a 2.35 acre site at 1121 NE Broadway, just north of Beltrami Park. Pierce first opened in a former church on Fillmore and Summer. The school moved to a permanent building on the northwest corner of Broadway and Fillmore in 1898. The two-story masonry and wood structure was erected in 1900. Five portable classrooms were attached to the building in 1923 and 1926. The school closed in 1967 and was destroyed by fire two years later.

**Sheridan**—Was built in 1896 at University and Broadway and served as an elementary school until it was demolished in 1932. A new building was built on the site, which has served as an elementary and junior high school. For awhile it contained a branch of the Minneapolis Public Library. Located on a 4.3 acre site at 1201 University Avenue NE, the new Philip H. Sheridan Junior High and Elementary School, a three story masonry and wood structure was erected in 1932

**Pillsbury**—The John S. Pillsbury Elementary School, a two-story masonry and wood structure was erected in 1908, with additions constructed in 1912 and 1923. It is located on a 2.63 acre site at 2255 Northeast Hayes, just south of Windom Park. Pillsbury closed in 1981. The building was demolished in 1990 and a new Pillsbury School was built on the site.

**Whitney**—The Eli Whitney Elementary School was erected in 1920 and burned September 18, 1962. It was located on a 2.42-acre site at 1843 NE Pierce Street. The enrollment in 1962 was 188 students.

**Lowry**—28th Avenue and Lincoln Street. Lowry began as a two room portable school on October 30, 1911. The first graduating class was June 1916 with 11 boys and 11 girls. A permanent school was built in 1916 at a cost of $130,000. In 1944 the school got new clocks and in 1950 each classroom had a radio. Beatrice Lowry donated 226 pictures to decorate the school. The school was closed in 1978. Two scrapbooks with newspaper clippings and photos are kept at the Minnesota History Center in St. Paul.

*left—Mrs. Florence Gustafson was a tiny gal with a fiery character.*

*right top—Auction for closing Lowry School in 1978*

*right bottom—Classroom door of room 202. Everyone loved Gusty. She was spunky and colorful and there was no misbehaving in her class. She taught Civics and History with vigor. Every afternoon she'd drag out the Philco radio with curved top and the class would listen and discuss world events, mostly World War II related. She still has a fan club today that meets pretty regularly.*

*Northeast Junior High, room 304 in the early 1960s*

*Ground breaking ceremony October 13, 1955
of Northeast Junior High*

**Waite Park Elementary**—The two-story masonry structure is located at 1800 34th Avenue NE. Dedicated in 1951, it was the first school and park board joint effort in the nation. It was also the first school on the Eastside since Sheridan was built in 1932 and the first Twin Cities School ever named after a living person, Judge Edward F. Waite. Edith Cavell, Alice Cary and Greshem Schools were consolidated into the Waite Park district. The projected enrollment of the modern, low maintenance building was 720. In 1954 the enrollment was 986. Since the limits of the district were no more than 4/5 of a mile, all students were required to walk to school. Because of his interest in the development and welfare of the youth of the community, the Board of Education and Park Commissioners named their project in honor of "The father of the juvenile court system."

**Northeast Junior High**—Is located on a 5.5-acre site at 2955 NE Hayes Street. A three-story masonry structure was built in 1956. An addition of pool and gym building were constructed in 1957 and 1959. The naming of Northeast School had several interesting developments. No other school had so many names suggested (there were 38), or so many people involved in the selection process. One of the names included was Davy Crockett, which has no connection with Minnesota history but at the time must have been influenced by a Walt Disney television program that had been aired in late 1954 and caught the imagination of some young viewer. The committee did not want to name the school after a section of the city, such as south, west, north etc. But after many months of deliberation on March 29, 1955 the board voted to accept the name Northeast Junior High School.

Edison—700–22$^{nd}$ Avenue NE, Edison High first opened Sept.5th, 1922, under the name Northeast High School. The new school built at a cost of more than $800,000 had 1,650 students in grades 7-11. Part of the students and faculty from Old Eastside High were moved to Edison when it was complete. The early days of Edison were noted for their vaudeville performances, sunlight dances and the two graduating classes, one in January and the other in June. Noted for many undefeated years in sports. The new gym building was added in 1977.

**Putnam**—1616 NE Buchanan was built in 1966. Named after Rufus S.Putnam, superintendent of Minneapolis schools from 1960 to 1967. Combined the enrollment from Whitney and Pierce.

## Winthrop School
1867–1888

The Winthrop school was a landmark in its locality. Since the days of early school buildings in the town of St. Anthony, it was an object of pride to the East Siders. Central Avenue was known as Bay Street in 1867, when the Winthrop was erected and is still so designated on the plats. It was built during the years when the late Winthrop Young was president of the St. Anthony school board. J.B. Gilfillian was treasurer and Charles Crawford was secretary. The Winthrop was replaced by the new East High School and the lots in "Block 18", that were earlier selected as educational ground, remained devoted to their original use.

Something of romance lingered around the building, and who can tell what scholars who studied side by side in the 70's ended up walking the path of life together reading the book of life's lesson. Not only did the pupils find mates in the school ranks, but also one of the members of the school board, Judge Gilfillian, found a bride in the corps of teachers. While he was connected with the St. Anthony Board of Education, he married Miss Rebecca Oliphant.

The records show that the school board in the town of St.Anthony was organized in 1860, and continued operating under its original charter until the spring of 1866. James McMullen and Dr.Ortman were also school board members. The school property consisted of three buildings, one occupying ground near where the Marcy School on Ninth Avenue Southeast now stands, and the "White School House", north of Bay Street in the Second ward. What is now the First

*Winthrop School near University and First Avenue SE in 1882, one of the first schools on the East Side*

Ward, the "Black School House" was so-called because it was unpainted and dulled in tone by sun and rain. It was located on University Avenue near where the Windom hotel was located.

Judge Gilfillian had been a teacher in both the white and black schoolhouses, before he became a judge and lawyer. The buildings were small, and in time they became inadequate for the number of children that clamored for admission. Finally a public meeting was called, and in May of 1866 the school board voted to buy two lots for which a consideration of $600 was to be paid to the St. Anthony Falls Water Power Company. A bare majority carried the vote. There were no funds to pay for the lots, so the matter did not progress until the following year. In May of 1867, three more lots were secured for $2,000. It was proposed to issue bonds and there was a great hue and cry among the people. But as prominent people began to donate money, others followed.

Ground was immediately broken and the building began. R.S. Alden became the architect; Weeks and Co. the masons; and Thomas H. Goodale, the builder.

Goodale was more familiarly known as "Sid" the carpenter. The material was native limestone quarried on the riverbank, and therefore had to be hauled only a short distance. Work progressed rapidly during the summer and the building was ready for use the following winter. It was immediately occupied, and was familiarly known as the Central High School. Nearly 500 children sought admission and the rooms were soon filled to their capacity. Mr. Gorrie was principal of the new school, and had his residential quarters in the basement. After a year or two, in compliment to the president of the school board, the name was changed to the Winthrop school, by which it had continued to be known.

The building was put up at an approximate cost of $40,000. It was constructed to leave the upper floor free for an entertainment hall, and was used as assembly room for the graduation exercises and public gatherings. It was the lecture hall for speakers who came from great distances to address the people of St. Anthony. When more space was required for school purposes, the assembly hall was cut up into recitation rooms.

In 1875 the Water Power Company turned over the deed to the Board of Education for the rest of the block on which the Winthrop school stood. This gave the city the entire square and the value of the bonds was exceeded twice over. In the summer of 1899 the Minneapolis Improvement League established its experimental public playground in the Winthrop schoolyard.

The Winthrop school housed a primary department, an intermediate department, a grammar school, and a high school when it opened in 1867. The grammar school was divided into three grades that indicated the scholarship of the pupils. "Under this rigid classification, age has no claims to place " a newspaper noted, "Small boys journey with large ones, and little girls with those nearly out of their short dresses on the road to learning."

The number of little feet that passed through the halls and over the doorsills have pressed the woodwork in hollows and worn away all rough edges. Fondly regarded by many that have grown from childhood to maturity, for was it not the first good school building in Minneapolis, the progenitor of a long line of worthy successors?

Its three early contemporaries have long since disappeared; the Winthrop School will live again in the new East High School that will occupy its place and ground.

*Times, Tuesday Morning Aug.15,1899*

## Webster
1880–Present

A center section of the building on Monroe and Summer St. NE, a brick two-story structure boasting six schoolrooms was begun in 1880 and named the same year. The pioneer school administration might be described as somewhat rigid. The records of 1883–84 tell us that 82 of Webster's 507 pupils were suspended, 69 were eventually restored. No record is shown of what happened to the remaining 13. Expenditures for the 1886–87 school year include $2.65 for supplies and $2.58 for furniture. In 1888, another 4-room addition was made to the building, at a cost of $17,000.

*Classroom at Webster School learning basket weaving, 1901*

By 1908, Webster also had an evening school; grades 1–8; directed by 20 teachers and no less than 4 principals. The enrollment of 567 consisted of adult immigrants learning the ways of their new land, and children were excused from day school by labor permits. Child labor still flourished and children who worked by day were required to attend school at night. The final wing was added to the building this year.

The neighborhood surrounding the school continued to grow. Throughout the Gay 90's, the NE Literary Association met at the House of Faith and the Scandinavian Debating Society at Hagan's Hall, 617 Monroe. One debate centered on "What causes the hard Times?" Webster families bought Virginia-cured ham at the Monroe Packing company, 358 Monroe, for 10 cents a lb., and took their grain to the Fisher Feed and Mill Company on Monroe. Riviere's Family Drugstore on Adams and Broadway installed a button on the Washington streetcar tracks, which would ring in its store when the car was approaching.

In the 20th century, Webster and other Minneapolis Public Schools began their School Patrol. Sometime in the 1920s Webster became the location of the Special Learning and Sight-Saving Classes, which were transferred away only a few years ago. Blind and partially sighted children learned Braille with special equipment, then went back to their other classmates for other subjects and recess. Famous schoolyard landmarks were the "Boys' side and the "Girls' side".

In 1931, Webster was condemned as a fire hazard by the Minneapolis Fire Department, but continued to serve as a school. During the war years, Webster pupils conducted copper and paper drives, bought U.S. savings stamps, and sent clothing to the "Save the Children Federation".

In 1963, the Michigan State University survey team identified new Webster as one of "the most urgent first building needs" of the Minneapolis schools. The St. Anthony East Urban Renewal Program began, a federally funded effort to rehabilitate an aging neighborhood whose school needed replacement. But still Webster continued to serve the area and its children. PTA carnivals and ice cream socials were popular. Balloonist Dr. Jeanette Piccard honored Webster's Science Fair by her visit. And while we found no national hero who attended Webster, no other school can boast that one of their little girls grew up to marry the Lone Ranger, Clayton Moore!

In June 1934 old Webster's doors closed for the last time. The wide golden oak stairway, worn hollow by 93 years of Northeast children, will wait in the dust and the sunlight of the wrecker's ball. A new building will be built.

*Yesterday and Tomorrow*
*Anniversary Closing*
*Webster School 1880–1974*

## Prescott
### 1884–1974

The closing ceremonies for Prescott were held Sunday June 2nd, 1974. No one quite remembers why the school was named after William H. Prescott of Salem, Mass., who was an author of Spanish history books. He was born in 1796 and died in 1859. Prescott School opened in 1884 with 129 pupils. The original building was two stories and contained four classrooms. The property was purchased for $2,100, and the building was valued at $16,000. Additions were made in 1887,

1901, 1909 and 1931. Teachers made a top salary of $650 and principals $800, depending upon years of experience.

A former student, Dr. Stella Bartsch Carroll, sent a parcel of memories to school when the 75th anniversary was celebrated in 1959. Her father had a small grocery store across from the school over 65 years ago. She wrote:

"The school yard was rather sandy and at recess we all rushed out to get a drink of water that had been set out in large tin pails on long benches. Each pail had a tin dipper in it. With the sudden rush the sand created quite a bit of dust that gently settled on the water. We were none the worse for it.

In those days children really wore clothes. For instance, in winter I had red woollies, home knitted stockings, two red woolen petticoats—each were trimmed at the bottom with red crocheted woolen lace. On top of these a red woolen dress with high neck and long sleeves. This material was called Henrietta cloth. Over this dress was a cute white pinafore to keep the dress clean. When dressing for school, woolen wristlets were a must; a woolen scarf around the neck; a pussy bonnet made of angora yarn; then another scarf was folded over my forehead, crossed in back and brought to the front and tied, and of course, woolen mittens. I wore four-buckle overshoes, which came just to the bend of my knees, and a good warm coat; then my brother carried me across the street on stormy days. By the time I got there I was just about roasted.

There was a hill at the East End of Lowry Avenue, then Twenty-fifth Avenue, where the boys and girls used to slide down past our store on bobsleds. Most of these were homemade bobs. Two small heavy sleds were fastened under a long plank which was raised about eighteen inches and were long enough for about ten or twelve youngsters. This bobsled had a steering stick fastened in front, and there were no springs, so sliding was pretty rugged when the streets were icy. There were no automobiles to interfere. The slide was about ten blocks long and when walking back to the top of the hill, the youngsters would stop in the store to warm up and perhaps dry their mittens on the sheet metal guard around the coal stove. What a noise and what a mess!"

Mrs. Emma Watson has many vivid memories of Prescott School. She came to America from Denmark when she was three years old. Her older sisters started school at Prescott in 1886. Now living near International Falls, Emma Watson writes:

"I shall always remember the first few months of my school life, as in my home we spoke only the Danish language and I could read and even write some in Dane as my mother had taught me. My first teacher was Miss Porter and I loved her after I wasn't afraid of her.

Several months after starting school my oldest sister had promised me a penny if I got 100 in my spelling and I would have, only I spelled Kate wrong. I spelled it in Danish. I'll never forget how I cried but Miss Porter came to me and told me not to cry as we all make mistakes and in a way I spelled it right, but I lost my penny.

How different schools were then compared to now? Children really respected their teachers more than they do today. My most beloved teachers were Miss Ida Allan and Miss Sullivan, an Irish teacher who was wonderful. She even pinned a green ribbon on me on St. Patrick's Day and told me I looked like a little Irish girl. I kept that ribbon for many years.

Every spring in April, we planted a little tree. This was Arbor Day and every room put their name in an envelope and a boy put them under a tree. Those trees were pretty big when I left dear old Prescott. I still love that school and hate to think it's going to be torn down as it's an old landmark."

*Down Memory Lane*
*Prescott School 1884–1974*

## Schiller School

### History

About the year 1888 Mr. Joe Ingenhutt and Mr. Robert Graham appeared before the Board of Education asking for a school in what is now the Schiller district. The school board was loath to comply with this request saying, "You have not enough children," Mr. Graham's reply was, "You give us the school, and the Irish, Germans, Russian, and Polish will soon fill it." This was convincing to the Board of Education and the request was granted. The late Joseph Ingenhutt, who was a great admirer of the poet, Schiller, was influential in giving the school its name. The residence at 2636 Grand Street NE was a temporary quarters, under the direction of Miss Wheeler, while the school was being built on its present site. The six rooms at the East End of the building on California Street were the first to be built. The entrance was on Grand Street. Additions were built in 1909, 1916 and 1960.

In 1918–1919 Schiller was in the outlying district of Minneapolis. A survey of 25 blocks showed there were 292 families of which 63 were American and 229 were foreign born, mostly Slavic. Most understood or spoke no English. At this time there was a visiting or home teacher whose job it was to get the children to come to school. This was a difficult task, as children were kept home to help with the gardening, herding cows, washing clothes and taking care of the younger children in the family.

Many Schiller grads will remember the many assembly programs with Principal Mary Martin, where the school song was sung and the school cheer could be heard. The school was truly the center of the community in those days. Class plays and musicals were a regular part of the school program and involved many people. Field Trips were often taken by use of the teacher's car, and the running boards were used to carry extra students.

### Graduations

In January 1910, fourteen pupils assembled at old East High School to receive diplomas. This was the first eighth grade class to graduate from Schiller School. The girls were dressed in white and carried large bouquets of flowers.

### Closing

Schiller was closed on May 5, 1974. The closing of a school is never easy. In the early 1970s, all of the pre–1900 school buildings in Minneapolis were closed.

*Ideal Diner, 1999*

# Northeast Diners

In the 1930s and 40s Northeast diners were very much a part of the landscape. Many of them had hearty and hot noon specials for under a dollar. The Band Box and the Candlelight Café were on 40th and Central across from each other. Gus and Peter Mangos opened the Central Avenue Café at 2403 Central in the 1920s. Business boomed during the war. The Soo Line Shoreham Yard crew and workers from the nearby factories poured in at lunchtime. Saturdays and Sundays were extremely busy. People called the Central Avenue Café, "The Greeks" when the Mango Brothers owned it. Gus Mangos died in 1945. After that the family ran it for a few years and they sold it in 1949.

Ted Pappas ran the Pig and the Bun, which served just hot dogs and hamburgers on 2431 Central. Gertrude Statig owned the Elmwood Café on 1846 Central and was a super cook. Her daughter Ann later joined her in the business. The Elmwood was famous for their lingonberry pancakes and family style dining. The waitresses brought out bowls of potatoes and vegetables to the table to be shared. People came from miles around to enjoy Swedish pancakes on Saturday mornings. Swedish pastries and home baked bread were also popular items. A group from Northern Pump came in to eat there every day.

Ron Clair's Diner opened at 1841 Central and was owned by Ron Cornelius. Ron sold it to his brother in 1948 and it became Freddy's. Freddy's was open round the clock and served a hamburger and soup special. Ron and Freddy's sister, Donna Stevens got her start as a waitress at the age of thirteen when she worked at Ebert's Hamburger Joint and then at the Band Box. Her mother told her she didn't want her slinging hamburgers for a living. So she took a job in the office at Coast to Coast.

Then when her brother Freddy asked her to come in and help during the Beer Run after the bars closed at 1:00, she said yes and stayed on for eleven years. When Freddy sold the place to his brother Jerry who sold it to a body shop, Donna leased the café space from the body shop owner in the 1960s and turned it into Donna's Café. Most of her customers came from General Mills, the Soo Line and Minar Ford. She served all homemade foods like liver, meatballs and meatloaf. Inside there were four booths and a horseshoe counter that seated twenty.

Donna closed her restaurant in 1969 and got a job at Ideal Diner. Zelda, the owner asked her to help out. Thirty-one years later, she's still there. Zelda Daniels owned the place for 17 years. Eddie Engels was the original owner and started the restaurant in 1949. When Kevin Kelzenberg bought the diner in 1981 it was open 24 hours a day. He is now open until 2:00 for seven days a week. Donna's daughter, Kim Robinson has worked there for 13 years.

Ideal Diner is one of the last of the old time diners. Some of their specialties are pork tenderloin; goulash,

*Inside Ideal Diner, 1999*

fast turnover in this small diner. Waitresses don't use slips; they just call out the order. It's like a family place where customers discuss what's in the paper and joke around a lot. Jerry Lauer and Jim Grausen are Ideal's longest standing customers. Jim came into the diner with his dad as a young boy. In July of 1999 Ideal Diner celebrated their 50th anniversary.

The Mighty Fine Diner began as the North Star Coffee Shop. In the early 1960s the décor changed from tables to a counter with stools when Gladys Kaste owned the place. She was said to be a sweet grandmotherly type. Truck drivers would order a stack of pancakes and coffee for 90 cents. Susan Lutz bought the café in 1990. Older customers say it served as a draft board during the war. Today they serve more young people from the University and families from the neighborhood.

When the factories and the breweries closed, many of the diners closed too. The Central Avenue Café, the Elmwood, and the Arion Café on 2833 Central all vacated in the 1970s. The Crest Café on 23rd and Central became a bank parking lot.

omelets and home made hash browns. A lot of people were brought up on Goulash and they get mad if its not served on Thursdays. They also love the home made mashed potatoes and great soups. They go through 50 pounds of potatoes a day. There's a pretty

*Crest Café on 23rd Central, 1952*

# Making Movies In Northeast

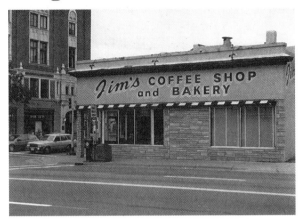

*Jim Kishush and Anjelo Tipe who emigrated from Greece started Jim's Coffee Shop. Jim's son George took over the business in 1936 and it closed in 1997*

Several years ago, in 1991, the former River Palace Restaurant and Hennepin Avenue Bridge hosted the filming of a movie called "the Bridge." Then in 1992, filmmakers began a local shooting of "Untamed Heart," a fictional story set in Northeast Minneapolis. The cast included Christian Slater, Marisa Tomei and Rosie Perez.

The movie was about a Minneapolis waitress named Caroline that was looking for love and a sickly busboy with a bad heart. They became close friends and later fell in love. Neither one of them had good luck with relationships.

Jim's Coffee Shop and Bakery at Fourth Street and Central Avenue was the setting for the all-night diner where they worked. The shop closed down for six weeks during the filming but some of his patrons became extras during the diner scenes.

Jefferson Street closed down between 15th and 17th Avenue while shooting neighborhood houses decorated in Christmas lights for one week during April. The location manager, Bob Graf, says he feels close to Northeast, as he spent a lot of time with his grandparents on Benjamin Street when he was growing up. His great grandfather was Henry Rosacker.

A house on Jefferson Street was chosen because of its interesting character that intrigued the filmmakers. They did have to remove one wall in the interior of the house. The house needed remodeling anyway. It's hard to find a house that's big enough to make a movie, but still make it appear to be an average size home.

People in the neighborhood were asked to leave their Christmas lights up on their houses because the movie was set around the holiday season. Snow was also added for effect. Some of the filming was done at night for the scene shot in the Riverplace area where Caroline walked from Lourdes Square to Nicollet Island. Graf said it was an interesting location but also difficult to light.

Although traffic remained open, there were occasional delays while cameras were running. Jim's closed from March 30th to May 1st during the actual filming and reopened early on May 11th. TBHC Production Company worked with MGM Studios on the film. Written by Tom Sierchio of New York who made his debut with his first produced screenplay. The director is Tony Bill and producers are Bill and Helen Bartlett and Boyce Harmon.

Other films shot recently in the Northeast Minneapolis area were "Little Big League," "Grumpy Old Men" and the bar scene of the "The Mary Tyler Moore Show" television series was shot in the Last Chance Bar.

*My Uncle Eddy with group of his buddies outside Little Jack's Restaurant, 1940s*

# 7 The Homefront During World War II in Northeast Minneapolis

**Northeast Neighborhood House**—The war had an important integrating effect on the neighborhood. People were brought together by common bonds. Red Cross classes were organized in first aid, knitting, sewing, surgical dressing, home nursing, nutrition, and food conservation at the Northeast Neighborhood House. Most of those who attended classes had relatives in the United States army, as well as friends and relatives in their native countries in both allied and enemy camps. The united effort to alleviate suffering helped to bridge the gulf between the various nationalities.

With the beginning of the draft, the Northeast Neighborhood House was able to offer practical assistance to young men in filling out their questionnaires. This might have been a seemingly minor matter to most Americans, but to the immigrant it presented great difficulties. Robin Gilman became a legal advisor of the first ward, and he was able to help the men avoid the fee that a notary public would have charged.

**Blackout Drills**—People learned how to make black out curtains and covered their windows with sticky tape to protect against flying glass. Some went to bed by candlelight, well away from the bedroom windows. Wardens patrolled the streets, banging on doors shouting, "Put that light out!" Pubs had plywood screens and blackout curtains at their doors so that you could go in and out without showing a light. City workers would come around and put out your lights. You had to cover all the windows. These drills were usually done at night in case of bombing or when foreign aircraft were spotted overhead. You had to have good shades and drapes. The block warden would check everything from outside to see if any light could be seen. They would check every block with one hour practice each week.

**Rosie the Riveter**—a fictional, symbolic poster character during WW II, became a publicity campaign to encourage women to join the workforce. Before that time most middle and upper class American women stayed home and took care of the house and children. Men leaving for war created a vacancy in many jobs. In addition, many more jobs were created as the war increased demand for food, clothing and munitions. Rosie was depicted as an attractive, rosy-cheeked woman dressed in men's work clothes. She was designed to make the idea of working outside the home attractive. She made it seem patriotic rather than unfeminine. With the help of Rosie the Riveter, more than 6 million women joined the workforce during the war. There was a popular song called Rosie the Riveter.

**Gold Star Mothers**—The American Gold Star Mothers, created in 1929, got its name from the practice of displaying a gold star, instead of traditional mourning

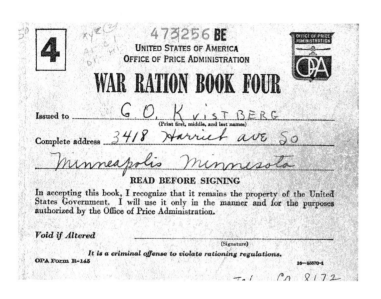

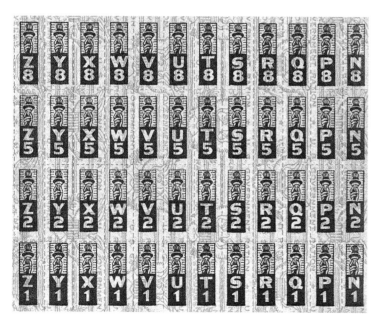

Northern Pump workers go all out for

## WAR SAVINGS BONDS

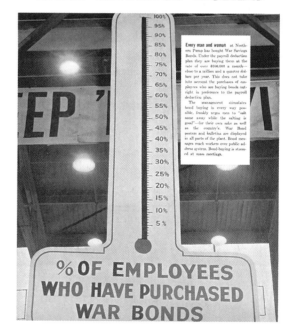

attire, by a mother whose son or daughter had made the ultimate sacrifice during war. A satin flag hung in the window about 8 by 10 inches. Blue stars on a white background and trimmed in gold indicated how many soldiers from that house were overseas fighting. A single gold star in the window meant that a soldier from that household had been killed. Gold star mothers were always honored. The last Sunday in September was dedicated to them and still is today.

**Victory Gardens**—Every scrap of land was used to grow food; parks and empty lots and rosebeds were dug out. "Dig for Victory" was the slogan. Also "Lend a hand on the land" became a slogan of public schoolboys. Thousands of elderly men spent their weekends tending allotments, using soot and manure. Americans dug for victory, and named their plots Victory Gardens. They bought seed catalogs and read the Department of Agriculture leaflets. Known as "Sunday Farmers," many discovered the sheer pleasure of eating home grown food. Victory celebrations were all over and Victory Gardens were planted along the railroad tracks. They were owned and tended by each individual family.

**Bond Drives**—The liberty bond drive was another project that drew a great response from the families of northeast Minneapolis. Subscriptions from the first ward exceeded $450,000. Solicitors found that the Polish and Slavic people in particular rarely refused to buy a bond. This same generosity had been demonstrated during the Red Cross drive. The Catholic priests of the neighborhood were active in urging people to express their patriotism through these drives. Bonds were also sold at the neighborhood theaters.

Often the immigrant's surge of loyalty went beyond the country they were from to a direct personal tie with the community and to the Neighborhood House. At St. Mary's Orthodox Church, a group of Russians gathered to learn the purpose of the War Chest drive. The Reverend John Dzubay, their interpreter, feared that many of the people thought such giving was compulsory. But during the presentation, one of the mothers jumped to her feet. She had heard that the quota for the War Chest was 2 per cent of the family's salary, but she and her husband wanted to give 3 per cent. Father Dzubay assured her that it was not compulsory, and then asked her why they wanted to give more than the suggested quota. "North East Neighborhood House," she said. "That's why."

By itself the war could have acted as a dividing point and negative force in Northeast Minneapolis. But largely through the influence of the Neighborhood House, which was already working on problems within the community and the long-range goal of Americanization, the war became a catalyst that brought about positive change. It provided solutions to problems and revealed problems that had not yet been recognized. It also led to the creation of new community programs that extended the influence of the settlement house.

## Rationing

During World War II everyone had to use ration stamps to buy everyday items, such as meat, sugar, and shoes. Even with stamps, food was often difficult to come by. Lines were long and quality was poor. Even ground beef was in short supply. It was not unusual to wait in line for hours, and then rush home with a large package of meat and looking forward to a mouthwatering supper, then biting into meat mixed with ground liver. All those precious stamps wasted on liver. The Northeast Neighborhood House was headquarters for the sale of thrift stamps in Northeast Minneapolis, which also had a social effect on the people.

Government–controlled rationing began in December of 1941, after the Japanese attack on Pearl Harbor. The emergency Office of Price Administration (OPA) was created, together with subsidiary local boards staffed by volunteers. Automobile tires led the list of items rationed, which by war's end included automobiles, typewriters, bicycles, stoves, leather and rubber footwear, coffee, sugar, canned and processed foods, meats, fats, gasoline, fuel oil for home heating, and coal.

A point system was set up for a number of articles that allowed customers to spend only a certain number of total points. The mechanics of rationing involved coupon books, stamps, or certificates; all three were used during World War II. Most Americans accepted it as necessary, although violations did occur and black-market or illegal trade existed in some items.

There were red, blue, brown and green stamps. Shopkeepers had to stick the stamps onto sheets of paper and take them to wholesalers who had to give them to banks. As America was not at any time near starvation, some people felt that food rationing was unnecessary. People traded rations according to their needs. One woman sent sugar to her mother in New York in exchange for toilet paper.

**Gasoline** was in short supply. "A" cards were used for gasoline. Each family was allowed only three gallons of gas for one month. There were special cards for people who worked at defense plants. It was common to see signs hung on the doorway, "Quiet please, defense worker sleeping." These employees worked strange hours around the clock. Later after the war, when gas was more plentiful, people began to take long drives just for the fun of it, a treat that they had gone without for a long time.

**Nylons**—Silk stockings became popular in the 1930s. They were first sold in Wilmington, Delaware and were advertised to "halve stocking bills without loss of glamour." It was the height of luxury for teenage girls to wear nylons. You couldn't get nylons during World War II because nylon and silk were used to make parachutes. The average silk stocking only lasted about 10 days. So stockings were mended. If you had no stockings at all, you painted your legs with suntan lotion, drawing a seam with an eyebrow pencil. Sometimes a soldier would risk court marshal and bring home a parachute. But everyone knew who you were going out with. A length of parachute silk could also be made into sets of undies. But you could tell who was wearing them because she rustled as she danced. It even helped to know an undertaker, because muslin was used for coffin linings. After the war people were lined up to buy nylons at Dayton's Department Store.

**Clothing** —Although clothes were not rationed, the stuff they were made of was rigidly controlled. Circumference of a skirt could be no more than six feet, belts two inches wide, and hems no more than two inches. The British zip-up siren suit became popular for men. Blouses and hats imitated uniforms; Tank Corps berets and peaked caps with glitter. Thus

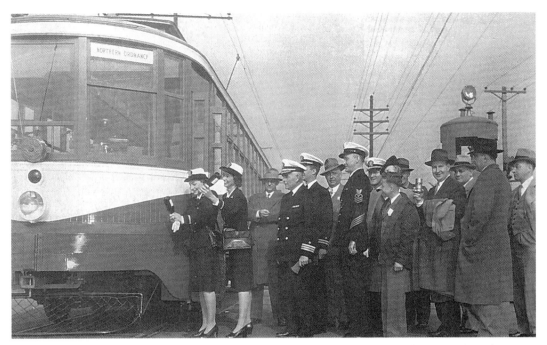

*Streetcar service exclusively for employees of Northern Pump Company began when two trolleys, painted red, white and blue ran between the plant and the Second Streetcar line. They were christened in proper Navy fashion, 1943*

*Signing up for the draft at Logan Park*

*Lady streetcar conductor during World War II*

*Customers lined up for boned beef in barrels in front of*
*Schmidler Meat Market on 1919 Central Avenue in 1946*

American girls who were not in uniform made believe they were. Even pajamas looked military.

'Make Do and Mend' became the slogan to live by and 'Mrs. Sew and Sew' explained how in publicity campaigns. Two dish cloths were turned into a jersey, men's old overcoats became tweed coats and skirts, patch-worked old pieces of knitting and unravelled woollens turned into warm waist coats, old cotton dresses were made into aprons, and curtains into skirts. And dressmakers advertised: 'Last season's dresses, coats etc. made to look new.' Wool was precious because it cost more coupons than rayon or silk and with conservation of fuel, it was warm. A popular design was the Victory Jumper, with V-neck, V-motif, and V-everything.

In 1942 "Utility" clothes appeared, in standard patterns designed to save cloth and buttons. They all carried the Utility mark, two crescents and a number. These were sold at controlled prices.

**Metal Salvage**—"Use it up, wear it out, or do without" was a favorite saying in the 1940s. Any old cans, old nylons, anything made of metal or rubber or paper. They could all be made into war materials and huge salvage dumps appeared in every town. The scrap drives caused Bing Crosby to croon, "Junk Will Win the War." Housewives donated aluminum saucepans with no prospect of getting them back. Kids collected scrap metal for recycling. They'd contribute the metal to a common fund and receive stamps. So instead of banking, people saved stamps and put them in a book. Then you could turn them in for one bond. Nothing new was made out of metal. You couldn't even get tricycles.

**Leather** was rationed to make combat boots for the soldiers. Each family member was allowed only one pair of shoes. With a child who outgrew shoes quickly, it was tough. You'd have to trade with someone older who didn't wear out their shoes, giving meat or gasoline stamps in trade. Women who were desperate to remain stylish would be seen wearing plastic or cardboard shoes. Going to a party in the rain made for some disastrous scenes of wearing wet shoes that fell apart. Unlucky was the girl who didn't have average feet. There were not many styles to choose from, all were heavy and 'sensible', with wedged heels and peep toes. They were worn on special occasions with silk stockings, or for everyday with leg make-up.

**Sugar**—The sugar ration was 12 ounces, but more in the jam making season. Sweets came with personal points equal to 2 ounces a week. There was a great deal of propaganda about how bad they were for your teeth. People saved ahead for special occasions like a ham for Easter or wedding cake. Neighbors and relatives pooled together their sugar rations so a special couple could have a wedding cake. You could make a cake out of flour, custard powder and dried egg. Carrots were chief ingredients of "wartime Christmas pudding."

**Spam (spiced ham) and dried eggs were introduced.** Also whale meat was announced to be safe to eat by the Department of the Interior in 1943. Grease was collected for grease points.

**Bandage making and care packages.** Red Cross Bandages and Care packages were made up at the settlement houses and churches. It was the Northeast connection to Europe. At the end of the war in 1945, rationing was generally eliminated.

The music during WW II helped with the pain. It

was the time of the Big Band era when Frank Sinatra started to become popular. There would be good looking sailors and soldiers that hung around Ft. Snelling, and the Naval Station by the airport. There was a USO on Hennepin Avenue by the Orpheum downtown. The place hummed with dances and pool playing. The depots became a big part of people's lives. Soldiers were constantly leaving and coming home from Europe.

*Bond drive for employees of NSP, 1944*

This recipe was created by the nutrition committee at General Mills and printed in a 1942 Betty Crocker booklet entitled *Your Share: How to Prepare Appetizing, Healthy Meals with Foods Available Today*. In this little booklet are 52 wartime menus, 226 recipes, and 369 hints including tips for using the government's newly created Basic Food Groups. This particular cake is, as the booklet says, "eggless, milkless, butterless," and "delicious uniced."

## Wartime Cake (World War II)

*Makes an 8x8x2-inch Loaf Cake,
about 16 servings*

1 cup firmly packed brown sugar
1 ¼ cups water
⅓ cup lard or other shortening
2 cups seedless raisins
½ ground nutmeg
2 teaspoons ground cinnamon

½ teaspoon ground cloves
1 teaspoon salt
1 teaspoon baking soda dissolved in 2 tablespoons water
2 cups all-purpose flour mixed with 1 teaspoon baking powder

1. Preheat oven to 325degrees F. Grease and flour square baking pan; set aside.
2. Mix sugar, water, shortening, raisins, nutmeg, cinnamon, and cloves in large saucepan. Bring to boil over moderate heat, then boil 3 minutes; cool to room temperature.
3. Mix salt and soda solution into pan, then blend in flour mixture.
4. Pour into pan, spreading to corners, and bake about 50 minutes until cake begins to pull from sides of pan and is springy-firm to touch.
5. Cool in pan on wire rack before cutting into squares.

*John Saba Ohad and Lebibi (Thanoos) Ohad, Shahid,*
*Mom's mother and John Saba*

# 8 The Ma and Pa Stores are All Gone Now
# Fifteen Interviews of Northeast Residents

## My Aunt Was Hit by a Stray Bullet and Died on Her Wedding Day

*By Shahid Ohad*

My father, John Saha Ohad (Hunnah Sabah Ahwaed in Arabic) was born on June 15, 1893 in Tullah, Bahtroon, Lebanon. And my mother, Lebibi Thanoos Elias was born in Lebanon in 1888. My father, in his youth was a very active person and a daredevil mountain climber and my grandfather owned olive and citrus groves. He was also the Mayor of their village. During my father's adolescent years, he and his mother immigrated to America. There were three children in his family. His sister was married in Lebanon and during the wedding shivaree, there was considerable feasting, drinking and general merriment. In those days every male had firearms. The revelers were riding their horses and jumping around while firing their rifles. My aunt was hit by a stray bullet and died on her wedding day.

When my dad was about nineteen, his mother decided it was time he took a wife. She shipped him back to Lebanon to marry my mother, whom he had never met until their wedding day. Sometime in 1913 or 1914, my parents immigrated to the United States. They landed on Ellis Island with very little money. A friend who they met on the boat assisted them in finding the proper train to Minneapolis. They arrived in Minneapolis with only $17.

My father found a house to rent on Fourth Avenue NE between Second Street and University Avenue. He then purchased a small suitcase and some sundries and tramped through the rural areas peddling to the farmers' wives. With the profits thus made, he purchased more and sold them. He eventually bought a horse and wagon, thus increasing his inventory and sales. My first lucid memory was when he had a Model "T" panel truck with shelves about a foot apart running the whole length of it. I recollect one fall I must have been about four when he came home from one of his trips. Upon opening the back panel truck doors, hundreds of big, red juicy apples came rolling out. My brother and I had a lot of fun gathering and eating them, with the tart, sweet and sticky juices running down our chins.

At this time he branched out. He acquired a briefcase fitted with wire-rimmed eyeglasses. The farmers and their families would try them on and purchase the pair that fit them. Ergo, he became the farmer's optometrist!

A few years later, he purchased a store building at 311 Main Street NE with living quarters upstairs. For awhile he had a pool hall in the store portion. Then later he rented it out for various businesses. My mother's youngest brother, Uncle Charlie, used it as a French Bakery. Did my taste bud's change? Nothing tastes like those French pastries and eclairs did then. They melted in your mouth, and that almond-sweet filling was nectar of the Gods.

I was born March 9, 1925, the baby of the family. Lebibi (Betty) was born in 1925. Betty was delivered by an inept doctor and his incompetence resulted in the untimely death of our mother. In those days all births were in the home. You went to the hospital only if you were on your last legs and were expected to die. I remember visiting Mom in the hospital during her last days and crying while she hugged us kids. The funeral wake was in the store building and lasted for three days. All the friends and mourners were seated in a large semi-circle facing the casket.

I remember my grandmother. The women then were always dressed in black. They wore voluminous skirts that reached the floor and wore ankle-height button-up shoes that needed to be laced with a buttonhook. These shoes reached at least six inches up their ankles. I must have been about six years old when grandma left to go to live with Mom's brothers in Brazil. We have many cousins in Brazil.

My father was determined to raise his children by himself. He advertised in the newspapers for a housekeeper. After many came and went, Frances L. Thompson came to us in February of 1927. Here was this tall, skinny, 27-year old Norwegian blonde. About two years later when I was twelve, my brother and I decided that we did not like her. She didn't cook the way we were used to. She made lutefisk ONCE. Lutefisk is fish the Scandinavians prepare for burial before they decide to cook it. It is a white fish that is immersed in a barrel of brine for ages, then dried hard as hell. A year or more later, they bring it into the house and boil, and boil, and boil it until the house from one end to the other has a putrid fishy odor. Remember now, here was a family that grew up on GOOD Lebanese food, being subjected to this foul smelling excuse for fish ('Nuff said). But that was not the worst. She insisted on weekly baths and disciplined us if we didn't obey. After two years of doing what I wanted, as dad was working and the people he had taking care of us were incompetent, I ceased getting my own way.

With Frances a permanent part of our home, Betty was brought back to us. In the next couple of years we moved twice. Dad bought a house on the south side but since we were too far from the Northeast, where most of the immigrants were, he next bought the home at 615 Quincy Street NE. This was our final home and the home we all, except Saba, were married in. It was also the home where Dad and Frances welcomed most of their grandchildren and the home they were buried from. Every so often we still think of it as back home.

There was a corner store on the same block as our home. My brother and I worked in it. Saba made the signs. He was the family artist and we both clerked, stocked shelves and delivered groceries. In those days all stores had free delivery. People would call and order groceries, we would fill the orders, stack them into folding boxes, and deliver them to their homes. It was not unusual to deliver 30 to 50 orders for both morning and afternoon deliveries. The middle of the 1930's was in the middle of the Great Depression. We had the only telephone in the neighborhood and also the only useable automobile. The neighbors thought nothing of giving our phone number to friends or anyone else. It was not unusual for us kids to call various people to the phone numerous times during the day or evenings. Also, whenever any of the neighbors had to be transported to the hospital to have a baby, Dad would have one of us boys drive them there. I don't know what would feed a family for a week. When most of the breadwinners were unemployed and welfare was not that great; it was rough on most people in our area. Dad would let them charge groceries, and the rare times they paid their bills in full, he would give the children candy or ice cream and the fathers a few bottles of beer. After Dad died, us kids went through his papers and discovered at least $50,000 in unpaid grocery bills. Nobody knows how many people he helped through the Depression. He never made a big deal of it. I remember he once took my brother and me to buy us winter clothing. My cousins, Dick and Joe came along. After buying what we needed; he bought them each a warm coat.

I was born in the home on Fourth Avenue NE. At five I was sent to Webster Grade School Kindergarten wearing either black shorts, or dark tweed knickers with long black stockings and black shoes. After the second grade we were sent to Parochial schools. In fifth grade I brought home a report card with an "F" in arithmetic. Dad blew his top and ranted and raved at me for hours. Dad whipped me only once, and that was when I was about five and he saw me run in front of a big old Mack truck. At any rate, never again through all of my school years, did I bring home a report card without an "A" for math. He would mildly scold me for poor grades in other subjects, but Math! Our ancestors invented the cipher, and they were the first mathematicians. Perfection in math was not only expected, but also demanded.

At this time my Uncle William's two children, Stan and Ann, came from Lebanon to Minneapolis. Since Ann was close to my age, for the next two weeks it became my duty to take her to school and to keep an eye on her. Can you imagine me shepherding this foreign looking girl to school? She spoke broken English, and for lunch she brought Arabic bread wrapped around greasy, oily, black ripe olives! She was an embarrassment to me. Needless to say, I took her to school and made myself scarce thereafter.

I remember my first pair of long pants. I must have been about twelve. Boy, did we strut around. Our parents made sure that we were always well dressed. From our teen years on, we received a new suit every Spring, usually for Easter Sunday. Our school and church attire was a starched and ironed white shirt, tie and a clean and well-pressed suit. Frances must have had a helluva time with all the washing and ironing.

While living on Fourth Avenue, I think we were the only immigrant family on the block.

## People Used Tar Blocks from the Street in Their Coal Stoves

### By Irene Spack

*Irene Spack was born in Northeast Minneapolis and lived there most of her life. Her mother, Angela Klempka was from Rapka, Poland and came to America in 1908. Her father was Raymond Lawicki (Laviske) from Grodnie, Lithuania. They left because of the bad conditions in Austria, Poland and Lithuania and met in Minneapolis. Angela's sister was already living in Northeast Minneapolis.*

There were all different groups in Northeast at that time. There was a Bohemian hall on the corner of Spring Street and Washington NE. The French school was on Washington and Fifth Street. There is a high rise there now. The All Saints neighborhood was from the River to Jackson (almost to Johnson St.) and from East Hennepin to Broadway. My Uncle Joe Surdyk had the Liquor store on East Hennepin for 62 years. His son, Jim now operates it. The Holy Cross people were from Broadway to Lowry and Marshall to Monroe going the other way. The St. Hedwig's group was past Lowry.

On Ramsey and Water Streets there were old houses and huge apartment buildings or flats. They were located on Seventh Avenue and Marshall Street. Logan Park was the hub of activity when I was younger. There were band concerts and community sing-a-longs. Harry Anderson had a souza band orchestra. About twice a month we'd get together and sing along with the orchestra. Bottineau, Windom and some of the other community parks had sing-a-longs too. A popcorn vendor sold popcorn for five cents a

*Irene's mother, Angela Laviske was named the Polish Mother of the Year in St. Petersburg, Florida in 1962. She went there every year during the winter. She catered many of the Northeast and North side weddings.*

bag. There were also dance recitals and marble tournaments. The football teams of Bottineau and Logan were long time rivals.

My family shopped at East Hennepin which was as busy as the Nicollet Mall is now. The Savage building was a huge store- kind of like Banks of today. The store clerks were on roller skates, so if they didn't have what you wanted-they'd skate out to another department. The money for payment would be pulled in a cup on a wire across the ceiling to the cash register.

There were about 35 stores from Third Avenue to Broadway on Monroe, Adams and Fifth Streets. This area was the start of many well-know businesses like the original Old Home Creamery, Sifo Toy Manufacturer that made wooden jigsaw puzzles and Wells Lamont Glove Factory. After school we could amuse ourselves for hours by standing outside the window of a Cigar Factory. We loved to watch the ladies make homemade cigars.

The meat markets over Northeast were Krawczyk's, Boydas on Marshall Street and Jedlinski's on 27th and Grand. The Polish bakeries were Blackeys and Semotiuks, which later became Carl Ludwig. My friends and I went to the Princess Theater for movies. Amateur night was on Fridays. The John Ryan bathhouse was on Second Street and First Avenue, 1 block off of East Hennepin. So about once a week they all had a shower for the cost of 5 cents each. We could also swim. It was cheaper than boiling water for baths in a galvanized tub. The Gerber Pavilion on Eighth Avenue and Marshall Street had free concerts and entertainment. Some children swam in the river or the pool. You could swim for about an hour or sometimes as long as you wanted. Times were hard. So people often used the tar blocks from the street in their coal stoves. Heating them up would save on coal.

There was a boarding house right across from John Ryan Baths that was just for men. The Sparta Ice Cream Parlor was on the corner of East Hennepin and Second Street. If we went downtown we'd walk over the Third Avenue Bridge, very seldom did we take the streetcar. We just didn't have the money. The stores downtown were Powers, Whitney's, McGreager-Leader, Starbard Clothing, Brown Clothing, Donaldsons, Daytons, Cordoza Furniture, and Boutells, Home Trade Shoe store, Moehller Barber College, and then there was the Gateway District.

We used to go to the movies at Old Eastside High School located on Fourth and Central, for free. They were educational movies filled with history and culture, kind of like channel 2. We went to public schools—Webster, Sheridan, and Edison, and my brothers went to Everett—because we didn't have a father and couldn't afford the tuition for private schools. Baby Face Nelson went to Edison. There were murders in the neighborhood back then.

We were advised to stay out of trouble because we didn't have a father to represent us. We were active in skating at Logan Park. My brothers helped out at the battery shop. They also did odd jobs including shoveling snow. Sometimes they washed dishes all day for 25 cents at the boarding house. We were taught from the time we were small to respect older people. We never called them by their first name. It was always Aunty or Uncle or Mister or Misses. My mother catered and did housework. Catering for weddings and club dinners for 300 to 500 people was not unusual. So on holidays, the kids would have to start supper.

We sometimes went to Sunshine camp, which was a special camp for poor children. We took the train to Forest Lake. We left from the Great Northern Depot, which was next to De La Salle High School at that time.

Christmas Eve was probably the biggest event when a roasted capon was served. The traditional Christmas Eve meal consisted of Oplatek (a holy wafer), which was passed to each other as a personal, loving blessing. We had mushroom soup, pierogis, baked fish, sauer kraut and peas, herring, mashed potatoes, homemade pickles, fresh fruit compote, fruit cake, coffee cake—poppy seed or walnut, Bopka-egg bread, Christmas cookies including Chopin cookies and butter cookies, Chrust-like Fatiman or Pig's Ears like Rosettes, cheesecake-Serowiec. We had people coming in to visit mostly relatives.

### Recipe for Golabki

1 head of cabbage
1 ¼ lbs. ground beef (freshly ground)
salt pork ¼ lb., fried a little, small cubes
1 cup rice uncooked, steam until half done
1 egg
onion and seasonings

Parboil cabbage until leaves are limp in salted water, Place filling on each leaf and roll by folding sides. Grease roaster or dutch oven and place golabki in it. Add a little water and pour 1 can of tomatoes over them. You may add a couple of strips of bacon or salt pork on top and place extra cabbage leaf on top. Cover and bake in 350 degree oven for 1 ½ to 2 hours.

My father was a violinist in a concertina and bassa (bass) band. They would go to houses after mass to play and sing carols. On Christmas day we had a tradition of coming in with whole walnuts in our pocket. Then we would throw them up in the air as we entered the house. It was also traditional to have a drink at the house you were visiting, usually a bottle of brandy.

The family Christmas gifts consisted of the essentials like slippers and clothes, especially woolen items and an orange or apple. Occasionally we were given a sled or wagon to be shared by all. Another tradition was for the mother and father to trim the tree while the kids were in bed. Some of our friends did this. The Polish people celebrated together with rituals, church and carols. The gifts received were often homemade, knitted or crocheted scarves and mittens.

When the war broke out there was the Polish Relief for Babies in Poland. We'd send over homemade things. All Saints church and the PNA hall had special rallies, "Rada Polonie" which means Save Poland.

My mother did all the baking of breads, cakes and cookies in a coal stove. The coal had to be replenished twice a day. There was a coal stove in the dining room for heat. We slept under a feather bed. It was always cold, with icicles in the morning. We wore flannel bed-clothes and filled a crock with hot water to put under the bed at night.

One of the Polish traditions was where many of the Polish ladies would get together to make pillows and down (feather) quilts. We would buy bags of feathers and strip them. These were often given as a wedding gift.

# 19th Avenue and Sixth Street
# Became the Nowe Targ of Minneapolis

*By Walter Warpeha*

My mother was born on January 20,1891 in Nowe Targ, Poland in the foothills of the Tatry mountains. At 16 she decided that she wanted to go to the United States to join her older sister Mary. She told us that her father promised to buy her dresses or anything she wanted just to stay home but she had made up her mind about leaving and nothing could change it.

My father often would reminisce about his early days in Nowe Targ, Poland. He was the second child in a family of six children, four born in Poland. This part of Poland was ruled by Franz Josef, a well loved emperor. He wasn't able to supply the people with food or jobs but he did the next best thing, he allowed them to migrate out of the country.

Given this opportunity, the Warpechas migrated to the United States. They arrived in Minneapolis in the spring of 1897. Their first home was on 14th Avenue and shortly after they moved to 1916–6th St. NE and they lived there until 1904. 19th Avenue and Sixth Street became the Nowe Targ of Minneapolis.

Some of the families that lived around 19th and 6th Street were Mrosczak, Hudoba, Watychowicz, Fafrowicz, Jeziorski. Others living within several blocks were Koscielniak, Lach, Swaja, Smialkowski, Majewski, Sporna, Jendrol, Batkiewicz, Mrugala, Krauzowicz as well as others whose names escape me. Most were good friends or shirttail relatives.

In the meantime my mother worked at the West Hotel on 5th and Hennepin and she liked her job and

*Walter's father in the army
in the Philippines, 1906*

apparently wasn't in a hurry to get married as many were. On Sunday the girls would go to Mass at Holy Cross Church and in the afternoon they would meet at the home of the Glodek family on 19th Avenue where the eligible bachelors would look them over. That evening they would go to a dance at the P.N.A. Hall. I don't know if this was a weekly occurrence but at least it happened often. My mother was a pretty girl, had many suitors. But she wasn't ready to get married until she met my father.

When my parents were married they first lived on the farm in New Brighton with his parents. He had to look for a job in Minneapolis so they rented the upstairs of a house just across from 2550 University Avenue and they bought this house later that winter. I was born on September 16, 1912 in this house. In those days practically all mothers had their babies at home, only the affluent went to the hospital. I was the first of thirteen children.

My mother and dad furnished room and board to

*Walter's parents, Frank and Sophie Fryzlewicz were married on October 20th, 1911*

several men, our uncles John and Joe and my friend Andy Lach's father and another man by the name of Ignac. Ignac hired me to buy his meat at the butcher shop and he would pay me 2 cents. As was the custom in that day, the boarder would buy his own meat, tie a string on it to identify it. And all these pieces would be put into the pot to make soup. Then each person would have soup and his own piece of meat.

The Warpechas struggled to exist, as did most immigrants. Generally around the turn of the century the men of the family either worked on the railroad in the most menial job or in the lumbering industry. In the fall of the year they were transported to the North Woods where they worked in the bitter cold, often 50 below zero. After the spring thaw, the logs were floated down the river to the various sawmills in Minneapolis. I can remember seeing the logs covering the west side of the river as they were guided into the sawmill on the west bank. The men would work in the sawmill until they were no longer needed and then wait until the fall to return to the woods. The pay was perhaps a dollar a day in the early days. There was no unemployment insurance or welfare help so that people would depend on their gardens and relatives.

On June 10th 1923, I made my first Communion and on the following day the Warpehas and their six kids moved to our new home on this beautiful tree lined street, 15th and Madison. This area was predominantly Swedish and Norwegian and I used to chide our Scandinavian friends later at the Athletic Club that when we moved into our home on Madison with all those kids, the neighbors didn't come out of their houses for over a week. They must have said, "there goes the neighborhood".

The names of some of our neighbors were Olson, Anderson, Hanson, Karleen, Modeen and several others. In the next block to the south there were four Scandinavian churches, one on each corner and on Sundays they were crowded. With four churches in the next block, one might wonder why we had to walk about a mile to get to school every day and to church on Sunday.

A big yearly event was the church bazaar at Holy Cross Church in the fall of the year. It lasted for four or five days and finished on a Sunday evening. The hall was filled with booths with a variety of crafts. But the big attraction was the raffling of live turkeys, geese, ducks, rabbits and chickens. It was great fun to see the winners wrestling with a goose or turkey that didn't want to go home with them. My father would on occasion win a turkey or goose and it was the greatest treat for the family because these were seasonal fowl, and they were expensive. My father earned under a hundred dollars a month in the mid 1920s.

In 1917 I started kindergarten at Schiller School. I was told to go to school by way of Lowry Avenue because there was a crossing guard on duty and he watched people as they crossed the tracks. On 26th Avenue there was no protection, and in fact, there was a fence to prevent crossing at this point. The kids cut a hole in the fence and all I did was to follow the other kids through this hole until my father found out. He convinced me that I had better not do it again. We got a small pig from my grandparents to raise and this pig became my pet. Several times on my way to school I forgot to fasten the gate and the pig got out and started to follow me to school. I had to get him back in the yard and it wasn't easy. You must remember how hard it can be to get a pig back into the pen when it has tasted freedom.

Every family in that neighborhood had chickens or ducks or geese and a few had a cow that they milked and there were a few others that had a pig or two. We had a flock of chickens in a fenced off area in the back of our lot and this was where the pig roamed when he wasn't in his pen. Those who had a cow would walk the cow to an open field around 27th and 3rd Street and one of their children would watch her and bring her back home for the evening milking.

Grandpa Warpeha lived with us during the time he worked at the sawmill just across the Mississippi near the Lowry Avenue Bridge. He didn't want to live in the house and although he came in to eat all his meals, he slept in a shed in our back yard, a sort of a bunkhouse. I guess that I was his favorite, perhaps because I was able to speak Polish and actually I didn't speak English until I started kindergarten. In February of 1918 he died. The reviewal was at our house and Kozlak Funeral Home took care of the service. I recall that my father's sisters, my mother and Aunt Mary wore dark clothes, a black veil and a black armband. A team of horses pulled the hearse and the carriages for carrying the mourners and because there was a February thaw the street was a quagmire. The wagons were stuck so the men had to wade in the mud to push so that the horses could get the wagons out to the main street. I can still remember how dirty they got.

When I started first grade there was an order from the Archbishop that everyone living north of Lowry Avenue would automatically belong to St. Hedwig Church and the children would go to their school. The pastor was Father Maximillian Klesmit, a crusty demanding

*Christmas time 1942. The last picture of entire Warpeha family before Brother Frank was killed on the last day of the war in Europe.*

man and he complained that the people on the border of Holy Cross-and St. Hedwig were not registering in his parish, as they should. They wanted to continue at Holy Cross and didn't want to join the new parish, thus came this order. Five of the affected families went directly to the Bishop and they asked my father be the spokesman since he spoke English. The problem was that they would have to send their children across the railroad tracks where there was no guard and since the distance was similar to both parishes, they felt that they should not have to belong to St. Hedwigs. They took the day off from work and rode a streetcar to see the Archbishop in St. Paul, an all day excursion. They were all very nervous, especially since Archbishop John Ireland was a hard-boiled man, powerful in the church and in politics. For these little people to ask that an order be changed seemed like impertinence on their part. They were pleasantly surprised by his reception of their problem. The Archbishop listened patiently and agreed with their concerns and said that he would notify the pastor of Holy Cross. So those five families were allowed to stay at Holy Cross

It was customary to advance the students to the next grade in September after the summer vacation and so the sister decided to have me skip the 4th grade and go directly into grade 5. I walked into Sister Hildegarde's fifth grade and she immediately stopped me and said in her loudest voice, "Warpecha, what are you doing here?" She had a loud harsh voice which was enough to scare anyone and I had heard her bawling out the kids in a combination Polish and broken English for several years and I really dreaded being so unlucky as to be in her class since there were two fifth grades. So in answer to her question, in a weak voice I said that Sister Veronica said that I was to be in 5th grade. She pushed me out the door and told me that I should go across the hall into the 4th grade because I was too small for 5th grade. So I walked into the fourth grade and sat down in an empty seat and joined in with the class as if nothing happened. There were no questions asked and I guess that I was relieved that I wouldn't have Sister Hildegarde as my teacher.

The snow seemed deeper in those days. And in the mornings the streets were not plowed until later because it was done with a horse drawn plow with a man walking behind steering the horse. I particularly remember the icicles and frost on the horse's face. About 1919 or 1920 electricity and sewer were brought into our area and University Avenue was paved up to 27th Avenue.

In 1918 you could find horse stables throughout the residential areas since horses were used for delivering milk, ice, coal, groceries, and furniture. It was interesting to watch these horses because they would travel much of their route without the driver, they knew where the next customer was and the milkman would carry milk for a number of houses. Even the doctor used a horse and buggy to get to the hospital or for housecalls. The police would take the streetcar to get to the area where they would walk their beat and many areas, especially in the business districts would be patrolled on horseback in addition to the police on foot. I even recall some covered wagons being pulled by oxen but only a few. But eventually the trucks replaced all horses and I had heard of at least one milkman who had to change jobs because he didn't know how to drive a car.

Many horses were frightened by the noise of the trucks and cars and the wise driver would jump off the wagon to hold the skittish horse. There were instances that a horse would get so excited that he would stampede and wreck the wagon. Later the horses became fewer and the remaining horses had become more tolerant. The milkman and the iceman were perhaps the last to quit using horses for delivery. Electric refrigerators replaced the icebox and the iceman. There were those who believed that food didn't taste the same and refused to change to electric refrigeration. They had to change their belief when the iceman would no longer deliver ice. In the early twenties, there were more and more cars around as the more daring young men would buy a new Model T Ford. They cost about 350 dollars and the proud owners were the envy of the neighborhood. As with everything new, the wise old heads would say that this was going to cause the ruin of the country.

My father started working for the Post Office. Because he was able to converse with the Polish, Slovaks and Russians, he was assigned a route from 2nd Street to 5th and from 18th Avenue to 27th. On Saturdays and days off from school I would meet him at the streetcar line and walk the route with him. I even helped by delivering the side streets so I learned the names of all the families on his route. To this day I can remember who lived in which house.

During the winter of 1922 the "Daily News" had a subscription drive and for 25 new customers you would get a Ranger bicycle, the very best of that day. With the help of my father, we got 30 new customers, mostly people on his route. For the extra 5 subscriptions I got a set of 25 Horatio Alger books. These books were among the most popular boys books and all had a common theme such as the hero was a young orphan or street urchin or something like that. He started out as a shoe shine boy or a baggage boy and through hard work eventually became a successful businessman. The scene was always in New York City and the names were like "Sink or Swim, " "Survive or Perish", etc. After you read a book, you could trade with someone that had a title that you didn't have. I traded some with Uncle Leonard. They were great books. I would often read on our front porch and some of the neighborhood kids called me a sissy since they must not have liked reading. But then many of them didn't finish high school.

The Ranger bike was a beauty, had a headlight, rear carrier and a front basket. It was the envy of the neighborhood and an older boy from 3rd street offered to teach me to ride the bike and he of course in the meantime also rode it. I learned very quickly and one particular evening I saw my father returning from work so I drove toward him to show him what I had learned. To impress him I showed how I could ride no hands and as often happens when you are showing off, I lost control and drove into a pile of construction trash next to the curb. My father had to untangle me from all this junk but there was no damage except to my pride. On the following Sunday afternoon I drove over to Bottineau to watch a baseball game. On the way back home I made a left turn from Lowry Avenue to 3rd Street and was hit by a car. I had the bike just 10 days. And my mother didn't say anything about my soiled shirt because she must have thought that I was lucky to not get hurt.

# Pizza in Minnesota was Unknown

## A *Tribute to Rose Totino*

*Plant kitchen at Totino's Finer Foods
73rd Commerce Lane in Fridley, 1980s*

Rose Totino is a legend in Northeast Minneapolis that will not be forgotten. She was a rare combination of the sensitive and the shrewd. She was also a woman of great faith and great love. During a time back in the 1950s when pizza was unknown in Minnesota, except in Italian neighborhoods and from those who had tasted it in Europe during World War II, she and her husband Jim built a multi-million dollar business. Rose accounted her success to the values instilled in her by her parents and complete faith in the ability of the people who worked for her. She never had any formal training in business management. She called it just common sense.

Fourth in a family of seven, Rose's parents, Peter and Armita Cruciani emigrated from Italy in 1910. Her father did not like working in the mines of Pennsylvania and moved his family to an Italian neighborhood in Northeast Minneapolis and in 1915 Rose was born.

Armita raised her children with strong values and affection. A great deal of care was put into planting a garden that would provide vegetables for the family throughout the year. She dried herbs and beans and canned tomatoes in late summer. They raised their own chickens and a few head of livestock. Every year they raised a pig and rendered lard from it. Peter supervised the sausage making. Rose's job was to sell milk to the neighbors at five cents a quart. This brought in $5.00 a week toward clothing and shoes for the growing Cruciani children. The left over milk was made into cheese to grate over the pasta, which was a household staple.

And when Armita put on her white kerchief, Rose knew it was bread making day. She had to hurry home from school to wash the big pan that her mother used for kneading dough. The Cruciani children loved breadmaking day because there was always a treat involved. There was enough dough to make individual thin-crust pizzas for everyone. The adult pizzas were topped in the usual way, but the children's were sprinkled with cinnamon and sugar. It was the only dessert the family could afford.

With a legacy of homegrown foods, carefully rationed meat, and limited sweets Rose Totino was blessed with good health and limitless energy. She also learned to make pasta and other Italian foods by her mother's side. From her father she learned to enjoy life. He was always happy go lucky and singing. When he came home from work he would go right downstairs to the wine barrel. And the kids grew up drinking small glasses of wine mixed half-and-half with water.

Rose quit school at the age of sixteen. She and her sister's salaries of doing housework for other people bought the groceries for their family. The brothers were allowed to stay in school. Before long she found a better job at the Hollywood Candy Factory and soon earned 37 cents an hour, which was almost $15 a week.

She met Jim Totino at the Viking Dance Hall near downtown Minneapolis and they were married in 1934. The Totino house became a favorite pizza-stopping place for kids from the elementary school across the street. Boy Scout and PTA meetings ended there too and before long, friends urged the Totino's to open a shop where they could stop and buy pizzas whenever they wanted.

They wanted to open a shop but were skeptical. Although there were pizzerias in Chicago and New York, pizza in Minnesota was unknown. They applied for a loan based on their used car for collateral. When the bank president asked what pizza was, Rose baked him one and took it with her when she went down to the bank. The banker was so taken with the taste that they got their loan.

On Feb.7, 1951, Rose and Jim opened the door of Totino's Italian Kitchen at Central and East Hennepin in Northeast Minneapolis. The response was phenomenal. They advertised their product by passing out samples in the new frozen food department of Donaldson's downtown department store, and almost immediately customers were lined up outside the Totino's door.

They had planned to sell hot and frozen pizzas and spaghetti for take out only with shelves full of dry pastas and imported foods. But when the boys from the filling station came in they asked for a fork and ate their spaghetti standing up. Rose and Jim brought in a few card tables and soon the place was full and they needed more card tables. After awhile they realized they were running a full service restaurant and the freezer and the shelving had to go to make room for tables and booths.

Rose was hoping to stay home with her children but never got the chance. On Arlie Haeberle's television show Rose demonstrated the mysteries of making pizza and Totino's Italian Kitchen became an instant success. In the early years they worked so hard and such long hours they weren't even sure if they were making money. Rose said, "All we knew was that after we paid the breadman, the milk man and the help, we had money left over."

The first employees were family members, including Jim's sister, Mary DeMay. She came down just to see the place and stayed on working part time at the restaurant. Thirteen-year-old Joanne Totino waited tables at suppertime and did her homework there too. Even two-year old Bonnie took her naps curled up in the corner booth.

Within three months, Jim Totino quit his job at the bakery and was baking more than 120 pizzas a day. The couple worked side by side, he baked the pizzas and it was her job to apply the topping. Instead of sliced cold sausage, Jim decided to cook it in open kettles and sprinkled it on the pizza. An opportunity came when the roofing contractor next door went out of business. They were able to rent more space and doubled their seating capacity. Later they bought the building.

In 1961 they used the $50,000 they had saved to make a down payment on a $140,000 frozen food plant and purchased the necessary equipment. They started with frozen pasta entrees, mostaccioli and manicotti and in the first year they were almost bankrupt. They had invested all of their lives' savings and ten years of hard work in the restaurant. But Rose refused to give up and file bankruptcy. Then Jim learned about pre-baked crusts at a frozen food convention in Dallas. Although Rose wanted to someday build her own bakery to make crusts like her mother did, they would start out with frozen crusts and new packaging equipment. It was the only way to salvage the company.

After they applied for a small business loan, Rose was one day driving to work when she heard an

*Jim cooking a pizza in the early stages of Totino's Restaurant in the late 1950s*

*Rose kneading pizza dough in Totino's Finer Foods Kitchen in the 1970s*

announcer on the radio. He talked about how God loved each and every human being in a personal way. The words moved Rose beyond anything she had ever listened to. In an act of faith, she vowed that if God would see them through this crisis, she would dedicate her life to serving him. When she got back to the office a man from the Small Business Administration was waiting to tell her that the loan was approved.

So Rose set about developing recipes and Jim Totino worked on a method for dispensing pizza sauce. He tried putting the crusts on the turntable of his record player; an old fashioned one that worked with a foot pedal. Pressing the foot pedal made the turntable spin as if there were records on it. As the crust turned Jim squirted sauce on it through a plastic tube. It took no time at all. That made it easy to prepare a lot of pizzas in a short time. There was only one problem: the foot pedal gave him an electric shock. They got a lot of shocks making those first frozen pizzas. Eventually they came up with more sophisticated machines but Rose continued to apply the topping by hand.

In 1970 after outgrowing numerous expansions, they financed a $2.5 million plant, which included a bakery in Fridley. After awhile Rose found people who believed in the business the way she did and the "Totino team" was formed. Most of the employees felt it was the best place they ever worked. Rose's management style was that of complete trust. The employees were always challenged because the company grew so fast.

Jim's health began to fail when the two of them were in their early 60s. So in 1975 when sales were more than $35 Million a year, they sold out to the Pillsbury Company. And Rose Totino at age 60 became corporate vice president.

Based on Armita Cruciani's long ago treats for her children, Totino's introduced "Crisp Crust." Rose went on a talk show tour of the country and introduced the new crust to the nation. She described it as "the most fun thing I've ever done."

Rose established a policy of giving 5% to charity and together she and Jim founded a foundation called Charity Inc., to help the people around them that were hurting. They had a special feeling toward a Catholic High School near their Fridley plant and Jim chose to give to them. They supported a girl's volleyball team, built a theater, tennis courts and softball fields. The school is now named after them, Totino-Grace.

Jim Totino died in 1981, her life long companion in work and play. They lived in the same house in Northeast Minneapolis for 37 years. Rose continued to be active in the business. A small woman with black hair, dark eyes and creamy white skin, she often wore a red and white checked apron. She offered her visitors coffee and refreshments, serving them herself. Her "office" in the Totino plant of Pillsbury's in Fridley was a kitchen patterned after an Italian Kitchen with a workroom, a warming room and a fireplace. She remembered her first extravagant purchase as a pair of red shoes and later in 1957 she bought a pink Lincoln.

Rose Totino had an uncanny ability to talk straight with everyone she met. She was genuinely interested in people. She brought her personal touch to the corporate world and even though she felt she wasn't knowledgeable enough to contribute, she continued to work hard. She also hand wrote most of her letters

*Jim and Rose at a celebration when Grace High School changed their name to Totino-Grace in 1980*

icYouth Center, Northwestern College, De La Salle High School, Prison Fellowship Ministries and many others.

Rose died in 1994 at the age of 79 leaving a beautiful legacy to her two daughters, nine grandchildren and five great-grandchildren.

*A special Rose Totino edition of "Continuum," the Totino-Grace High School newsletter, which came out just after her death in 1994. The photo was taken in Rose's backyard garden and used earlier for an American Express magazine ad that came out in the late 1980s.*

and they were always from the heart. She didn't understand dictating machines and calculators but could rattle off multiplication tables. Yet she had instincts about how numbers relate to one another. And her instincts and the way she used them were the basis of her success.

True to her faith promise, Rose literally spent her life serving the Lord. Leading among her many charitable works were commitments to the St. Paul Cathol-

# I Wasn't Catholic or Irish and My Father Didn't Work for the Railroad

## By Maelyn Hansen

*Maelyn Hansen brought me all the way to the top of the enormous Railroad Bridge that runs over East River Road, just to show me the view of all the trains and the railroad yard below. He also took me on a tour of all the railroad yards in the Minneapolis area.*

*Maelyn when he worked at the "Hump Yard", 1988*

Many of them are gone now. He was proud of working for the Northern Pacific Railroad, a place he retired from in 1992 after working there 42 years. He also seemed a little sad over the changes that had taken place.

"It's all gone now," he said. "The huge roundhouse and car shed was located on 35th and Main Street. The old yard office was torn down to make room for the new yard. They even took down the café that was next to the old yard office. The only thing that remains is the 35th Street tower. The huge concrete wall along the bluff is gone too.

Not too many people know about how big the Northern Pacific really was. It was much bigger than the Great Northern in the Twin City area. The Northern Pacific started in St. Paul with two tracks that came into Northtown. From the Northtown Yard in Northeast it went on to St. Cloud, Little Falls, Staples, Fargo, Valley City, Jamestown and later out west to Seattle. A total of 1,800 miles long. There were two main lines going west. This line followed highway #10 and the other line was from St. Paul along highway #61 to Forest Lake, Pine City and then north to Duluth.

The west side of the Northern Pacific tracks on 35th and Main Street belongs to Great Northern, which used to be the Anoka line that delivered supplies to Northern Pump and Minneapolis Waterworks. Shortly after the war they shut down the Anoka line. The #328 Engine they used for this line was built in 1934 and is on display at the Minnesota Transportation Museum.

The new Hump Bridge was built, starting in 1974 after the merger of the Northern Pacific, Great Northern, CB&Q (Chicago) and SP&S. In the early days there were 16 tracks from the University Bridge to 35th and Main Street that ran close to the East River Road to 43rd Avenue. This is where the road went across the tracks before the new bridge over the hump to East River Road was built. From there the yard was continual to old highway #100. The Northern Pacific was one of the last railroads to buy steam power. They owned their own coalfields and still do.

When the company first decided they wanted to build 64 tracks, all of the guys thought they were crazy. It seemed impossible; there would never be enough room for such a huge undertaking. It took 1½ years to take down the big bluff. After dynamiting the area, they discovered there was prime rock underneath. So they ground the rock up and sold it for great profit. The riverbed near the bluff was all sand. There were all kinds of caves in the bluff. When they cut down the bluff there were all kinds of fossils in there.

When they completed the HumpYard or Northtown Yard it was made up of 102 miles of track. It was a blessing. Imagine driving over 64 tracks. The computerized terminals below the bridge are so sensitive that even a snowflake could throw the switches off in the yard.

There were several yards located in the Minneapolis area; most of them were in Northeast. The West Yard was called the "A" Yard, which is on #694. This was designated for trains coming from the west. When working the west end of this yard, we would pull 29 cars over old highway #100 (now #694) and switch them out to the tracks in the yard. Just imagine how the traffic would pile up today if we switched a train over #694.

The "B" Yard on 43rd and Main Street is where they made up the trains going west and where the Road Crew went to work. We had engines working both the East end and the West end and over the crossing at 43rd. The third yard was called the "T" Yard, located on St. Anthony Boulevard. This was the transfer yard. The last steam engine I worked in May of 1960 was in the East end of this yard, Number 1172.

My very first job as a Fireman was working at the "Watertank" Yard on 30th and California. The water tank is gone now. The Republic Elevator on 27th and Main Street that burned in 1974 is part of this yard. This is where we would make up our train for Lower Northeast Minneapolis. It was from this yard that we delivered coal to the Northern States Power plant. We also delivered to two lumberyards and Marshall Blocks. Between Lowry Avenue and 22nd was Elevator R. This one also burned.

The fifth yard is on 20th to 22nd and Grand Street. We called it the pocket yard. It had a small yard office and Yardmaster. It was the Yardmaster's job to go and talk to the industries in the area. We moved the freight with a little steam engine #1169. It was a 060. These numbers indicated how many drivers were in the front.

I started with the Northern Pacific on July 19, 1950 in the Northtown Round House as a laborer. That night going home, over the radio came the word that my Reserve unit in the Marines was being called into active duty in Korea. I was #108 on the Seniority Roster. When I came back from Korea in March 24, 1952 the next day I went to the Roundhouse Foreman. He looked at me and said, "What am I going to do with you? You are now #8 on the Seniority Roster and no one has ever seen you." Then he asked me if I would like to become a Fireman. Of course I said yes.

He said you will be the first one put on as fireman this summer and he kept his word. He made me a fire-lighter in the roundhouse and on July 16th, 1952 I made my three student trips to Staples and White Bear Lake. Almost all firemen had to have a father working there that was the only way you could get in. The duties of the fireman were to shovel coal into the firebox of the engine, 30 ton a day. We worked 16-hour days and were paid 12 to 15 dollars per day.

Seniority was pretty important to the guys on the railroad. So when I became an engineer, this was quite a change. And the guys didn't like it. The guys all asked," How did you get on? How did you get past Murphy?" Now Mr. Murphy was the master mechanic. I wasn't Catholic, I wasn't Irish, and my father didn't work for the railroad. And you could never get on without one these three connections. They said I moved up too fast.

I took my test for Locomotive Engineer in 1960 and in 1965 went full time as an engineer. My route as an engineer was from Minneapolis to Staples. I got to know the route pretty good. I took my dad on a trip to Staples in the fog. He wondered how I could see the track. I didn't need to see it; I could have traveled it in my sleep.

My last seven years I worked the Grove Yard Job in the afternoons. On July 23, 1992, I retired from the Burlington Northern, a merger of Northern Pacific and several other railroads. They were going to send me to Kansas City for Engineer training. No way! I loved my work as an Engineer. I can honestly say that I never killed anyone at a crossing. We still get together with

the former Northern Pacific employees every year in July and have a picnic at Paul Bunyan Land. There are helicopter rides and a toy train for the kids. And the guys sure know how to tell stories.

*Maelyn taken after his retirement, 1993*

## I Held a Run on the Streetcar Mainline out of East Minneapolis

*By Bill Olsen*

*Here are the memories of Bill Olsen, a Minnesota Transportation Museum member who used to operate the streetcars out of Eastside Station.*

*Bill Olsen inside of a streetcar, 1999*

In the fall of 1943, as a fifteen and a half-year-old high school junior, I had the best of all worlds. Before and after classes, I held a run on the streetcar mainline out of old East Minneapolis Carbarn. After a few months of training as a conductor, I returned to high school at De La Salle on Nicollet Island and found I could still take both a morning and evening rush hour run from nearby East Side.

Only the old timers were left as trainmen. The company had tried hiring college students as conductors; but kept losing them to the draft. It was now up to our set to avoid the three cardinal sins: losing a fare, causing an accident, or delaying very tight schedules.

There was always a hassle around the super's cage where we all "plugged in" on the assignment board. If someone missed, there was always a quick scramble to cover the one-man runs. We high school student conductors would sneak a motorman's spot if we could. I waited for a year to try it and got my Como-Harriet car out to the 44th Street loop at France Avenue before the inspector caught up.

The hot summer glare soon softened into a pastel canopy of leaves covering our tracks—beautiful but deadly. We could easily slide half-a-block beyond any stop. Spinning our wheels over those oily leaves produced clouds of ozone smelling dust that seeped in everywhere "up through the cherry wood sills, into the yellow rattan cushions, and soaking into my sweat." Still, the grime gave me the seasoned look I needed to keep the crowds moving.

Acceptance came in stages. "Number four, you ought to go visit the first number four. Ask for Joe Walsh over at 23 Southeast Fourth Street." It turned out old Joe was laid out in state at Washburn-McReavy's Mortuary. "You have to be agile with your change," cautioned my instructor. When a token broke loose from his cupped hands, he did not "pull" one bell to stop and recover. Even at only 85-cents per hour pay, he would rather lose the coin than suffer embarrassment. "It's okay kid." Finally I got the nerve to ring my first four bells, the emergency signal to skip all stops. Our football special was jammed up to the rear gates in a bumper-to-bumper line-up outside Memorial Stadium. Down the line we passed Inspector Christensen, who signaled thumbs-up. We were on time, the others were not. I had made the team at last.

For those of you who are unfamiliar with the background of this story, World War II regulations had imposed a heavy burden on Twin City residents. Speed restrictions were an absolute 35-MPH even cross-country. You were rationed only a few gallons of gasoline per week—and then only if you had an essential job beyond public transportation. There were no new cars, few repair parts, and all tires had to be recapped over and over.

Twin City Lines soon found itself transporting almost 75% of the city population on its aging fleet of more than 700 electric trolleys. Because the system had been well designed, the cars were much bigger than present day busses, and the maintenance program and hydro-electric power supply were low-cost enough to have survived the previous depression.

Operation of the standard, two-man, gate car required a motorman enclosed in his private cab up front. He listened to his conductor's bell signals to perform all driving functions. One bell meant stop and open rear gates. Two bells meant close those gates and start. Three bells meant it was okay to back up. Four bells meant we are too full to accept any more passengers.

The cheapest ride was by token, sold six for 45 cents. All coin fares had to be dropped into a hand cranked fare box, then scooped out of the bottom compartment and juggled back into separate tubes of our belt hung money changer. Pads of paper transfers were pre-punched just before each one way trip. Four punches would establish the date, time and direction. We had to inspect each transfer received from another conductor and punch once again if the passenger required a second transfer. In rush hour as many as fifty passengers might board at once. Our schedules required thirty-second spacing between cars within the "LOOP" (downtown transfer points); and we had to maintain a five-mile per hour speed still making all stops. Seventy-eight seated and standing passengers was considered a full car.

*Bill Olsen, 1999*

*East Side Station 317 First Avenue NE, 1920*

When they pulled the heater fires out early in 1944 to save coal, I hung a "This car heated" sign on the outside of our electrically heated gate car.

The worst run, always left to new men was #66 that somehow hit all theater closings on Saturday night and caught the last ride for sailors avoiding AWOL/curfew at the University. It was listed as the baby owl because it ran between the hourly Owl car after midnight. It was a universal curfew for both students and navy training programs, and usually found the dates sitting on their escort's laps to double up in the wide spaced seats.

We often had head counts exceeding 200. Then totaling up the cash forced me to miss the Owl car home, which meant sleeping overnight at the station. Sleeping upstairs at East Side was nothing short of traumatic. There were no sheets; just gray blankets on army cots thoroughly stained by the snoose chewers. The old wooden barn would shudder as each car rumbled in or out, and the thought of all those trolley poles still on the wire, with the fire warnings, made deep sleep impossible.

Our pay was 66 cents per hour with all the free rides we wanted. How different from being isolated in today's angry freeway gridlock, wondering if we will ever get home again.

## What Kind of American Farm Is This with No Potatoes and No Cows?

*By Francis Siwek*
Reprinted with permission of "Project Challenge," *Eastside Neighborhood Services*, 1978.

My parents came from Europe in 1903. In 1905 they were married at Holy Cross Church. I was born at home in 1907 at 14th Avenue NE. There were five children in our family and I was the oldest.

*John and Mary Podgorski with their children Sophie (Vlach), Frances (Siwek), Mary (Chmielewski), Sister Claudia and James Podgorski, 1926*

When I was growing up, Northeast was quite different from what it is now. For instance, there was no plumbing, so each home had an outhouse. For water everybody had an outdoor pump where we pumped water then carried it to the house where it was heated on the wood stove if we wanted hot water. Clothes were washed by hand in a tub with a washboard. Instead of bleach for whitening and disinfecting, we boiled clothes on the stove. People used to wear their clothes much longer back then and didn't change as often.

Everybody baked their own bread. For larger families that meant baking three or more times a week. When gas became available people put the new gas cooking plates on top of the old wood stoves. We were all so fascinated by the beautiful blue flame given off by the burning gas. Nothing else around gave off such a pretty flame.

Neighbors helped each other much more before. Many more things were done by hand too, like digging out basements. It would take a group of men with shovels about a week to dig out a basement for a house.

I went to Holy Cross Church School. There were no kindergartens then so I went right into first grade. It was difficult at first because I didn't know a word of English. At home we spoke only Polish. Classes were taught in English and Polish, the Polish classes being grammar and religion. They discontinued teaching in Polish at about 1940, unfortunately. At any rate, I soon learned English with the help of the other children.

When I was twelve years old I got my first job. It was on a vegetable farm. I planted, hoed and picked green peppers, carrots, onions, beets and watermelons. I also washed, bunched and boxed them. The pay was 10 cents an hour, and the workday was 10–11 hours long. My mother used to say, "'What kind of American farm is this with no potatoes and no cows?"

You see, in Europe every farmer had cows and potatoes, If nothing else. My second job was at a box factory - B. F. Nelson, one of the larger employers of Northeasterners. At one time B. F. Nelson maintained a community center in Northeast but it was burned down and never replaced. There I worked stapling boxes together for 25 cents an hour. Next, I worked for Northern Bag Company inspecting flour sacks, making sure that the seams were well placed and strong. I received 25–35 cents an hour. The workday was about nine hours long plus five hours on Saturday. For Halloween we didn't go from house to house like they started doing here later. Most of the neighborhood families had parties at home for the children. Those that did go out usually played pranks like tipping over outhouses and waxing and soaping windows. Baptisms were a big "to do." After the Church Baptism there was a big lunch and reception with music and dancing.

*Frances Siwek in 1986*

In 1930 I was married at Holy Cross Church. My husband had come from Poland in 1923 at the age of 14. During the Depression my husband lost his job, like many other people, so we started a wood yard. With the money we had we bought an old truck and a used saw. We went into business selling scrap wood. Eventually, we became a lumber company - Siwek Lumber, which still operates at 2536 Marshall Avenue NE. My husband died just two years short of having lived in America for 50 years - half a century! He had always been very proud of America and very proud of her flag and what that flag represented.

In the past many people chose to forget their culture. It's great that they don't do that now. It is good that the high schools are teaching more about the different nationalities.

In Northeast many of the Polish Americans still speak Polish daily. If you know Polish you can understand Ukrainian and Slovak without too much trouble. The recent immigrations, especially, like speaking Polish.

## Don't Build a House, Unless It Is on a Hill

*By Helen Peake*

*I met with Helen and her long time friend, Clara Newberg, in her home. Helen enjoys keeping up the Norwegian customs. Throughout the house are examples of Hardanger, Rosemaling, and her entire kitchen is decorated in Fjord Blue. Fjord Blue signifies the ocean and water and is a very traditional Norwegian color. There are paintings in the hallway of Viking ships. She also has a small collection of troll statues. Clara says that people who travel to Norway often bring back Troll dolls. It is the typical souvenir. Trolls are mythical mischievous characters who are much like the Irish leprechaun. There are trolls in the story of Three Billy Goat's Gruff, an old favorite fairy tale. Here is Helen's story.*

My father, Soren Hunstad came to America in 1912 from Aarnes, Norway. His real name was changed at Ellis Island. He came because he was not the first born and would not inherit. He also came for an adventure and to look for his brother, Ole who hadn't been writing home. He probably was one of the many who died in the Alaska Gold Rush. My mother, Gerda Marie Ageson, came from Namsos, Norway in 1912. She came on the Lysitania, which she said was a beautiful ship. She was bound for Montana, where she would work as a cook on her brother's ranch. She didn't really like this type of life and went on to Minneapolis where she met my father at a Norwegian dance at Dovre Hall.

My father worked as a lumberjack and in various foundries in Minneapolis and St. Paul. It was hard for

*Gerda and Soren Hunstad taken, 1919.*
*They immigrated to Minnesota, 1912.*

new immigrants to get jobs because they didn't know the language. He later became a master iron molder for Crown Iron Works.

Their first house was on a corner lot on 32nd and Johnson. Norwegians like hills. My father always said, "Don't build a house, unless it is on a hill." I was born in 1918. We moved away from there when they started to plow the avenues. So my father built a house on 33$^{rd}$ and Cleveland.

My mother would go out to auctions where they would sell lots on Sundays. At that time there was nothing but open fields in that area between Johnson Street and Stinson Boulevard. My father loved to build. He would sit for hours drawing floor plans, even late into life. My mother always said to keep him happy all we had to do was keep him supplied with pencils, a ruler and paper. When the Depression came and the foundries were closed, he could still build houses on the lots bought at the auction.

While I attended Thomas Lowry School the principal, Mrs. Sand, sent a letter home to all the parents. She said that they should discontinue the use of the Norwegian language in their homes. Because it was difficult with so many different languages spoken in the classroom. My parents being the good citizens that they were of course complied and began to speak less Norwegian and more English. Eventually they spoke nothing but English and their children did not learn Norwegian until later in life.

I also went to Alice Cary School on 33$^{rd}$ and Cleveland, a portable school, which was built on coal cinders. It was difficult to play on this type of surface. I remember the ice being quite rubbery. When I was in second grade I did some tutoring and also did a great deal of baby-sitting. This was usually during the summer. Later I went to the Edith Cavell School and finished my education at St. Anthony Village School and graduated from Edison. Later I went to business school. The old Hart Lake was on a hill on Stinson.

My friends and I kept ourselves amused by playing Annie, Annie Over and Jax and made lots of mudpies.

We also played dolls and swam at Silver Lake. My mother would say, "Don't go in over your knees." We also swam at the Salvation Army Camp, across the lake where they had a diving board, but my mother didn't know about that. We frequently walked down to the big stone library on Central Avenue. My bosom friend, Marian Davis and I would come home with about seven or eight books. We also went to the Arion Theater for a double feature on Saturdays. One of the things I remember fondly, are the variety shows that we put on in the open field. Each kid would take their turn performing, kind of like the "Little Rascals." Some children did cartwheels, and some sang or danced. It was a real gambit of talent. Sometimes these shows would even draw kids from closeby neighborhoods. You had to have a safety pin to get in. This was in the late 1920s and we sure had a great time.

We went to Mt. Carmel Church. Some of the grocery stores in our neighborhood were Sexton's on 33$^{rd}$ and Johnson and there was also one on 32$^{nd}$ and Arthur and another on 32$^{nd}$ and Ulysses. Sometimes we would get a nickel to buy something. We shopped at the Misses Johnson's Store and once my family walked all the way downtown to the Maurice Rothchild Store on Fourth Street. We bought a coat and chocolate chunks.

We shopped on Central Avenue mostly. It was so nice back then. I enjoyed riding the streetcars. There was Egevist Bakery and Strandene's Meats. We shopped at Johnson's Meat and Grocery Store and another store on 30$^{th}$ and Johnson. We went to Columbia Park for sliding and tobogganing in the winter. And we skated at a small lake on Cleveland. There was never a warming house. Sometimes the older boys would make a fire. We also traced a large pie in the snow and played tag. We would have large bonfires in the fall during harvest time.

The area that lies from Arthur Street to Stinson Boulevard and between 33rd and 37th Avenue was known as "Liberty Heights." Immigrant families from all the European countries lived there. Despite the many languages, they were friendly and always helped one another. They were all poor, hardworking, but determined to become good Americans. The area from 33rd to 35th from Ulysses to Arthur was a farm owned by the Rachels. There was a brother and two sisters. They had cows and chickens and raised their own corn, hay and vegetables. The two sisters were often seen in their old-fashioned long dresses and bonnets while herding cows. They never mingled with the neighbors. One day a girlfriend and I went to their house hidden in the trees. They were very nice and treated us to cookies and milk out in the yard and invited us to come again, so we did many times.

During the summer there were weekly early evening band concerts at Windom Park. Most of Northeast was there; both grown ups and children came to join the sing-a-longs. These concerts should be revived. As I remember someone sold popcorn and it was fun for all, big and small.

Also we never missed the downhill races held on Norway Hill on St. Anthony Parkway. The races were for boys who built small soapbox cars with a little help from their fathers no doubt. We cheered for the ones we knew. It drew quite a crowd!

My parents would sometimes have parties where

*Soap Box Derby races on St. Anthony Hill*

they would roll up the rug and dance. When we went to visit people we were to sit quietly and never to ask for anything. And also we were not to touch anything.

Our car was a boxy Ford, and later an open touring car. Once my father tried to teach my mother how to drive. While he was cranking it she screamed, let out the clutch and the car went into the curb. We had a vegetable garden and my mother made homemade bread. She was famous for her rye bread. We made our own root beer in a crock during hot summer days. We could never wait long enough for the root beer to mature and always drank it early. Was that good!

In the deep Depression days of the thirties, my father started a backyard foundry in his spare time. World War II changed all of our lives. When my younger brother, Gene returned home from the Pacific, he and my father decided to build a gray iron foundry in Columbia Heights. They called it Hunstad Company. It ended up being quite prosperous and ran for 44 years. They were noted for the quality of their castings. My parents died in 1979 and 1980. Gene sold the building in 1993.

My older brother, Oscar, became a carpenter and built many of the houses in the Twin City area, including Northeast Minneapolis. Later he became an expert wood carver.

My Aunt Kaspara was famous for Norwegian weaving and once demonstrated to Mrs. Kruschev. Another aunt received gold and silver medals from the king of Norway because of her 50 years of service as a druggist.

Our Norwegian Christmas lasts for twelve days. You don't have to give a gift on Christmas Eve; you can give it on any one of the days. This custom has somewhat faded with Americanized customs. A typical Norwegian Christmas Eve Dinner consists of Lutefisk at about 4:00 P.M. Although many like it, there are also those who strictly endure it because of tradition. After 6:00 the real dinner is served which consists of:

Meatballs in brown gravy
Roast
Midagpolse (Norwegian sausage)
Lefse
Rollapolse (lamb rolled or pressed)
Fattigmann (poor man's cookie)
Rommegrot (dessert made with boiled milk, flour and whipped cream)
Eggadosi (eggs beaten with vanilla and sugar)
Jula Grot (rice cooked in rich milk with cinnamon and sugar)
Sandbakkier, Berlinner Kantz and Spritz cookies.
Fruit cake

### Recipe for Fattigmann
6 egg yolks, 3 egg whites
6 Tbs. sugar
6 Tbs. Cream
2 Tbs. melted butter
6 cardamom seeds
flour

Beat egg yolks and whites together until thick and lemon colored. Add sugar and continue beating, add cream and beat again; blend in butter. Crush cardamom seeds to powder and add with enough flour to make dough firm enough to roll. Roll thin as paper, cut into diamond shapes about 5 x 2 1/2 inches. Deep-fry in hot fat 2–3 minutes or until golden brown. Drain on absorbent paper and sprinkle with powdered sugar. A slit is made in the dough and pulled through. There is also a fattimand cutter with serrated edge.

Our family was close. My parents were hard working and honest as were most all the immigrants in Northeast. My mother had a wonderful sense of humor. I don't remember her ever scolding us. She encouraged us all to not be afraid to try new things.

*This picture was taken for Helen's husband Charles who wrote and asked for a picture. He served in the army during World War II in the Battle of the Bulge. Those were the hardest years.*

After graduating Helen went to business school. She worked in Student Affairs at the University for 15 years. Her interests include Calligraphy, collecting old books, flower gardening, painting watercolor eggs with miniature scenes or floral designs. She has taught crochet and is very interested in English Literature and Scandinavian Studies. She learned to speak Norwegian as an adult and would like to someday translate Norwegian books into English, especially two books about her Norwegian relatives.

# We Used Magazines As Shin Guards, Long Stockings and No Helmets

*By Donald Moss*

*Don Moss is my oldest brother and the rock of our family. He was quite a star athlete in his day and we are all proud of him. He is married and has five children. In fact they just celebrated their 50th wedding anniversary. He worked for the City of Minneapolis Water Department, fourteen years as a pipe layer and 23 years as an inspector. In 1984 he retired after 37 years. He loves to tell about the old days and when nobody could beat the teams from Northeast.*

I was born in my grandparent's house on California Street. We lived on Marshall Street and then next to Henne's store on Main Street. There were small yellow one-bedroom houses all in a circle with one yard. They had no hot water and no lights. We used kerosene and gas lamps. We moved around in Northeast a lot. Then later when I was in high school, I lived with Grandpa and Grandma Koniar again on California Street. I spoke Polish until I was four years old because everyone around me spoke it.

Grandpa Koniar rolled his own cigarettes. He was a quiet guy and hard working. Grandma controlled everything. She would give him a shot on payday. On Saturday nights everyone in the family would line up and she would give them a dollar. Even those that didn't work got a dollar. Grandma, my mother, Aunt Vicky and Frank's Ann would do all the cooking. And it was quite a large group of about fourteen people. My cousins, Carol Ann and Bobby were living there too.

On Sunday we had chicken and dumplings. Monday was round steak and gravy, Keeshka on Tuesdays, sauerkraut and pork hocks on Wednesdays, Thursdays was Golabki, potato pancakes on Fridays. And Saturday was fend for yourself. We had pierogis on special occasions and sometimes headcheese with vinegar on rye bread. We grew our own vegetables in a garden across the street. And the potatoes were stored for the whole winter in a bin in the basement. Grandma was one of the best bakers around. She would make white bread, but sometimes gingerbread or donuts.

Grandma Koniar was hot-tempered but very nice. She died when I was twelve. And her body was shown in the house in the front window. Stanley Kapala was the undertaker. It was customary for someone to remain with the body at all times. So Teddy Eskierka stayed awake with the body all night.

I liked all of my uncles but probably got to know my Uncle Frank the best, because he didn't go into the service. Grandma had five stars in the window for her four sons and one grandson that served during World War II.

Some of our neighbors on California Street were Kubinski, Dziedzic, Romik, Eskierka, Matusek and Gomuleks. The stores we shopped at were Yablonski's on 27th Avenue, Gonsiors on 27th and Grand, Koscieleks on Lowry and Grand, and Biernats on Lowry and 3rd Avenue. Jedlinski's Store on 30th and California made the best Polish sausage. Our neighbor, Mrs. Dziedzic would give me ten cents to go down to get poppyseed for her at Maslow's Store. Makowiec is Polish for poppyseed. There was a hardware store on Lowry and Second Street, with Brandt Drugstore next door and Ptak's Drygoods. We bought our shoes at Kanta Matushek's Store on Washington and Lowry. They were high top shoes with lace hooks that were supposed to be good for your feet.

Some of my friends were Gigi Eskierka, Jimmy Schach, Ted Karkula, Hank Schmuda, Johnny Chrystofiak, Yashu Jakubiac, and Jerry Koniar. Some of the games we played were, pom pom pullaway, prisoner's base, kick the can, run sheep run, Annie, Annie Over, and stickball. We played ball in the backyard and in the streets. We also played at the B.F. Nelson Settle-

*Hockey at Marshall Terrace Park midget division 1939.*
*Top-Babe Melich, Don Zurek, Mike Homa (coach),*
*Uncle Eddy Koniar (coach), unknown coach,*
*Jackie Kauth Bottom-Donnie Moss, Barry Mularz,*
*Dick Murlowski, John Garbett and John Jakubiec*

ment House and the parks, mostly at Bottineau, Logan and Marshall Terrace. We used whatever we could find. Sometimes we even used a wooden banister or a stick for a bat. The baseballs were different than they are today. We used huge cotton filled balls that were all beat and taped up.

The schools I went to were Schiller and Everett for kindergarten. We moved in the middle of the year. At St. Hedwig's, my favorite teacher was Sister Eustasia. There were three rooms. Grades 1 through 4 were in one room, 5th and 7th, 6th and 8th in the others. We walked to school and carried a bag lunch, which was pretty skimpy. Sometimes syrup or even lard sandwiches. In the eighth grade there were six boys who would go to the cottage with Father Klesmitt. They were Ted Karkula, Max Zurach, Stan Slonski, Mike Truchinoly, Gene Klesmitt and myself. I was Valedictorian at St. Hedwig's, only because that Lunewski girl (Lulu) didn't want to do it. I had to wear Uncle Eddy's jacket and make a speech.

Uncle Eddy helped me to be good at sports. He used to hit grounders to me in the back yard. Then I made the St. Hedwig's team. St. Hedwig's always had good baseball teams. We would play against all the other Catholic Schools. One year we were Division champs and Father took us out for ice cream.

I never skipped school until I went to Edison. Me and my buddies, Milt Chapman and Goose Gonsior would go down to the railroad tracks and smoke cigarettes. Goose Gonsior could get Sensation cigarettes that sold for ten cents a pack from his dad's store. They used to call us "the Sensation smokers."

The most influential person in my life was Pete Guzy. He taught sports for fun and competition, but he always said studying was more important than sports.

He used to say "Right bunch at the right time" makes a winning team. Composition and public speaking was not my thing in school. I was better at math. I was on the National Honor Society at Edison.

Every Saturday a group of guys would play basketball down at Bottineau Field. We played half court then, with some really good ball players that went on to the U of M, like Baldy Romanoski, Willie Warhol, Marty Rolek, and Don Carlson. For baseball I played infield, second or third base. And for football I was the quarterback.

But my favorite sport was hockey. We never had ice hockey through the schools. But Marshall Terrace Park had three hockey teams. Each of them won the championship. We didn't have good equipment like they have today. We used magazines as shin guards, long stockings and no helmets. Barney Malarz was our goalie. Al Burman sponsored a team in the senior league.

I used to shine shoes to earn money for Saturday nights. We went to John's Bar and the Friendship Club a lot. Uncle Joe and Uncle Red met their wives at the

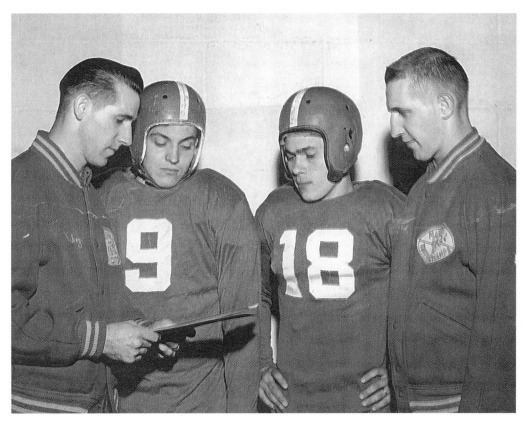

*Walter Karkula (Uncie), Greeley, Donnie Moss, Ted Karkula looking at the playbook, 1952*

*Marshall Blocks Football team 1947, top; Bailey, John Piwaschuk, Gene Eskierka, Bill Tamm, Moose Wallace, Dick Rodin, Mich Arduser, Jimmy Lottie, unknown. Middle; Walt Eskierka, Walt Piwaschuk, Butch Norton, Dick Wilder, unknown, Ken Kirberger, Ted Karkula (coach). Bottom; Harold Kelvig, Butch Kocon, Bill Stanoch, Val Mus, Oscar Rasmussen, Don Slarks, Donnie Moss, unknown, Bobby Sopcyk (coach) and Ted Krystofiak.*

Friendship Club. You could get there by streetcar for one token. The bridal dances in those days were different. There was always plenty of food and drink and anybody could go. Even if you didn't know the bride and groom. For the dollar dance you could only dance if you threw money. And each person would throw a silver dollar at a plate. If you hit the plate you would get a shot. And the wedding lasted three days, including Papravena.

Some of the places my friends and I hung out at were the Ritz, Bijou, Princess and the Arion Theaters. Nobody had cars so we walked to the movies. We liked going to John Ryan Baths, but it was always crowded. For three box tops you could go to a Minneapolis Millers game for free on Saturday afternoon. We all collected Wheaties box tops and went almost every week. Mostly my hobbies were sports and stamp collecting.

After high school I played Football for John's Bar and Gawron's Liquor in the late 1940s. I played football for Marshall Blocks for eight years and we took the championship six times. Then in 1952 to the 1960s I played fast pitch softball for Danny Buchneck's, which later became the Wig and Bottle, 1029 Bar, Cozy Bar, Marshall Terrace, Logan Park, and Bottineau Park.

I met Alice Olson at Valentine's Hamburgers on Washington and Lowry. She was living at 47th Gerard North. I was seventeen when one of her girlfriends gave me her telephone number. Then we saw each other a few times and went out when I was on leave from the service.

I joined the navy when I was seventeen. My mother had to sign. Glenn Flannegan, a friend that lived by Logan Park joined up at the same time. He and his brother became professional boxers. My basic training was at Coeur d' Alene, Idaho. During boot camp I was welterweight champ. I had to be in wrestling or cross-country. My manager would say "Maslowski if you don't win, you're back on cross country." I was stationed on the USS Elkhart in the Pacific in 1945. Later I was in the Invasion forces as a gunwatch on deck. I was in Japan right in the heat of things. Then on our way to invade Japan in the third fleet, with troops—Truman dropped the bomb, and Japan gave up.

*Alice and Donnie on their wedding day, 1949*

Alice and I were married in 1949 when I was 22 years old. Our neighbor, Mrs. Kubinski made sandwiches for our wedding. Teddy Eskierka played the concertina and Volek played the sax.

## Aunt Leda Became a Dressmaker in a French Shop on Nicollet Island

*By Claire Gaudette Faue*

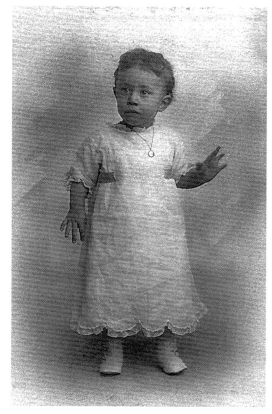

*Claire about 18 months old, 1918*

*Claire lived in Northeast and Southeast Minneapolis all of her life, except for about five years. Her home is filled with photographs of her family and embroidered pillows and lace work that she has done herself. One of her favorite pastimes is embroidering tablecloths, dresser scarves, and pillowcases. They are donated to the church where chances for a drawing are sold once a year. She also enjoys making homemade gifts for family members. The special tablecloths and pillowcases that are stamped for embroidery are hard to find now. But they still can be ordered from Hershner's Store in Stevens Point, Wisconsin. She also paints ceramics. This is Claire's story.*

My mother Rachael Gaudette immigrated to Minneapolis from St. Germaine de Granthan, Quebec with her family in 1889. They bought a house near Second Street and East Hennepin, and my grandfather worked in the nearby sawmills until his death in 1897. My grandmother then began taking in boarders to support her family of four daughters. Laura, the oldest, had studied music in Quebec and taught Mother, who gave private piano lessons to families in the area. Another sister, Leda, became a dressmaker and worked in a French shop on Nicollet Island, "Miss Bissett's of the Isle." Laura later married a University medical student who boarded with the family, Dr. Dumas. My mother also married one of the family's French boarders and raised four children of her own.

I was born at home when we lived in Southeast Minneapolis in 1916. When I was about ten we moved to where St. Constantine's Church is now on 6th and University. We did a lot of things with our neighbors; most of them worked at the sawmills. Later immigrants settled in the area and started businesses like the Laliberte Hotel on Second Street and First Avenue or DuLac's Grocery on Central and Broadway. Our neighbors that lived from Third to Sixth Avenue from University to Fourth Street were the founding families of

*Claire's aunt and uncle, Leda Malboeuf and David Bernard*

each baker used a different spice. So to make a uniform taste and appearance they adopted one recipe and began to bake them at the church. The recipe remains a secret. The church now houses six freezers to hold the pies, which are baked a half-dozen times a year. The sale of these meat pies has helped with the building restoration of the church. And now even though the restoration is completed, they continue

*Claire's mother and dad,
Rachel and Philip Gaudette were married
at Our Lady of Lourdes Church, 1914*

Our Lady of Lourdes Church. They were all French. These families were Broad, Carpentier, Pronerose, Lapierre, Paquette, Pomerleau, Malboeuf, Guillemette, O'Connell, Gaudette, Bolduc, Hashe, Rainville, and Bourbeau.

The women of Our Lady of Lourdes Church began baking "Tourtiers" for an annual dinner in 1953. Then they decided to sell them after Mass. At first the pies were baked at home. But no one made them in the same way. They came in different shapes and sizes and this tradition. It is a way of preserving the French-Canadian heritage.

We always spoke French at home. So I was used to hearing it. I couldn't even talk English when I started school, but I received very good grades in French. I attended Our Lady of Lourdes School, which went up to the eighth grade. The Gray Nuns taught us. Sister Paula, my eighth grade teacher was my favorite. She was strict but I liked her. My family didn't own a car until I graduated from Edison High School in 1936. My uncle, David Malboeuf was a policeman and he drove us around quite a bit. Sometimes he would even pick us up from church in a Paddy Wagon.

Our whole family would take the streetcar to Excelsior or Wildwood Amusement Park in St. Paul. Sometimes we went to the Minnehaha Falls Zoo or had picnics at the lakes in Minneapolis. My dad worked for the Soo Line Railroad so we could get special passes for free trips. My brother and I took the train to Chicago and other cities. We also visited our relatives who had a farm in Jefferson, South Dakota.

We didn't go to the theater very often. But we did go to Camden Park for picnics. We also went tobogganing at Columbia Park and skated at Logan Park. Afterwards my friends would come over for home made soup or baked beans. My mother made the best chicken and vegetable soup. She made these in a pressure cooker and used the vegetables that we grew in our backyard garden.

We bought our bread from Jim's Bakery on Fourth and Central, which recently closed in 1998. Harasyn's Store was on Sixth and University and Guillemette's was on Fourth and University. We would buy convenience items there but we did our main grocery shopping at National Tea on East Hennepin. Our mother made most of our clothes and we also had hand-me-downs from our cousins. We would all walk downtown to buy our shoes at the Home Trade Shoe Store on Lower Nicollet Avenue.

We played softball in the backyard and broke windows in both our house and the neighbor's house. If the ball went over the fence at the neighbor's, she would keep the ball. If there were a lot of kids, we would try to play on an empty corner lot. We also played a game called, "Nip the Stick," where you put a stick into a hole in the ground and then tried to knock it down. Hide and Seek was also a favorite since we had a lot of good hiding places at our house. We also played with yo-yo's and went to watch the Millers play ball almost every week. You had to have three Wheaties boxtops to get in.

I sang in the children's choir and belonged to the dramatic club at church. We had fun putting on plays. Most of that stopped during World War II when there were no men around. At the Margaret Barry House and Logan Park I took cooking and dancing lessons and played games on Saturday. All five kids in our family took piano lessons. I also took violin both at home and at school.

As I got older we would go out to the Friendship Club and dances at the Uptown about four or five times a week. I loved the old time music of Glenn Miller and others. We danced the Schottische, Polka, Three Step and the Waltz. I met my husband, Reinhold Faue at the Friendship Club and we were married in 1944. We moved out to Hamel, Minnesota and tried farming for awhile. After about five years we moved back to town and he worked for Scherer Brothers Lumber.

*Barbara Flannegan visits the ladies from the 500 Club including Lydia Dropps, Emma Paquette,
Rachel Gaudette is seated on right and Martha DeMeules and Laura Paquette are standing.*

I became a beauty operator in 1938 and worked in a shop on Broadway and Monroe, next door to Amble's Confectionery. There were two of us in the shop, Alice and I. When Alice retired, I managed the shop and hired Madge. The owner was John Amble. I retired in 1959 but continued to do people's hair in my home for a while.

Since the spring of 1925, a group of Frenchwomen met every two weeks to play the card game "500." My mother, Rachel Gaudette and Mrs. Dropps were two of the original members. They played 500 instead of bridge because they could talk more while they were playing. And they did like to talk. Mother even drove a car-pool to make certain twelve players were always on hand. She drove until age 92. The women were all of French ancestry—some Canadian born. At the card ta-

bles they use both languages, mostly French. At every meeting, each player paid 50 cents and they raised $1,500 to build the shrine on the church lawn. Some of the favorite topics were talk about families and good food. All of the women learned to cook in the French style. They all knew how to make "tourtiers" and pea soup and a good ragout or stew. These corps members of the "500" club were: Lydia Dropps, Emma Paquette, Martha DeMeules, Rachel Gaudette, Leona Durand, Corinne Coulombe, Lizzie Labrie, Lois LaMere and Mrs. Smith. For many years the DeMeules family operated a French language newspaper, "L'Echo de l'Quest' (Echo of the West) in Minneapolis. The "500" Club ended in the early 1980s when many of the members had passed on.

# Five Generations Were Raised in This House

By Lois Theilmann Buchinger

William Kampff, George Kampff, Dora Kampff Wachsmuth, Vivian Kampff Theilmann, Mina Kampff Warneke, Lois and her brother Glenn Theilmann are sitting in front, 1936.

Dick and Lois Buchinger live in the original homestead on the Mississippi River. They are proud of their German heritage and very interested in history. The Kampff house dates back to 1861 and is one of the oldest in lower Northeast. It was part of a group of houses on land called the Kampff addition. Five generations were raised in this house. The beams are 14 inches square and the floor joists are made from rough white fir 18 inches wide. The original key to the front door is hanging on the wall of the front porch, enclosed in a glass frame. It was found in an old miniature trunk that belonged to the Grandmother. The house remains much like the original except for new siding and the front porch is now enclosed. Lois began to tell me about her family.

My great grandfather, Louis Kampff was born in Germany and came to America in 1854. He started the St. Anthony Pottery Company in 1857. With his workshop in a log shanty he mined the clay from a nearby claypit. Making flower pots, jugs and vases, he used horsepower to grind the clay and hand and foot power to make his merchandise. To bake his pottery he made his own kiln. The pottery business grew fast and in 1870 he sold the business to Jonas G. Swahn because of health reasons.

He and my great grandma Mina Kaylberg Kampff had six children. Their descendants started their own businesses in the area. When each of his four children got married he would build them a house as a wedding present. Four of the buildings are still standing in the 2200 and 2300 block of Marshall Street.

One of Louis' daughters, Mina Kampff married Edward Warneke in 1896. Her father and husband went into business together. They started the Kampff-Warneke Store on 2201–2203 Marshall Street NE. It was a combination store that sold dry goods, notions, men's furnishings, hats, groceries and shoes. They also sold furniture and did re-upholstery.

Louis Kampff Junior owned a horseshoe shop and machine shop. He also owned the first automobile in Minneapolis. George Kampff built a drug store in the 1920s. Second Street Pharmacy, and later called Theilmann Pharmacy. George's daughter, Vivian was one of the first female pharmacists in Minneapolis. Vivian married Paul Theilmann and they took over the business.

*The Kampff-Warneke Store, which sold furniture, groceries and hardware on 22nd Marshall Street NE in 1936. Mina, Dora and George Kampff are in front.*

The Kampffs were neighbors and good friends of the Gluek family. At one time there were many German families from 13th Avenue to 30th Avenue on Grand and Marshall Streets among the Orth, Gluek and Grain Belt Breweries. Many of the houses dated back to the Civil War. Most of the people worked for the McVoy Tub Factory and the sawmill on Lowry and Marshall Streets. The family doctor was Irving McDonald who delivered all the babies. Encompassed in this area was Pulaski's Palace at 2128 Marshall. Matt Theise built the bar and Ferdinand Borchardt ran it.

Many of these families came from Barnshaven, Germany and the surrounding communities in about 1885. Some of the German families and other nation-

# New Capitol Store
## Quality Meats and Groceries
### 2207 Marshall Street N. E.

Special Fresh Baked Bread, Large 1½ lb. Loaf each 13c

We have arranged with one of our Best Bakeries for a Supply of this Delicious FRESH HOME BAKED BREAD to be delivered at our Store twice a day, giving our trade a strictly Fresh Loaf at all times, a Bread just like Mother Makes-a real Home Made Loaf always uniform, the finest of quality guaranteed to please or your money back on every Loaf-try one and enjoy good Bread there's a Difference. Remember this is an every day special 6 days a week, Fresh to us twice a day these Large 1½ lb. Nut Brown Loaves at 13c each, Rye or White.

FRESH PASTRY Real Cinnamon Rolls Plenty Spice and Sugar Large Size just like Home Made Fine for Lunch or Breakfast Special dozen 19c.

FREE One Sample Package of Post Tosties FREE Saturday only with each Cash Purchase or 2 pkg. Post Tosties 25c and 1 Sample Package FREE.

### 3 Day Special Sale Thursday, Friday, Saturday

| | | | |
|---|---|---|---|
| FRESH BUTTER, Dandelion Brand, lb. | 47c | POTATOES, Minnesota White, Peck | 63c |
| Nut Ole, Holly Brand lb. | 22c | Head Lettuce, Large Crisp, each | 10c |
| Fresh EGGS, Guaranteed, doz. | 31c | Fresh Carrots, 2 lbs. | 10c |
| SUGAR, Fine Granulated, 5 lbs. | 35c | Fresh Parsnip, 2 lbs. | 10c |
| Powdered Sugar, 3 lbs. | 28c | Apples, Ben Davis Extra Fancy, 6 lbs. | 25c |
| Home Brand, Pork and Beans, 3 cans | 29c | Oranges, Sweet Juicy Medium Size, doz. | 35c |
| Chaska Bell Peas, 2 cans | 25c | Fresh Fig Bar Cookies, 2 lbs. | 29c |
| Home Brand Sauer Kraut, 2 cans | 25c | COFFEE, Atwoods Special, lb. | 43c |
| Home Brand Jello asst. Flavors, 3 pkgs. | 25c | Oat Meal, 5 lb. Bag, | 25c |
| Sliced Pine Apple, large can | 25c | Karo Syrup, 5 lb. Pail, | 29c |
| Toilet Paper, 7 Roll | 25c | Large Sea Foam, pkg. | 23c |
| Table Salt, 10 lb. Bag | 21c | Oil Sardines, 5 cans | 25c |
| Macaroni, Spaghetti or Shellets, 2 lbs. | 25c | Matches, 6 boxes, | 25c |
| Hand Picked Navy Beans, 3 lbs. | 25c | Large Oregon Prunes, 2 lbs. | 25c |
| Apricots, Large can | 25c | Raisins, Seeded or Seedless, 2 for | 25c |
| Fresh Weiners, Standard Made | 20c | Hormel's, Pork Link Sausage, lb. | 25c |
| Beef Pot Roast, | 15c | Fresh Pork Steak, Sliced, lb. | 25c |
| Fresh Pickeled Herring, lb. | 25c | Fresh Leaf Lard, lb. | 15c |
| Creamed Cottage Cheese, lb. | 15c | Smoked White Fish, | 28c |

Do You know we redeemed Cash Tickets on over $600.00 worth of Cash Business last Week, are you getting your 2 1-2 per cent discount on what you spend, if not, why not, we give it on all cash sales. Save the tickets we redeem them.

We Deliver---Dinsmore 0665.          ALLEN & DEISS

alities that lived in the neighborhood were: Ackerly, Barno, Buczak, Borchardt, Bloch, Buchinger, Bauer, Behles, Fitting, Finke, Gonko, Gozola, Gullen, Haspert, Ingenhutt, Jungnukel, Knealing, Lietzke, Mely, Navarra, Oberlie, Ray, Rusinko, Seiler, Schonebaum, Sery, Schagun, Stommel, Swahn, Scheffel, Schroeder, Tschudy, Theis and Wachsmuth. The Rusinkos on the corner of 23$^{rd}$ and Marshall had an outdoor oven in their backyard in the 1930s. It always smelled so good. We'd eat our home made bread with lots of butter. Most of the families attended St. Paul's, St. Boniface, and St. Anthony churches.

I went to Schiller School and was taught by both Lennon sisters, Ester and Mary. I played the clarinet in the school orchestra. We put on regular concerts for the PTA. For Home Ec class we would cook lunch for the teachers, once a week. I always felt sorry for them having to eat our concoctions. As I recall we made a lot of salads and creamed dishes, like creamed chipped beef. Miss Dunning was our teacher. I remember the truant officer, Mrs. Teckla Murlowski. She was rough. If you said you were sick, she would go over to your house to make sure you were telling the truth. The year I graduated was the first year that the Schiller ninth graders were transferred to Edison and they would be part of the high school.

On Christmas morning, I remember going to visit relatives. We would sing to the tree and look at the gifts and were served a drink and cookies. Then we would go on to the next house. This is called Yulebuching, a German custom. Many of the people around us belonged to the neighborhood Smear Club. Once a month they would play cards. At Christmas time the club members would sing songs and ring out the bells. They'd also have summer picnics. A big ice cream container from the factory would be purchased. It was a special time for kids because it was the one time we could eat all the ice cream cones we wanted.

Here are some German foods we used to eat. Lebkuchen, a cookie or honey cake, sauerkraut, pfeffernuesse, a cookie, kaffee kuchen, saurbraten, a meat, pumpernickel bread, and wienerschnitzel, a breaded cutlet served with vegetables.

### Recipe for Kaffee Kuchen

½ cup shortening
¼ tsp. salt
2 beaten egg yolks
1-½ cups sifted flour
1 tsp. baking powder
1 cup sugar
½ cup milk
2 stiff beaten egg whites

Cream shortening & sugar, add egg yolks. Add flour sifted with baking powder & salt, alternately with milk. Fold in egg whites. Pour into greased 8x8x2 pan. Blend 6 Tbs. flour, ¼ cup brown sugar, 2 Tbs. butter & ½ tsp. Baking powder. Sprinkle over cake. Bake at 350 degrees for 40–50 minutes.

## The Grain Belt Beer Sign Had An Arrow That Pointed to Friendly's

*A Tribute to Sophie Abraham*

Friendly's Bar and Bowling Alley was an important fixture in the Northeast community. It was more than a bar and bowling alley. It was a place where friends gathered and always felt welcome. Sophie Kania, an immigrant from Poland started the bar with her husband in 1927. During the Depression Sophie served hot meals for 25 cents. Her grandchildren and descendants keep her memory alive by reminiscing about what a strong yet gentle woman she was. I was invited to their home where I met with four of her descendants and was treated to a traditional Polish meal, while they eagerly told me the story of their grandmother.

Sophie Kania came to Minneapolis via Ellis Island and Philadelphia at the age of 18, from the village of Siedziszowie located in Rzeszow, Poland. Austria-Hungary occupied Poland at the time she left. Her sister Mary was already living in Philadelphia and sent money over for Sophie's passage. She also had a job lined up for her. Her first two jobs in America were baby sitting for a wealthy couple who lived on the ocean and also working for a Jewish bakery. The owner was a kind man and didn't make fun of her the way others did for not knowing the English language. He taught her by using demonstrations. Built on steep hills, Philadelphia was a congested and polluted city filled with mills and sweatshops. A stopping place for many Polish immigrants, Aunt Mary or Ciotka sponsored many of them.

*You are cordially invited*
*to attend our*

**GRAND OPENING**

*Saturday, December 3rd, 1949*

*of*

**THE NEW FRIENDLY BAR & CAFE**
**309-311 MAIN STREET N. E.**

MRS. SOPHIE ABRAHAM  ·  LOUIS  ·  WALTER  ·  TED

*Wally, Sophie, Mamie and Teddy during*
*Grand opening of bar, 1949*

Sophie's allergies caused her to move to Minneapolis. Doctors told her to leave Philadelphia because of the heavy smoke and pollution. She came to Northeast Minneapolis and lived with cousins in 1914. She soon met Louis Abrahamowicz (Abraham), who was a friend of her brother, Frank. The two men were both stationed at Fort Snelling. Sophie and Louis were married at Holy Cross Church on Jan.21, 1918. Three

*Louie and Sophie's wedding in 1918*

days after the wedding, Louis was deployed on army maneuvers. Sophie's wedding dress was stolen from the car she rode in the day of her wedding. So the dress that she wears on her wedding photo was on loan and the picture was not taken until he returned from maneuvers. They lived at several places in the Northeast area; Adams, Monroe, and then Quincy Streets, until they purchased their first home on 616 Monroe Street. They had four children: Mary Helen, Louis, Walter and Teddy.

Louis and Sophie purchased the building at 311 Main Street for $5,000 with a down payment of $350 from the sale of a farm they owned in Anoka and with the money Sophie saved. This was purchased during prohibition and the depression years. Friendly's Bar opened its doors for business as the Main Street Tavern in January of 1927. During the prohibition years the business was listed as many different types of establishments; 1927 listed it as a billiard hall, 1930 as a garage in the Minneapolis City directory, and in 1932 as a restaurant. As prohibition lifted the name was changed to Friendly's Bar and Café in 1937 and in 1940 the bowling alley was added. There were also two banquet rooms, a dance hall and a bar downstairs.

It became a very important connection for Northeasters as well as other Twin Citians. A place where you could quench your thirst, play a little cards, hang out with the guys and even get a bite to eat. Even the old Grain Belt sign on the river had an arrow that pointed to Friendly's. Friendly's Bar and Bowling Alley served three generations of customers, from World War I, the Depression and World War II. It was a place where people from Northeast got out together and a working man's bar. Many of the guys from the Grain

Belt and Gluek Breweries, B.F. Nelson and the other mills hung out there.

During the depression family and friends helped each other to survive. Sophie Abraham helped people with their rent and house payments, supplied diapers, and even loaned them money. Sophie would feed and give clothes to those in need. She'd also let homeless men sleep in the basement of the bar. Often she would hire them on as pinsetters, always mindful of people's pride. Meals at Friendly's were just 25 cents and consisted of mashed potatoes and gravy, salad, meat, soup, dessert and beverage. During the depression it was often the only meal of the day the workers had. For many years on Fridays she served a free meal of pig hocks and saurkraut. At the same time she was a lifeline to relatives in the Old Country, sending clothes, soap, money and canned meat.

All of her life Sophie referred to the bar as the Main Street Tavern. The Main Street Gang was made up of local boys. There were twelve or thirteen guys who swam in the Mississippi River and came into the bar regularly. It was a group that Gram Sophie took under her wing. Most of them called her "Mom." Many of the single guys addressed Sophie as Mother. One guy, Jimmy Tigue, even sent her flowers every year on Mother's Day. Many of them worked at the bar when they were older. These guys were so close they would cover for each other. One of the wives would call and say "Is Wally there?" The guy answering the phone would say, "No, he left five minutes ago." Everyone knew they covered for each other. Even the wives knew that their husbands were still there!

When all the boys went off to the service the gangs

*Part of Main Street Gang, Mel and Mamie Lipski, Jim Joseph, Stan Partyka, John Gable, Ed Joseph, Ed Gromek and Woody Swentek. Ed Partyka is in front with Sophie's dog Buster, 1943.*

were broken up. And when they came back the bar was a place to go to be with friends. It was a connection for those who came home from the war, a home for vets. They came back with all kinds of problems. At that time there was no treatment for flashbacks, depression, etc. They wanted to forget what they'd seen and heard.

Sophie was very religious; she contributed to the building of All Saints Church and supported it all of her adult life. She was a strong but gentle woman. She had a great sense of humor and was game for anything. Before she was widowed in 1948 she was fashionably dressed. But in her later years she usually wore straight skirts and a checked plaid apron, and *al-*

*ways* open toed high heels. She would take dresses apart and sew them together by hand, paying no attention to whether the prints matched. The only luxury she kept in her later years was her mink coat and high-heeled boots for winter. She'd be busy sweeping

*Sophie sweeping the bar in her high heels, 1950s*

or on top of ladders, painting and varnishing alleys and cleaning at 8 AM. Complete in her high heels. She would never sit down to eat with you; she would pick at her food while cooking. She almost always had a cup of coffee in her hand. Her coffee consisted of ½ cream, ½ coffee and loads of sugar. She was very conservative, thinned everything down, and always turned off lights. She bought meat at Blue Ribbon Meats on East Hennepin—5 pounds of ground beef for a dollar. One cook wanted to use parsley and other trimmings.

She got rid of him in a hurry. Her ways were not fancy. She'd leave the bar late at night with the cash and receipts in her purse under her arm, walking home in her high heels. She didn't trust banks and wasn't afraid of anything. Her sons would follow her in the car to watch over her. If they tried to give her a ride even in the winter she would scold them in Polish. The bar was robbed twice. Everyone said, "It's a good thing Grandma wasn't there during the robbery—she would have fought them off in her high heels."

The bowling alley and restaurant made it an ideal outing for the ladies to get together. Bowling was socially acceptable as a sporting event for them. They could get something to eat, have a few drinks, bowl and socialize with friends, neighbors, boyfriends and husbands. The Abraham's organized bowling banquets downstairs. Spring was the bowling banquet dinner with prizes and dancing and awards for the women's teams, mixed doubles and men's leagues. They also had a Mother/Daughter's league. Saturday and Sunday afternoon was a good time for family bowling. In the summer they had short league season, summer picnics and family fishing trips and large groups of family's would rent most of the cabins at a resort for the week. In the Fall there would be Halloween costume parties. Christmas was a big affair, all of the mirrors were hand painted and sprayed with artificial snow by daughter-in-law Irene. Sophie put a huge tree up with ornaments from the Old Country. A New Years Eve party would end the season with hats and horns for everyone. The regulars never missed a party.

Easter was reserved for church and family. She cooked for a week making Polish dishes for her family and their children. Most loved and remembered dishes are her Polish bread, pierogis, cabbage rolls, blood

*Ladies bowling team, 1962*

*Grandpa Louie's car in front of Friendly's Bar and Bowling Alley. Building on left is original restaurant with apartment above, 1943.*

*Men's bowling team, 1960s*

*Grand opening of back alleys Lois, Sophie, Marion, and Mamie*

are her Polish bread, pierogis, cabbage rolls, blood sausage and homemade root beer-made in the bathtub.

It was very hard to walk away when Sophie was forced to close the doors of Friendly Alleys due to Redevelopment's seizure of the property in order to build a new freeway. The freeway never materialized in that location which added insult to injury. But she laughed when the City offered her a chance to rebuild again years later when she was much too old.

She traveled to Philadelphia and Poland. After retiring she went to South America. She died at age 102 in 1998 leaving a beautiful legacy; she outlived all of her four children. Her grandchildren remember her as a Polish immigrant with only a third grade education, who came to America with it's language and custom barriers, owned a business and even though a woman couldn't have her name on a liquor license, she expanded the business. She loved her family dearly and passed on the spirit with care and love. She'd give you the shirt off her back. She taught us all unconditional love.

Grandma always used to say, "You could be whoever you wanted to be when you came to America."

*Teddy Abraham is behind the bar of Friendly's and the customer is Leroy LaSota, 1950s*

# The Ma and Pa Stores are All Gone Now

*By Ted Biernat*

*Biernat family store in 1928, Ted, Frank, clerk, Florence, Pete,*
*Victoria, clerk, Steve Wasik and Jane (little girl in front)*

My parents, Victoria and Peter Biernat were born in Tanochuk, Poland. They each came separately to this country in about 1913 and met at the Polish dances at Holy Cross Church. They were married shortly after. I was born in 1918 when my parents rented a house on 24th Avenue and Fourth Street NE. My dad worked for the Soo Line Railroad for twelve years before he saved enough money to buy a grocery store for $1,000. The store was located next door to where we were renting. And my mother worked at the flourmills down by the falls. She worked as a laborer for about ten years.

We used to sell groceries on one side and liquor and wines on the other. The only stores that were allowed to sell liquor were Sentryz and Biernats. This happened because the laws changed. When we owned the store there were eight holdups. There was a robbery at the store when I was fifteen years old. I was peeking around the corner and I almost got shot. The guy took $150 and that was a lot of money at that time—today its peanuts. It was rough growing up in the depression years. We didn't have everything we wanted, but we got by. The people charged their groceries. The customers kept their own books and dad trusted them. They would bring their book every time they came to the store and paid their bill weekly or monthly, but not much each time. There was no payment schedule. The people who wouldn't or couldn't pay were forgotten. I remember a time when I was ten years old, my dad had figured up these charge accounts and they totaled over $10,000 to $15,000. He threw the books away. Dad said, "How can these people pay us when they aren't working. And things are just too rough for them. They can not pay."

Our customers came from the immediate locality. In the early years they were primarily Polish and Russian but that changed over time. They bought groceries every day because they had no refrigeration. We kept things cold by using large amounts of ice. The deliveryman would bring ice twice a week. And there was sawdust on the floor. We didn't get an electric refrigerator until the 1930s.

I helped out as a clerk in the store when I was fourteen. I started driving when I turned fifteen and delivered groceries in our Model A Ford. All of my brothers

*Biernat family Dairy Store on Lowry
and Third Street NE, 1980s*

and sisters worked in the store. There were four children in our family, Frank, Jayne, Florence and myself. We carried the groceries in wooden boxes. The "Ma and Pa" stores are all gone now. There used to be a store almost every other block, Russinik Meats, Janda's Store, Stakowski's, Huskak Grocery, Bauch's and Koscieleks. And the funny part, they all made a living. Nobody got rich but they all made enough to stay in business. It was never the purpose of one store to drive others out of business.

My father learned the butcher trade by himself. He made his own Polish sausage in a smokehouse out back using a special mixture of his own spices. At Easter time he would have a lineup of people waiting to buy sausage and ham. I helped him but I never learned how to be a butcher. There were quite a few butchers in the area. Other items in the store we sold in bulk like beans, rice, sugar and flour. They were packaged in one pound brown bags tied with string.

When I was growing up we were allowed to go as far as East Hennepin but not beyond. We used to walk across the river to Camden Pool for a swim. We also swam in the river. That was almost our second playground. Some kids fished in the river. We went up to Johnson Street to the Hollywood Theater. Lots of kids would hang out on Central Avenue.

We had our recreation from the local settlement house, the Northeast Neighborhood House. I went there quite a bit as a kid. We played basketball, football and indoor sports of all kinds. They had organized leagues where we played against people from other sections of town and other schools like Ascension, Schiller and St. Hedwig Schools.

We didn't have radio or TV. I got a Crystal set in 1925 and the whole family would listen to it. This device used a silicon crystal and a small metal wire to detect radio waves. Some of our favorite programs were Amos and Andy and Charlie Chaplin. For a nickel you could go to the show at the Arion and the Ritz Theater.

I went to Holy Cross for grade school and graduated from Edison High in 1939. There were so many kids in our class that they had two graduations, one in the Spring and the other in January. My dad and I were both active in the church. I belonged to the Usher's Club and the Holy Name Society. I went to catechism at Holy Cross when I was 8 or 9 years old. Today they have first communion at age 7. This is too young.

Northeast was a good, healthy place to live. Love for your fellow man was a lot greater and the associations were stronger. We always said hello to our neighbors. We have a lot to be thankful for. There are people today who are putting money in the bank on their social security checks and other pensions. No, I don't want to go back to the 1930s. That was rough. It is better now. We have inflation but still we manage some way. We are lucky we are living in America.

When I graduated from high school in 1939 things were beginning to change in Northeast. There was a lot of defense work and things were looking better. People seemed to have more money and they were happier. A lot of homes were being built right after the war and it was hard to get the materials. Certain items in the store were starting to get scarce, like sugar and liquor. All you could get during the war and after the war was rum. Once in awhile you could get Brandy or Scotch. But this was rare.

After high school I went to the "U" for a couple years and studied insurance, real estate and business courses. But then the war broke out and I went into the service on March 3rd, 1941. I was one of the first ten men from Northeast to get drafted. My brother and I were inducted at Fort Snelling and ended up in the same division in Fort Crook, Nebraska. There were a lot of men from Minnesota there. I was in the 63rd infantry as a rifleman. There were quite a few guys from Northeast in my division. Some were butchers and we even had some undertakers. My brother was killed overseas in Luzon, about a month before the war ended. I was first in England and then later traveled all over Germany. I met Mother Teresa in Czechoslovakia. Our colonel knew a lot of the guys were Catholic and that they would want to see her. So he gave us time off to go. He had a special love for the men in his outfit.

I met my wife, Sophie, in Weyerhaeuser, Wisconsin when my dad ran a butcher shop there. Later she lived on 27th and Marshall Street with some friends. There was a hamburger shop right across from the Ritz that was "some place" in the 1930s. I think it was called the Hamburger Shop. It was quite a hangout when we were dating. We were married on October 27, 1941 while I was in the service. We had a big wedding, with 40 cases of liquor and about 400 people. There

*Ted's father, Peter Biernat with*
*family members in Poland—*
*Ta sa Biernato we Wnucek*

were always a lot of relatives in those days. We got married while I was on furlough. She joined me in California and we lived there for a short time. After awhile things got rough in Minneapolis, there was not enough help in the store. So she went back to help my folks out. I got out of the service in 1945 and we bought the house from my dad. We have been here ever since.

*Sophie, 1947*

We had a daughter while I was gone. People were glad to see the GI's come home. There was a lot of drinking and parties. They don't drink as much now. There were lots of bars in the area. We used to go to a bar and sit there half a night. What else was there to do? A lot of the bars had music. So we danced. Then when TV came out, people stayed home more. We would entertain families at home. You couldn't afford to go out. Today you see a family and all their kids go out to restaurants. We never did that. We still have Christmas Eve and Holy Saturday lunch at home for the family. Those two holidays we keep up.

When I was growing up, people who shopped at the store were primarily in the neighborhood. You wouldn't cross Central or shop further away. But all that changed after the war when people started getting cars and the economy got better. They started building supermarkets. Our first supermarket was the Red Owl in St. Anthony Village. That was such a gorgeous store. The store is still there but it is little compared to the big new ones. After that people bought smaller amounts of groceries at our store, last minute items, more odds and ends. Business changed in the late 1950s. We couldn't provide as much variety as the big stores could. We belonged to the Off Sale Liquor Dealers Association and the Grocery Store Association. We sold the store in 1988. My folks lived in the house on 24th and Fourth Street until they retired in 1964 when I took over the business. The building is still there but we don't own it any more.

I started speaking English when I was about eight years old. My family often spoke Polish. My wife and I both speak Polish and still speak it with each other, but we never taught our children to speak it. They are all mad at us over that. We would speak in Polish when we didn't want them to hear. I can remember they all hated that. Our children went to De La Salle, St. Margaret's and Edison. Our boys played hockey. They were in school plays. Our kids were always in the house by 8:00 or 9:00.

I served in the state legislature for eight years in the late 1950s. You had to be a good union man to get in the legislature then. I was also active in the Knights of Columbus and Polish White Eagle. They provide scholarships to college kids.

# Our Uncles Would Tell Us Wild Tales

*By Vince Walker*

*Tom and Vince Walker taken about 1920*

I was born in 1913 and raised in Northeast Minneapolis. My parents owned property at 33rd and Tyler, and also at 33rd and Central Avenue. My father, O.J. Walker was a grocer. In the old days, a common way to get groceries was to call the local grocery store, give the order, and the store would deliver the groceries within an hour. My dad maintained this service. And I was a delivery boy. So I kept busy delivering groceries on foot, all over the neighborhood. Even to the Ostranders who lived at 3314 Pierce Street. Holy smoke, I got the exercise.

I should mention that while I was going to Edison High School I also had a paper route. I delivered the *Star/Tribune* from Central Avenue to Fillmore Street and from 19th to 23rd Avenue. I had about 100 customers. This kept me busy, especially on Sunday, when the papers were about an inch thick and weighed about 3 pounds each. I walked with a sled or coaster wagon, starting at 4 A.M. to do this job. And every month I had to carefully collect the fees for the papers. Going from door to door. Times have changed.

In the late 1800s many of my relatives emigrated to the U.S. from Ireland. They came with no money and little but the shirt on their backs. So they went to work doing housework, etc. Then they sent their earnings back to Ireland to transport other family members to the U. S. Soon there were a dozen or twenty more relatives here. Minneapolis-St.Paul was a favorite gathering place. There were the Fitzpatricks from Ballaghaderreen, Ireland, and the Foley and Roddy people from central Ireland. These people, many of whom were related, congregated in the Twin Cities and began working and setting up households.

Many of these Irish people settled in Northeast Minneapolis. The men applied for jobs at the Soo Line Railroad, which had a large repair facility for steam locomotives, called the Soo Line Shops. Some of the jobs were horrendous. I remember my uncles coming out of the repair round house after a day of work on steam locomotives. They were black as the ace of spades. And with no facemasks it is surprising that they survived.

But they loved visiting and telling "wild stories about the old country." My mother was one of them. We youngsters were fascinated about the stories they told. Often our hair stood up as the stories unfolded. So we paid extreme attention. But every now and then the story would terminate with a big joke and a loud thunderous laugh, which took minutes to end. These Irish relatives were "real characters."

One night my uncle, Thomas Fitzpatrick was baby-sitting the Walker kids. And when they weren't behaving and wouldn't go to bed, he snuck outside. He threw a sheet over his head and stood in front of the window. They were so scared that they ran to bed immediately.

We also got together for square dances in people's homes. We'd go down the basement and play the victrola, and square dance. The Irish people ate a lot of corned beef and cabbage and of course potatoes. Although the Irish meal here would be quite Americanized, a typical meal in Ireland would be like this. For breakfast—black pudding, blood sausage and Irish soda bread, fried in a pan. For lunch—a cold plate would be served with ham, turkey, tomatoes, spring onions and potato salad. Lots of tea would be consumed during afternoon tea. For supper—baked or pan fried lamb chops or slices, with potatoes either boiled or mashed with scallions or raw eggs mixed with potatoes. Another favorite is beef barley soup or Irish Stew made with lamb, potatoes and vegetables. This is made with a medium thickness of chicken or beef stock. For dessert there would be bread pudding or custard, made with caramelized jelly hardened in the bottom of the glass and then mixed in with the custard and cake and topped with whipped cream.

St. Clement's Church on 24th and Jackson Street is where all my relatives and friends went. When we were parishioners there, a tall (6'6") priest with a shock of white hair ran the church. When he sang he would drown out the rest of the singers with his loud baritone voice. He was a super fellow and had control of everything. He was going to build a school between the church and Lowry Avenue but the property is still vacant. The stained glass windows on the side walls are out of this world. Fr.Fitzgerald put them in about 1920. You will never see such beautiful stained glass anywhere in the world.

But the fondest memories I have were when we had a family gathering like a picnic in Columbia Park. Story telling was always a special feature. So we kids gathered at a spot and our uncles would tell us some "wild tales". What a great experience. Our uncles were special in our lives. And "Nordeast Minneapolis" was a gathering place for these people. There was also a substantial group of Italian people settled in Northeast in the vicinity of 33rd to 35th Avenue and Polk Street to Pierce Street. Edith Cavell School was in the center of this area. Families included the Colianis, the Gioncolas, etc. They were great people. I grew up with them. I went to school with Rose Cruciani; she owned a top-notch restaurant. One family, the Marchiafavas lived on the northwest corner of 30th Avenue and Tyler Street. They were active in all kinds of "northeast" events. Roy Marchiafava was a super person.

Also I should mention the Peltier family who settled at 3307 Taylor Street about 1915, or before. "Old Man" Peltier worked for the Soo Line Railroad. They owned many lots of property so they always had a large garden. And our family received lots of vegetables as a result. "Old Man" Peltier was a great storyteller. He would keep us on the edge of our seat for awhile, and then he would wind up his story with a funny comment, which would bring down the house with a great laugh. Dolph, Felix, and Wilfred (Wuz) were the boys and Helen, Mildred and Gen were the girls of this family. Helen and Genny still occupy the house.

In those days I was a skier. I had a super pair of skis and Columbia Park was a great place to ski in the winter. The park board kept some hills covered with snow. But when I left and went south, I left my skis in the rafters of the garage at 33rd and Tyler. They're probably still there. I was also a skater and loved going to Audubon Park, near Lowry School. I could cut all kinds of corners and figure skate all over the place. I still have my skates. And I love to watch the skate programs on TV. It makes me want to get out there and skate. I'll bet I could put on a show. Occasionally I skate yet, and have no difficulty on the ice, backward and forward.

*Vince standing next to his Wurlitzer 105 Band Organ. He uses this machine, which was made in 1905, to play old time music for picnics or special occasions. It plays music rolls.*

## Stay Away from the Tracks, the River and the Clay Pools

*By Jude Abraham Honigschmidt*

I was born the first of eight children, five girls and three boys on November 21, 1946. A post war baby boomer delivered by Doctor Leonard Borowicz at St. Mary's Hospital. He was Polish and delivered many

*Lois and baby Jude in 1946. Monroe Street Bakery is in the background across the street.*

Northeast babies. My parents, Louie and Lois Abraham lived at 611 Madison Street NE in a duplex that was later converted to a single family home. Our large

home was jacked up and braced while hired men jack hammered and blasted a hole through the river bed shale with dynamite to create a basement. It was a big event. We belonged to All Saints Church and also went to school there. My parents were married there.

My father was a bartender at Friendly's Bar and Grill. His parents immigrated here from Rzesnow, Poland and Russia. My mom's grandparents immigrated from Ireland and Germany. My mother worked many jobs of housekeeping and then for the Ambassador Sausage Company till she retired.

Nannie Lizzie Rosenberger always lived a few houses away or nearby in a Senior High Rise. She smelled of Desert Rose Bath Powder. She embroidered, crocheted, made aprons, pillowcases, and pillows that she gave as gifts to people. Along with the gift she gave scissors with a penny in the box for good luck. On Fridays, which was payday, I'd meet her at Monroe and Spring Street to help carry her groceries. Then she'd give me a nickel to spend. She was arthritic and rubbed copper pennies in her hands, while she sat watching TV shows.

My Grandma Sophie Abraham lived with us for awhile. Before she left for work she would divide her change between whichever grandchildren that were awake. We seldom slept late. We learned the denomination of coins and what they could purchase at a young age. It was a thrill spending our coins at LiLa LaHood's Groceries on Madison and Spring Streets. Our grandmothers were both involved with us daily. However, we did not know our grandfathers.

Grandma Sophie owned the corner lot adjacent to my dad's. Every kid in the neighborhood used this field as a playground. We kept the grass (whatever could grow) and weeds beaten down with our activities. Baseball, marbles, forts and games. Even the dads and moms would "get up a game of ball with us." It was especially fun if the Partyka's and Risk's joined in. Our near neighbors were Wojack, Sularz, Kraska, Salem, Chido, Leon, Kritches, our Abraham cousins and the Colgurie families.

The term Northeast to me was Hennepin Avenue, Old Highway eight, St. Anthony Village to Columbia Heights, across to the Mississippi River and back to Hennepin Avenue. It divided into "the Hill," "the Valley," "the Village," and "Dogtown," or Little Italy. They had a low crime rate in Dogtown and people said they had no crime and their own laws. The Valley cut off at Lowry Avenue was given a great credit rating once and the Hill had nice new cars and homes. The Valley was integrated and ethnic, words we didn't use!

People said if you lived Northeast, you could go anywhere and meet someone who knew you, which happened because of the multiple generations and large families and tight connections with schools and churches. Another saying was "If you get in trouble, don't do it Northeast." It was for sure your parents would find out through the Northeast Hot Lines of moms on phones and across back yard fences. "If you want to have a good time or good food, go Northeast. There's a bar on every Northeast corner and a good restaurant down the block."

Mom shopped at the Monroe Street Butcher Shop, Monroe Street Bakery, Jim's Shoe Repair, Ambles Confectionery, Dinsmore Cleaners and Ludwig's Bakery, the home of the "Lemon Meringue Pie" that Dave Moore of Channel 4 News made famous by mentioning it during an interview. Most had tin roofs, ceiling fans, screen doors that banged and bells that rang on their doors and rental apartments above. On Madison and Spring was our favorite little store LiLa LaHood's, previously LaHood's Pool Hall. They had an ornate cash register and armchairs that the women sat around in the winter to share gossip. She had string to wrap packages with, a scale and bags on her counters. There were awnings on the windows and she sat on a wood box with cushions behind the counter.

The men shopped at Eklund's and the gals went to the Columbia Department Store where regulars had store accounts in slots behind the counter and you also could put purchases on lay away and make weekly payments. We loved lay away! People in our neighborhood lived for the day that the Polish paper came out. They would go down to the Avenue, to a little newsstand that was next door to Eklund's Store. It was like a Shinder's filled with newspapers, magazines and comic books. Fern Alexander, a Lebanese man stood on the corner selling papers, rain or shine. In later years people would pull up in their cars and he would hand them the paper. My parents would circuit the meat markets and stop at Sentyrz Grocery Store. They'd patronize their own.

Walgreens was a must stop for lunch of hamburgers, fries and malts, or pharmacy items. Prescriptions were filled while we ate. They served breakfast every day too. On Sundays they drew large crowds. Some folks ate breakfast every Sunday after Mass. The older folks, like Grandma Sophie was always anxious for news from home [Poland] and the latest copy of the Polish newspaper, the Pravada. Dad bought the local paper and Mom wanted Time or Life magazine. And we kids bought comic books. 10 cents a piece, we couldn't get enough of them! Dick Tracy, Archie and Veronica, Superman or whatever the favorites were. Alexander had them. Later when we had a car, we'd just pull up to the stand and he would hand in our purchases and off we'd go.

Women would get together and permed each other's hair. All of the neighbors got together at my Aunt Mamie's house. She would cut all our hair into tight frizzy perms. I was always fascinated with the colorful permanent rods. We'd also give our dolls a perm. The "Tony Doll" came out in the early 1950s. It was sold as a set, including a doll with home permanent and shampoo. We would bring our dolls to the Fairy Dolly Hospital to get new hair every time I'd cut or give her a bad permanent.

We'd go down to Woolworth's with our Christmas money every year. We always got the same amount, which was 15 cents for each gift. The gifts were always the same, hankies and Desert Rose bath powder for Grandma, Evening in Paris perfume for mom plus lipstick, emery boards, writing paper or bobby pins. We'd buy a package of nails and screws plus a back scratcher for my father. I never saw him build anything. But he always made a big deal out of this gift, saying it was just what he wanted. Every woman in the parish must have gotten Evening in Paris perfume! It permeated the church on Christmas morning or Midnight Mass, whichever you attended.

One of the scariest events in the 1950s that I can remember was on Memorial Day when planes crashed on the A Field on 18th and Johnson, near the quarry. Two planes collided and pieces dropped into people's yards with propellers and everything. After hearing the crash, people from the neighborhood ran to see what happened. It became complete cayous as people were running up Broadway and sirens were blaring. Kids who weren't allowed off their block had taken off. Parents were worried and went off searching for their kids. This incident was talked about for weeks. Many families checked their insurance policies to see if they were covered in the event of falling objects from the sky.

On Sundays we often walked to the Ritz Theater on 13th Avenue or Dad dropped us off for a show. Abbott and Costello, Laurel and Hardy, the Three Stooges, Zorro, Cowboy shows with Roy Rogers, Hoppalong Cassidy, Tarzan, Lucy, Ma and Pa Kettle, Spanky and our Gang were some favorites. We had other things to keep our eyes on too! The back row! We spent a lot of time looking away from the silver screen, laughing and spying on the older couples that were hugging and kissing. Sometimes it'd get wild. Boys put gum in the girls' hair and popcorn flew, candy shot through the rows and then the usher silently "spotted" each one of the culprits. That meant "Out" (of the theater). We liked to see the matinee twice, then re-enacted the show on the way home. We liked running up and down the hills in front of the houses on Washington Street. Another route was through Logan Park where we'd stop and swing if we felt like it, or ran around the rim of the pool and up and down the curved stairways, through the balcony of the park building, a great spot for Robin Hood or Cinderella.

Sunday was a day Dad was home, so you better be good. It could mean a ride in the station wagon, most times with Nannie Lizzie. We'd take turns sometimes laying our heads on her lap and with her finger she'd softly trace the folds of our ear which tickled and soothed at the same time. We'd go to Lake Johanna,

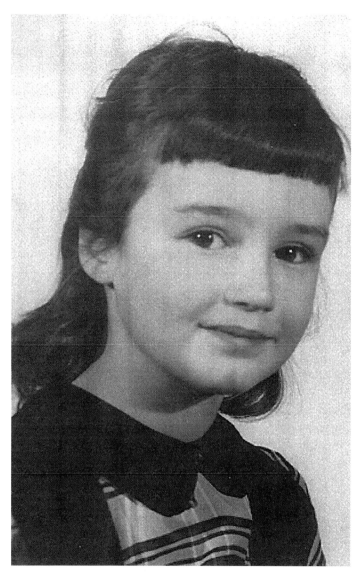

*Jude age 6, 1952*

*Jude with her brother Richard and
Sister Jan Easter time, 1952*

*Jude with cousins Susie and
Carol with their dolls, 1950*

Como, and Minnehaha Park or down Victory Memorial Drive. When on the drive or at Minnehaha, my mom would point out with pride the beautiful WPA works of stone and tell us that one of her brothers worked on those projects. Uncle Joe Rosenberger worked during the Depression to help support the family.

Ethnic food was not in our vocabulary. We grew up eating it as every day fare. However, for a few years we too ate what we thought of then, as foreign food. Chow Mein from Roger's Take Out near Sheridan School. We loved it, especially the egg rolls and fortune cookies. It was a special treat in the hot summer, as it meant a real break for mom, no cooking and no dishes. Another of our favorites was hamburgers and fries served on waxed paper with Dad's Root Beer Floats. And again no dishes to wash! Though we had no fast food chains, we had something better, the popcorn wagon and the ice cream truck. They traveled the neighborhood ringing bells with strings of children running down the street after them.

When we had TV, there was another special meal, lunch with Casey Jones. Peanut butter and potato chip or peanut butter and banana sandwiches and you could crush up potato chips in your soup. Really up scale and trendy.

On Memorial Day, we drove to St. Mary's Cemetery and Fort Snelling to pay our respect to our dead family members. We'd pray and leave flowers. Grandma Sophie was very superstitious and would caution us not to step on a marker. Do not take a stick or a rock or anything from the grave site or you would be haunted, and she had someone in the family take pictures of the dead in their coffin then discreetly put it away. It was serious business. My Nannie Lizzie on the other hand told of picnic lunches where she and her children took the trolley there, made a day of it trimming the grass and scrubbing the markers. Nannie would always walk us to the baby section at St. Mary's to pray for all the babies that died during epidemics.

As we grew old enough to leave the yard and expand our horizons "Logan Park" became the key word in our social lives away from home. The order of the packs was the oldest child was responsible for all of the younger children in the family and several families ran together. The oldest children were the leaders in every game or decision and you did what they said, or you had no life. We told them things like if you snitch to mom and dad, remember we "hang stool pigeons by their toes to bleed to death." We had learned that fear taught a good lesson.

Logan, the land of the free, year around fun was "our park." The building was a grand ornate indestructible fortress of thick stone walls and high ceilings. With curved stairways and porch balconies large enough to hold an entire concert band and sheltered from the elements, which it did many Sunday afternoons and evenings.

Staffed Monday through Saturday and closed on Sundays. There was never any graffiti left on any of the walls. It smelled of Pine Sol and a crew maintained the buildings and grounds. There were restrooms, warming house and office in the basement with a phone to call home, no charge. Office, gym court, library and activity room upstairs. A police officer was assigned to our park and we called him officer and said yes sir, no sir as our parents taught us. He was friendly and low-keyed. Occasionally parents would be at the park or see him on the street and ask, "Kids behaving?" and he'd answer, "Yes." That was important to us. He was our safety net and we wanted to be able to go to the park.

Fall began every season with sign up time for all the activities that were geared to each age group. Basketball, baseball, tap and ballet, Friday after school movies, arts and crafts, and board games in the library. Holiday parties, hockey, figure and speed skating, volley ball, tennis, trampoline, field trips and camp for a day at Theodore Wirth Park. Swimming, ice cream socials, concerts, touring plays and puppet shows. Each park participated in the big summer event, the pre parade show, held at Parade Stadium for the Aquatennial Evening Parade with costumes, songs and dances. Your parents delivered you, you'd meet your friends at a designated spot, performed, then joined your parents for the evening parade. You were a star performer that evening—lights, glitter, applause, great costumes, it was exciting and you got to stay up late!

On a good day in the summer you could stick your swimsuit on, grab a lunch and spend the day in free activities. Swim in between, spread a towel on the tennis court and sun till dry and return to an activity. Break for lunch, and resume playing. All the while being supervised the whole day. Yet they were park instructors, not baby sitters, whose job it was to lead you in constructive fun and entertainment. If you misbehaved you were sent home, kicked out of the park for the day or week. At suppertime we'd jump on our bikes, ride home, eat, and throw the dirty pots and pans in the oven, to hide them. Then we'd ride back to

the park to play and take a last dip in the pool and be home at 8:00 for street games, the popcorn wagon or ice cream truck. And of course, mom would have the dirty pots and pans lined up ready for us to wash. She always found them too!

Maple Hill Cemetery in Dogtown removed all the caskets and renamed it Beltrami Park. They staged the 4th of July fireworks and carnival, a big family and neighborhood event for many years. Sometime in 1972 while the street crews were working on Central and Monroe Streets, they unearthed a coffin of French design, as it had a glass top and the body still intact of an unknown person. All work was halted. We all wondered why it was found there, at least 1/2 mile from the old cemetery. And we never heard any more about it. After Maple Hill quit hosting the 4th of July events, Central Avenue had the parade, carnival and coronation of the queen.

A lot of odd things were buried Northeast. Grandpas buried money, afraid of another Depression. Grandmas buried fish heads under tomato plants for fertilizer and children buried pets. And to keep you away from the river adults told us to stay away from the tracks, the river and the clay pools, least we find a dead body. Fear tactics again. Along with don't make a face or stick out your tongue or God will freeze it that way. Or when we caught snowflakes on our tongues and then made snow cones and licked icicles, they'd remind us not to eat the yellow snow. Making snow angels was relatively safer.

One day while eating lunch at the park picnic table, men came and sprayed the entire park lawns with we were told "perfectly safe DDT." We did not have to pack up our lunch or leave the park, so we sat in a cloud of chemicals eating our lunch. Many years later we read it was cancer causing.

The original swimming pool at Logan was used as a watering spot for horses to promenade around and to hitch to a post to rest. I wish I could have seen that. They entered the park on Broadway and Madison Street on an unpaved bridle path; it was left that way for maintenance vehicles to use through the later years.

In the evenings we all got together to play games—statue maker, red light, green light, one o'clock the ghost is out, bacon and eggs in the frying pan, captain may I, Annie, Annie over, hop scotch, jump rope, marbles (steelies were the best prize) war games, pom, pom pullaway, kick ball, and red rover.

The sheeny man coming down the alley with his horse and wagon excited all the boys from the neighborhood. They collected and stripped metal and wire to give to him and he paid cash. Naughty boys stole the wire back from him at his next stop and re sold it the next time he came around. The girls just wanted to see the horse and look afar at the sheeny man. He was frightening to us because when we misbehaved we were told to "shape up or they'd give us to the sheeny man."

Another adventure would be a trip to B.F. Nelson Roofing Company on the river. Vast storage areas were loaded with newspaper and magazines to be converted into roofing material. One bin contained comic books and colored paper. These were several room sized bins with very high walls and huge loud metal rolls that crashed into the bins, rolling across the paper and up and down the length of the area, then up to the roof and back again. This was a restricted off limits area, that was infested with bugs and rats. The employees had rifles hung on the wall to shoot rats with. The key word here is "comic books." You had about 10 to 15 minutes to climb the wood slat walls, jump in, find comics between the magazines and climb the wall before the rolls hit again. No one was watching this process and the rolls were automatic so there was no help for you if you didn't get out.

Swimming in the river or clay holes, carp fishing by the NSP plant and walking the railroad ties were forbidden. But we did play on the bridges. We liked the Monroe Street Bridge the best. Between the road and pedestrian walk there was a cast iron structure that we walked across. If you fell a car would run you over. Added to the thrill, the cars would honk and people would wave, but anyone of them might tell your mom. Sometimes the trains would pass underneath the bridge and the smoke would fill the air and you couldn't see. If you just walked across the wood slats on the pedestrian walk you could see through to the tracks below and though there was no danger of them breaking, we pretended there was. You could also scale the concrete structure down the embankment to the tracks, sometimes finding hobo camps abandoned by day.

# Ma the Streetcar is Coming

*By Walt Dziedzic*

*An ex-cop, who grew up in the shadow of the NSP smokestacks on Marshall Street, Walt Dziedzic excelled in sports and was nicknamed "the Polish Rifle" when he played in the Brooklyn Dodgers minor league. He joined the police force and was honored Eastside Policeman of the Year in 1968. But he is most well known for his tireless effort as a city council member for 21 years. Sometimes fighting to the wire to give Northeast a fair shake. Not long after his retirement in 1997 they named a street after him and three others who were long time city council members. Dziedzic Avenue runs for six blocks near the old quarry on Johnson and Stinson Boulevard.*

My parents were John Dziedzic and Sophia Storwa. My father came to this country in 1907 with his younger brother George and Frank Wolinski's father from Przemysl, Poland, which is near the Russian border. My mother came from Miedzabrodzie, which is near Krakow. They were married at St. Hedwig's Church in 1916 and later bought a house on 27th and Randolph. He worked for the American Brake Shoe Company on 40th and University.

I was born in the living room of that house, delivered by a midwife. We had seven kids in the family, Paul, Catherine, Helen, Alice, Genevieve, Walter, and John. It was difficult for us to learn English because there was only Polish spoken in the home. In fact, I was held back in second grade because I sometimes confused the two languages. Later I skipped the sixth grade. I remember my uncles used to say "Ladny Chlopiec" which means nice boy.

*Walt, age 4 playing ball in the yard with his brother John, age 2½, 1937*

I was only two years old when my father died so my mother raised all of us alone. I was amazed at how she could make something out of nothing and feed all of us kids. She used to make potato soup with dumplings, home made bread with butter. We sprinkled sugar on it. We also ate squadkis (fried bacon scraps). One of my favorites was left over piecrust topped with cinnamon and sugar. My mother worked most of the time I was growing up at the Emerick Bakery in Southeast

*Walt's father, John Vincent Dziedzic and*
*Uncle George Dziedzic about 1912*

on a treadle machine. She was kind hearted and would feed the bums that came to our back door asking for food giving whatever she had. Sometimes it was only a cup of coffee or a crust of bread. Then she would sit and talk with them. I suppose she remembered that someone had once helped her.

*Mother Sophia in her apron, 1950*

Minneapolis. She rose early in the morning and I would watch for the streetcar that parked with its lights off at the end of 30th and Grand. As soon as he turned his lights on I'd run to get her and called out "Ma the streetcar is coming." She had her hands full with work and all the household duties, sewing all of our clothes

*First communion on the steps of St. Hedwig's Church, 1940. Walt is in third row on right.*

When I was young one of the things my friends and I did to amuse ourselves was we always used to play "Mass" in the house. Someone would be the priest and some had to be the altar boys. We'd set up an altar and draped a towel over ourselves. We had to learn Latin to become an altar boy. It was always quite dramatic when we'd sing out "Dominus Vobiscum" and "Et cum Spiritu tuo" imitating the priest in his bellowing voice.

I found a love for sports at a young age because there was plenty of opportunity for it in the neighborhood. Marshall Terrace was close to home and there was a warming house for ice-skating and an instructor during the summer that helped us with baseball. There were always people in the parks in those days.

We also played other games at the park too. We played a little basketball, hockey, rough house football, volleyball and a modified version of cricket. I remember once when Red Koniar took me down to see an all star baseball game at Nicollet Park on the streetcar in the 1930s. It was thrilling to see all the guys from the big leagues.

We'd play ball every chance we could. Someone would go over to the park early and whoever got to the field first could use it. We'd chose sides and then palmed off on the bat with our thumbs up to see which

*1945 Northeast Neighborhood House junior boys championship. All went on to play at Edison.*

team would bat first. Sometimes we'd walk over the bridge to the north side and play at Folwell, North Commons, or Fairview Park. It was kind of scary to walk over that bridge. I became a pitcher and threw the ball so hard, that nobody could hit off me.

I went to school at St. Hedwig's and played baseball there too. They had good teams and some real good athletes came out of that school. Johnny Gorbett became an outstanding pitcher at Edison. Others that played were the Novitski Brothers, Gary Worwa, George Wojack, Frank Kubinski, John Ptak and Don Yablonsky.

Logan Park had a special track for speedskating. I'd go down there in my hand-me-down skates and stay until dark. One time I fell at Logan Park during a race. The prize was a pair of long bladed skates that I wanted to win so badly. I was leading the race by almost double when I took a bad tumble. It was a hot day and there was water on the ice.

*Speed skating at Powderhorn Park 1947 and 1948*

Later I belonged to the Eastside Skating Club. Bobby Adamson was the coach and he was quite a guy. One day he said to me, "You have some real potential, but we have to get you some speed skates." When I answered that we couldn't afford it, he said he'd see what he could do. A little while later he sent me down to Billman's Hardware Store to buy a new pair of speed skates. I found out that a man by the name of Art Gobel, who was top salesman for Minar Ford had donated the money. Later I had the opportunity to meet and thank him in person. Once I got those new long blades, I could really fly on the ice. I was so proud that someone I didn't even know believed in me.

I finished third in the nationals for speedskating held at Como Park for Junior Boys at age twelve. We had lots of tournaments on the weekends. Some of the other good skaters that came out of Logan Park were Jimmy Stevens and Tom Awod. 10,000 people would come to Powderhorn Park for speedraces on Sundays. Minneapolis became a hotbed for speedskating after the war. Olympic skaters like Kenny Bartholomew and Bob Fitzgerald lived in Minneapolis at the time.

Immigrants would push themselves to learn to read so they could read the paper. They wanted to read about their kids in the sports page. It was a great incentive. The Northeast Neighborhood House had classes for them to learn to read and write.

Everyone thought that I would naturally go to De La Salle. But we couldn't afford it. I went to high school at Edison. Pete Guzy was my gym instructor for ninth grade. He also coached football and baseball. Here I was a fatherless youngster looking for a role model. And along came Pete Guzy. In those days after the war, he had obstacle courses in gym class. We would always work toward getting below 40 seconds. One day I finally got 39 in front of the whole class. What a day that was!

Pete Guzy had a way of setting you up to look good in front of the group. He knew how important it was for your self-esteem and how it made you try even harder. He was noted for taking a young player that hadn't nearly reached his potential. He would put him in with the other better ball players. Then he'd say "See how he did that," to the rest of the guys. Frank Rog and Jack Neumann were players at Edison. Some of the other players were Dick Yates, Emil Alexander, Goose Gonsier, Dick Dank, Dick Anderson, Jim Stevens and Vern Jasewski.

*Edison played football against South High at Nicollet Park for featured game of the week, 1949.
Dick Dank, Walt Dziedzic and other Edison players.*

*Walt with his mother and aunt, Sophia Dziedzic and Angela (Mrs.George) Dziedzic*

I am still a great believer in sports for kids as a way to better themselves. It's a great way to improve their self worth. We took in two Polish boys that were exchange students at Edison in 1988. They lived with us for one year. I felt it was a chance to give something back to repay the chances I was given.

After I got out of high school I played in the minor league for the Brooklyn Dodgers in 1953. I fought in Korea in 1955. Then I came back and I graduated from St. Thomas College, majoring in History and Physical Education. In 1960 I taught one year at De La Salle and was married in 1961. I joined the police department and had the opportunity to work with young kids. I was shot twice in the line of duty. I was in a bar in South Minneapolis when one of the customers got unruly and I had to escort him out of the bar. He pulled out a gun and shot me twice in the leg. After I recuperated for a while I was promoted to sergeant and then lieutenant. Later I ran for the city council and stayed for twenty-one years. Harold Kauth and Frankie Wolinski were city council members at that time and were influential in my life.

*Bus trip on the way to a ball game at Met stadium, 1972*

# Photo Credits

Courtesy of Pam Velander, cover

Doug Kieley, Photographer, 4, 14L, 15, 50, 54, 56, 59, 60, 71, 82, 83, 85, 87, 88, 91, 92, 94, 96, 110, 133, 137, 138, 145, 146, 148, 153, 166, 167, 189, 196, 198

Author's Collection, 10, 14, 17, 18, 18, 20, 24, 26, 200

Minnesota Historical Society, 16, 30, 37B, 39, 39L, 39R, 40T, 41, 42, C. J. Hibbard-43, 45B, Mpls. Star-Journal-28, 45BR, 184T, Norton & Peel- 46, 107, 108, 110, 112, Moore & Retzke-122, 124, 125, 125R, 110, Lee Brothers-174, 182, 184B, 190, 192, 198, 204, 208, 230, C. P. Gibson-233, 238

Minneapolis Public Library, Minneapolis Collection, 40B, 89, 102, 104, 106, 114, 126, 144, 202, 206

Jerry Nelson, Photographer, 22T, 22B, 111, 154, 164,

Hennepin County History Center, 31, 33T, 33B

Riverfront News, 44

© 1999 StarTribune–249

Mpls. Board of Education, Facilities Department, 185, 186T, 186B, 188T, 188B

*Trinity United 100th Anniversary* Book, 63, 65

*St.Michael's Ukrainian Orthodox Golden Jubilee* Book, 72

*St. Hedwig Golden Jubilee* Book, 75

*Mt. Carmel 70th Anniversary* Book, 78, 79

*St. John's Evangelical Centennial* Book, 97, 99

Minnesota Chronicle and Register, August 12, 1850-113

*Over the Years at Logan Park*, 121, 204

Minnesota Transportation Museum 123, 205

Northeast Sun Press, 134

Building Production Morale at Northern Pump Company, Wiley, 200, 202

Courtesy of Gary/ Josie Kvistberg, 202L, 202R

*The American Century Cookbook*, Anderson-209-Reprinted from *Your Share*, General Mills

Courtesy of Grace Sharp, 22, 49T, 76

Courtesy of Rudolph Ptak, 23

Courtesy of Marjorie Szykulski and Lorraine Niziol, 24, 158, 176, 177, 180

Courtesy of Joe Bishop NSP, 27

Courtesy of Ken's Barber Shop, 34

Courtesy of Lorraine Levandowski, 36, 37, 37

Courtesy of Roger/ Betty Rodengen, 45T, 135, 136

Courtesy of Art Boike, 48

Courtesy of Walter Warpeha, 49B, 151, 217, 218, 220

Courtesy of Irene Spack, 52, 214

Courtesy of Curtiss Johnson, 67, 69

Courtesy of Diane Wutsch, 117, 118, 119, 120

Courtesy of Ethel Arnold, 128

Courtesy of Carol Engler, 130T, 130B

Courtesy of Marlene Manshak, 131L, 131R

Courtesy of John Dady, 132

Courtesy of Dick Eklund, 134

Courtesy of Andy Zurbey, 138

Courtesy of Virginia Schnabel, 139, 140

Courtesy of Island Cycle Supply 141L, 141R

Courtesy of Jacob's 101, 142

Courtesy of Joe Kolodjski, 143

Courtesy of Dick Maczka, 147L, 147R, 168

Courtesy of Carl Ludwig, 149

Courtesy of Ann Cisek, 155, 156

Courtesy of Ready Meats, 157

Courtesy of Grace Schwerdfeger, 159

Courtesy of Roxanne Jorgenson, 160, 161

Courtesy of Cecilia Jakacki, 162

Courtesy of Betty Wykrent, 163

Courtesy of Mary Katzmarek, 165

Courtesy of Abraham family, 170L, 170R, 171, 253L, 253R, 254, 255, 256, 257L, 257R, 257T, 257B, 258

Courtesy of Bill Volna, 187L, 187R, 187B

Courtesy of Robert Kishush, 199

Courtesy of Shahid Ohad, 210

Courtesy of Totino family, 223, 225T, 225B, 227L, 227R
Courtesy of Maelyn Hansen, 228, 230
Courtesy of Bill Olsen, 231, 232
Courtesy of Judy Siwek, 234, 235
Courtesy of Helen Peake, 236, 240
Courtesy of Donnie Moss, 242, 243, 244, 245
Courtesy of Claire Gaudette Faue, 246, 247L, 247R

Courtesy of Lois and Dick Buchinger 250, 251L, 251R
Courtesy of Sophie Biernat 259, 260, 262L, 262R
Courtesy of Vince Walker, 264, 266
Courtesy of Judy Honigschmidt 267, 270L, 270T, 270B
Courtesy of Walt Dziedzic, 274, 275L, 251R, 276L, 276R, 277, 278, 279L, 279R

# Bibliography

## General History

Richard Soine and Lee Hanson, *Northeast,* sponsored by Project Challenge, Northeast Area High School Students, Northeast Neighborhood House, Chris Skjervold and MPS Ethnic Cultural Center, Minnesota Folklife Society, A. Miskell and Jiffy Print, 1978.

*Northeast: A History,* Sun Newspapers, Inc., Bloomington, MN, August, 1976.

Jo Ann Rice, "River Road: Where It All began Years Ago," *Minneapolis Argus,* November 19, 1975.

Marion D. Shutter, *History of Minneapolis: Gateway to the Northwest,* Minneapolis, 1923.

Isaac Atwater, *History of Minneapolis,* Isaac Atwater and John H. Stevens, editors, *History of Minneapolis and Hennepin County,* New York, 1895.

## Streets Named After Presidents

"A Look at 13th and University," *Northeaster,* April 20, 1994.

Gail Olson, "Old Osa's Central Avenue Landmarks," *Northeaster,* February 24, 1997.

Scott Korzonowski, "Central Avenue Development," *Northeaster,* August, 1981.

Gail Olson and Margo Ashmnore, "Remembering East Hennepin's Heydey," *Northeaster,* December 16, 1996.

"Streetlife and the River fill Bill Surdyk's Memory of East Hennepin," *Riverfront News.*

Kerry Ashmore, "Many Businesses, Some Brief, Some Long-lasting, operated in Historic Buildings on East Hennepin," *Northeaster,* February 23, 1991.

## Churches

*St. Michael's Ukrainian Orthodox Church—Golden Jubilee—1925–1975,* 1975.

*A Memento of the Dedication of All Saint's Church,* Minneapolis, MN, February 19, 1939.

Most Reverend John F. Kinney, *Souvenir of the Blessing of All Saints Parish Center,* November 1, 1979.

"All Saints Northeast Minneapolis: It's Like Coming Home, *Catholic Bulletin,* March 15, 1991.

*Golden Jubilee of the Church of All Saints, 1916–1966,* Minneapolis, MN, August 21, 1966.

George V. Wiberg, *This Side of the River: A Centennial Story, 1888–1988,* Salem Covenant Church, 1995.

*Trinity United Methodist Church, 1883–1983,* 1983.

*Centennial Celebration—St. Paul's Lutheran Church, 1890–1990,* 1990.

*St. John's Evangelical Lutheran Church Centennial, 1867–1967,* 1967.

*Mount Carmel Lutheran Church, 70th Anniversary, 1926–1996,* 1996.

*Gustavus Adolphus Lutheran Church, Guest Information,* 1992.

*Waite Park Wesleyan Methodist Church Dedication,* September 18, 1966.

Doug Davis, "Mt. Carmel Rises," *Waite Park Voice,* July/August, 1997.

"A Golden Pastorate," *Church of St. Hedwig—Golden Jubilee Yearbook—1914–1964,* 1964.

*Church of St. Hedwig, Early Recorded Minutes.*

*History of Elmwood Evangelical Free Church,* undated.

Tim Fuehrer, "They're All Catholic but Customs Give Distinct Flavor," *Northeaster,* December 3, 1986, page 9.

"Sacred Heart of Jesus Parish," *Straz, the Polish National Newspaper,* 3 items.

*St. Cyril's Church Centennial Commemorative Book,* 1991.

Curtiss D. Johnson, information on Salem Covenant Church.

## Immigrants, Steamers, Trolleys and a French Explorer

Steven Gerber, editor, "Immigrant Room Reflections," *Depot Quarterly,* Volume 1, Number 1, July to September, 1986.

William Loren Katz, *The Great Migrations, 1880s–1912* Raintree Steck-Vaughn Publishers, Austin, TX, 1993.

Hans Olaf Pfimnkuch, "A Lost Lake Reconsidered," *CORA Reports,* June 19, 1981.

Mike Kaszuba, "Northeast's High Hopes for Lake Sandy Haven't Dried Up," *Minneapolis Star and Tribune,* 1985.

Jeanette May, "Northeast Should Rediscover Its 'Lost' Lake Sandy," *Minneapolis Star,* May 3, 1973, 12A.

Karen Boros, "Who is Pierre Bottineau? And Why is His Name All Over Northeast?" *Minneapolis Argus-Sun,* March 14, 1973.

"When a Steamer Sailed Five Miles Through Minneapolis Loop and Didn't Get Stuck," *Minneapolis Journal,* March 4, 1927.

Carol Linders, "Gerber Baths," *Northeaster,* January 28, 1987.

Stanley L. Baker, "Great Northern Depot was a Link to Adventure," *Minneapolis Tribune,* July 1, 1978, 5B.

Jay Walljasper, "When the Trolley was King," *Minneapolis/ St. Paul,* April, 1981.

Tim Fuehrer, "From Streetcars to Light Rail, There's a Family Connection," *Northeaster,* June 24, 1987.

Joseph Zalusky, "Fares, Transfers, and Other Pertinent Facts about Streetcars," *Hennepin County History,* Winter 1961.

Aaron Isaacs, Bill Graham and Byron Olsen, "Twin City Lines—The 1940s," *Minnesota Transportation Museum,* 1994.

Larry Fitzmaurice, "Clamor over Trolleys goes Back to 1907," *Minneapolis Star,* January 12, 1953.

Alan R. Lind, *Twin City Rapid Transit Pictorial,* 1984.

Amy I. Clements, "Streetcar Man Thomas Lowry had Vision of Future for Northeast," *Northeaster,* May 21, 1986.

## Connections, The Places We Remember

"Jerry Grohovsky, Mayor of 13th Avenue," *Modern Maturity,* August-September, 1974.

George Grim, "I Like It Here," *Minneapolis Star-Tribune,*

"Northeast Mourns Passing of Mayor of 13th Avenue," *Minneapolis Argus,*

Ambassador Sausage: "Ethel Arnold Led Firm Through Wurst of Times," *Star Tribune,* December 2, 1979. Dick Youngblood, "Sausage Company's Savior, 71, Still Done All She'd," *Star Tribune,* October 19, 1986. "Diligent Sausage-Maker Grinds Out a Healthy Profit," *Star Tribune,* April 28, 1989.

Amble's Confectionery, Interview with Carol Engler.

Andrew Manshak, Interview with Walter Warpeha.

Dady's Drug, Interview with John Dady.

Dusty's, Interview with Dusty Stebe.

Eklunds Clothing, Interview with Dick Englund. Newspaper Accounts.

Frances' Fairy Doll Hospital and Gift Shop, Interview with Roger and Betty Rodengen.

Frederick Janda Store—Poppyseed Man, Interview with Walter Warpeha.

Grumpies Bar, Interview with Pat Dwyer and Andy Zurbey.

Hans Rosacker Company, Interview with Marv Saline.

Island Cycle Supply: "We've Been Waiting 50 Years," *Minneapolis Argus,* November 29, 1972.

Jacob's 101: Kay Miller, "Lebanon…a Tradition of Closeness," *Minneapolis Star,* March 28, 1979.

John Ryan Public Baths: "We Want a Bath," *Minneapolis Tribune*, June 9, 1954. *Minneapolis Star and Tribune*, 1921, 1923, 1932, 1955, 1961 and 1964.

Last Chance Bar, Interview with Marty Kubik

Laura's 1029 Bar, Interview with Jim Purcelm. "River Road: Where It All Began Years Ago," *Minneapolis Argus*, November 19, 1975.

Linda's Hair Affair, Interview with Linda Petroske.

Ludwig's Bakery: Dean Mosiman, "A Master Steps Aside," *Northeaster*, December, Kate Perry, "Twin Cities Bakeries: Authentic Ethnic," *Minneapolis Star Tribune*, December 18, 1980.

Marino's: Menu and Ad from "Taste" Section, *Star Tribune*, October 24, 1990, provided Ralph Mathes. Ad in *Northeaster*, March 9, 1998.

Northeast State Bank: Dee DePass, "50th Anniversary Video, Socials and Service," *Star Tribune*, March 31, 1998. *A Legacy of Community Partnership*, pamphlet. Assistance of Sue Sjoselius.

Olson Hospital: Tim Fuehrer, "'Capsular Treatment' Drew Many to Olson Hospital on Central Avenue," *Northeaster*, January 29, 1986.

Polish Palace: "River Road: Where It All Began Years Ago," *Minneapolis Argus*, November 19, 1975.

Rabatin's: "Here's the Scoop on Twin City Ice Cream, *Star Tribune*, July 27, 1986.

Jim Fuller, "New French Gets Face Lift, Rabatin Turns Modern," October 21, 1994 Star/Tribune

Jeremy Iggers, "Dining Out," *Star Tribune*, September 13, 1991.

Jeremy Iggers, "The Year in Restaurants in Local Eateries '94 was Year of Noodle," *Star Tribune*, December 30, 1994.

Jeremy Iggers, "Modern Café Maintains Features of Coffeehouse While Improving Menu," *Star Tribune*, November 11, 1994. Jim Klobuchar, "A Woman of Her Time Goes to Rest," *Star Tribune*, May 4, 1991.

Ready Meats: Jerry Anderson, "Fifty Years for Ready Meats," *Waite Park Voice*, July/August, 1996.

Red's Grocery: Rita Deyo, "Red's Grocery, a Local Landmark," *Waite Park Voice*, November/December, 1996.

Rolig Drug, Interview with Loraine Niziol and Marjorie Szykulski.

Schwerdfeger Meats: "Biography of August and Karl Schwerdfeger," in *History of Minneapolis and Hennepin County*, by Holcombe and Bingham, Henry Taylor & Company, Chicago, 1914. Interview with Grace Schwerdfeger.

Stasiu's, Interview with Roxanne Jorgenson and Marlene Hiltner.

Steve's Bar, Interview with Cecilia Gromek Jakacki.

Stillman-Schmidler Market, Interview with Betty Wykrent and Dick Parlow.

Tony Jaros' River Garden, Interview with Dan Jaros.

22nd Avenue Station, Interview with Glen Peterson.

331 Club, Interview with Steve Benowitz

Wig and Bottle: Ken Wisneski, "Of the Wig and Bottle and Things Polish," *Midweek Sun*, April 8, 1972.

## Alleleluia! Nazdrowie

"Minneapolis Parochial Schools," *Minneapolis, City of Opportunity: A Century of Progress in the Aquatennial City*, T.S. Denison & Company, Minneapolis, 1956.

*School Fact Book: Facilities Study*, Volume II, Chapter 5, Michigan State University, Minneapolis, August, 1963.

"Early Schools: From Green Lumber to Covering the Cost Overruns Even Then," *Northeaster*, October 18, 1989.

"East Side Schools Adequately Served," *The East Side Argus—Anniversary Edition*, June 18, 1926.

*Down Memory Lane, Prescott School, 1884–1974*.

*Schiller School, Farewell to Schiller, 1890–1974*, May 5, 1974.

*Anniversary and Closing Webster School, 1880–1974*.

"Historic Associations Cling to the Winthrop School," *Minneapolis Times*, August 20, 1899.

Mike Anderson, "Where the Bars Are—in NE: 'Centers of Drunkeness and Vice' Were Restricted to Northeast and Downtown," *Northeaster*, April 20, 1998.

Peter Leyden, "Northeast Bars Reflect Neighborhoods in Change," *Star Tribune*, March 25, 1991.

Kerry Ashmore, "Movie: It'll be Christmas Season in April," *Northeaster*, March 25, 1992.

Tom Clark, "Just What the Doctor Ordered: Hennepin Country Drug Stores." *Hennepin County History*, Winter, 1989–90 and *Minnesota Pharmacist*, October, 1990.

Gail Olson, "Many of Northeast's Old Diners and Cafes Came and Went with Wave of Workers," *Northeaster*, January 27, 1997.

## The Homefront During World War II... in Northeast Minneapolis

Allan Jenkins, *The 40s,* Universal Books, New York, 1977.

Sylvia Whitman, *V is for Victory: The American Front During World War II,* Lerner Publications, Minneapolis, 1993.

Kathleen Krull, *V is for Victory: The American Front During World War II*, Alfred A. Knopf, New York, 1995.

R. Conrad Stein, *World at War: The Home Front,* Regen Steiner Publishing Enterprises, Inc., Canada and the United States, 1986.

## The Ma and Pa Stores Are All Gone Now – Sixteen Interviews with Northeast Residents

Ted and Sophie Biernat, "Life History Interviews," Conducted by Harley Shreck, Ph.D., Associate Professor of Anthropology, Bethel College, Arden Hills, MN, 1994.

Shahid F. Ohad, *Smoke from the Lamp of Shahid F. Ohad: My Story,* May 15, 1997.

Carol Pine and Susan Mundale, *Self-Made—Stories of 12 Minnesota Entrepreneurs,* Doin Books, 1982.

"Rose Totino: Superstar of an American Success Story," *Business People,* March-April, 1984.

"A Tribute to Rose Totino," *De La Salle Prison Fellowship,* Unico National, undated.

Robert B. Pite, *Top Entrepreneurs and Their Businesses,* The Olive Press, Minneapolis, 1993.

Cynthia Furlong Reynolds, "The House That Pizza Built," *Minneapolis-St. Paul,* January, 1988.

Brother Milton Barker, *A Legacy of Faith and Love,* Totino-Grace, undated.

Susan Casey, *Women Inventors,* Chicago Review Press, Chicago, 1997.

Gail Olson, "Flower Pot Entrepreneur Left His Mark, but Apparently Not His Pottery, in *Northeaster,* January 26, 1998.

"Francis Siwek," *Project Challenge,* 1978.

Bill Olsen, *Times (or Walking Among the Redwoods),* 1995.

# Index

Abraham, Sophie 253
All Saints Church 50
Ambassador Sausage Company 128
Amble's Confectionery 129
Band Box 196
Bars in Northeast Minneapolis 168
Biernat, Ted 259
Bottineau, Pierre 102
Boundaries 29
Buchinger, Lois Theilmann 250
Candlelight Café 196
Central Avenue 35
Central Avenue Café 196
Connections—The Places We Remember 128
Dady's Drugstore 132
Diners and Cafes 196
Drugstores Hennepin County 175
Dusty's Bar 133
Dziedzic, Walt 274
Early Schools 183
East Hennepin 41
East High School 184
Edison High School 189
Eklund's Clothing 134
Elmwood Café 196
Elmwood Evangelical Free Church 85
Enterprise Steamship 112
Faue, Claire Gaudette 246
Frances' Fairy Doll Hospital and Gift Shop 135
Friendly's Bowling Alley 253

Gerber Baths 117
Gloria Dei Lutheran Church 92
Grace United Methodist Church 96
Great Northern Depot 126
Grumpies Bar 138
Gustavus Adolphus Lutheran Church 88
Hansen, Maelyn 228
Holland School 185
Holy Triune Lutheran Church 87
Honigschmidt, Jude Abraham 267
House of Faith Presbyterian 91
Humbolt School 182
Immigrants 107
Island Cycle Supply 141
Jacob's 101 142
Janda, Frederic Store—Poppyseed Man 137
Jim's Coffeee Shop 199
Joe's Barbershop 143
Johnson Street Market 145
Lake Sandy 114
Last Chance Bar 147
Laura's 1029 Bar 146
Linda's Hair Afair and Al's Barbershop 148
Lowry School 187
Ludwig's Bakery 149
Main and Marshall Streets 29
Main Street businesses 32
Making Movies in Northeast 199
Manshak, Andrew Shoe repair 131

Marino's 150
Marshall Street businesses 32
Monroe Express 121
Moss, Donald 241
Mount Carmel Lutheran Church 78
Northeast Junior High 188
Northeast State Bank 151
Northstar Café 196
Ohad, Shahid 210
Olsen, Bill 231
Olson Hospital 152
Peake, Helen 236
Pierce School 186
Pig and Bun 196
Pillsbury School 186
Polish Flyer 121
Polish Palace 154
Prescott School 193
President Streets 29
Princess Theater 44
Putnam School 189
Rabatin's 155
Ready Meats 157
Rolig Drug 158
Ron Clair's Diner 196
Rosacker, Hans Company 139
Ryan, John Public Baths 144
Sacred Heart of Jesus Polish Church 56
Salem Covenant Church 67
Salvation Army 82
Schiller School 195

Schwerdfeger Meats 159
Sheridan School 186
Siwek, Francis 234
Spack, Irene 214
St. Charles Borromeo 94
St. Clement's Church 59
St. Hedwig's Church 75
St. John's Evangelical Lutheran
    Church 97
St. Michael's Ukrainian Orthodox 71
St. Paul's Lutheran 60
Stasiu's 160
Steve's Bar 162

Stillman-Schmidler market 163
Streetcars 121
Tony Jaros' River Garden 164
Totino, Rose 223
Trinity United Methodist 63
Untamed Heart 199
Van Cleve School 185
Waite Park Elementary 188
Waite Park Wesleyan Church 83
Walker, Vince 264
Warpeha, Walter 217
Webster School 192
Whitney School 186

Wig and Bottle 165
Winthrop School 190
World War II Homefront 201
    Blackout Drills 201
    Gold Star Mothers 201
    Liberty Bond Drives 201
    Northeast Neighborhood House 201
    Rations 201
    Rosie the Riveter 201
    Victory Gardens 201
13th Avenue Businesses 47
22nd Avenue Station 166
331 Club 167

# About the Author

Genny Kieley grew up in Northeast Minneapolis and has written several short stories. She hopes to someday put them into a collection called *The Spinning Pie Case.* She also has plans for two other projects in her life-time. *Daughter # 5, Baby of the Family,* a non-fiction story and a fictional novel called *A Polish Girl,* based on her grandmother's journey from a Polish village to Minneapolis. Her first book *Heart and Hard Work: Memories of Nordeast Minneapolis* was published in 1997.

Genny has two children and two grandchildren. Her other interests include making baby quilts, genealogy and collecting antique dishes